THE VIRTUAL WORKPLACE

The recent pandemic has clarified the overwhelming connection between the workplace and technology. With thousands of employees suddenly forced to work at home, a large segment of the workforce quickly received crash courses in videoconferencing and other technologies, and society as a whole took a step back to redefine what employment actually means. The virtual workplace is the blending of brick-and-mortar physical places of business with the advanced technologies that now make it possible for workers to perform their duties outside of the office. Trying to regulate in this area requires the application of decades old employment laws to a context never even contemplated by the legislatures that wrote those rules. This book explores the emerging issues of virtual work – defining employment, litigating claims, aggregating cases, unionizing workers, and preventing harassment – and provides clarity to these areas, synthesizing the current case law, statutory rules, and academic literature to provide guidance to workers and companies operating in the technology sector.

Joseph A. Seiner is a Professor of Law and the Oliver Ellsworth Professor of Federal Practice at the University of South Carolina School of Law. Professor Seiner has been featured in a number of national media sources, including The New York Times, The Wall Street Journal, CNN, ProPublica, The Atlantic, and Fortune. He routinely gives presentations on labor and employment related issues, and teaches classes in the area of workplace law. Professor Seiner has published numerous books and articles on employment topics, and his work is widely cited in academia and by the federal courts.

The Virtual Workplace

PUBLIC HEALTH, EFFICIENCY, AND OPPORTUNITY

JOSEPH A. SEINER

University of South Carolina School of Law

CAMBRIDGE
UNIVERSITY PRESS

CAMBRIDGE
UNIVERSITY PRESS

University Printing House, Cambridge CB2 8CB, United Kingdom

One Liberty Plaza, 20th Floor, New York, NY 10006, USA

477 Williamstown Road, Port Melbourne, VIC 3207, Australia

314–321, 3rd Floor, Plot 3, Splendor Forum, Jasola District Centre, New Delhi – 110025, India

79 Anson Road, #06–04/06, Singapore 079906

Cambridge University Press is part of the University of Cambridge.

It furthers the University's mission by disseminating knowledge in the pursuit of
education, learning, and research at the highest international levels of excellence.

www.cambridge.org
Information on this title: www.cambridge.org/9781108483711
DOI: 10.1017/9781108652148

© Joseph A. Seiner 2021

First published 2021

A catalogue record for this publication is available from the British Library.

Library of Congress Cataloging-in-Publication Data
NAMES: Seiner, Joseph A., author.
TITLE: The virtual workplace : public health, efficiency, and opportunity / Joseph A. Seiner,
University of South Carolina.
DESCRIPTION: Cambridge, United Kingdom ; New York, NY : Cambridge University Press, 2021. |
Includes bibliographical references and index.
IDENTIFIERS: LCCN 2020058415 (print) | LCCN 2020058416 (ebook) | ISBN 9781108483711
(hardback) | ISBN 9781108718028 (paperback) | ISBN 9781108652148 (epub)
SUBJECTS: LCSH: Telecommuting–Law and legislation–United States.
CLASSIFICATION: LCC KF3557.S45 2021 (print) | LCC KF3557 (ebook) | DDC 344.7301/25–dc23
LC record available at https://lccn.loc.gov/2020058415
LC ebook record available at https://lccn.loc.gov/2020058416

ISBN 978-1-108-48371-1 Hardback
ISBN 978-1-108-71802-8 Paperback

This book is dedicated to all of the frontline workers who helped save our country during the time of pandemic crisis. Thank you to all of the doctors, nurses, grocery store workers, delivery drivers, and everyone who put their lives on the line to keep our country safe and to provide a sense of normalcy during times that were anything but normal.

Contents

Preface

The outbreak of COVID-19 caused our society to rethink the fundamental meaning of "work," and the extent to which employment has any physical boundaries. With literally hundreds of thousands of workers required suddenly to work from home, the perception of virtual employment radically changed overnight. Indeed, many employers that were previously strongly and openly opposed to allowing workers to perform their job duties outside a brick-and-mortar facility quickly required such work-at-home relationships. The law, which often takes decades to refine with respect to employment doctrine, could not keep pace with these changes. Indeed, in my vast experience in this field, I can recall no singular event that has had a quicker, more substantive impact on the workplace.

This text seeks to tackle some of the core issues now evolving in this area, focusing on how the law is struggling with a changing technological landscape. This work provides clarity and simplicity to this area, synthesizing the current case law, statutory rules, and academic literature to provide substantial guidance to workers and companies operating in the realm of the technology sector. While no work can provide an exhaustive review of all emerging issues in the platform-based economy, this text addresses the primary topics with which courts and businesses are currently grappling. In particular, this book examines closely the core definition of what it means to be an employee in this sector. The battle lines were drawn early on over this question, and the line between "employee" and "independent contractor" in the technology sector has created much consternation as the courts attempt to apply decades-old employment laws to workers now using highly advanced modern technologies. In addition, there is also confusion over how workers can attempt to vindicate their claims in the federal courts. Access to justice is a critical factor here, and workers must be able to actually bring viable claims against their places of business if the laws are to have any real meaning. Similarly, aggregation of claims often comes into question in this area. Many workers in the technology sector have had similar experiences with the same company and bring related employment claims in court. These workers must be able to band their claims together if they are to effectuate any meaningful change with their employers.

In this same vein, collective action is a critical area being discussed in the gig economy. It can be difficult for workers to unionize in the technology sector where there is often no physical place of business and where coworkers may never even meet one another. This book proposes an alternative arrangement – a "union light" – type approach that could be highly beneficial for both companies and workers in this evolving sector.

One other employment-related question that must be addressed in the technology sector is the high prevalence of harassment that occurs. This book looks squarely at that question, examining why this industry sees such a large number of sexual harassment claims. This work takes the next step of identifying possible solutions to this ongoing problem, or offering suggestions that can help alter these existing inappropriate behaviors.

The *virtual workplace* is no longer something from the world of science fiction and it is not limited to a select few employees or companies with tremendous resources. COVID-19 has forced the virtual workplace on almost all employees to a certain extent, as many job responsibilities have been moved online with workers performing their duties either at home or remotely. The employment laws in this area, which are already in need of updating, have struggled to keep up. This book takes this struggle head-on, identifying the areas where technology and traditional workplace laws collide, and explains the best way that the courts and litigants can now address these difficult and evolving questions.

Acknowledgments

I would like to thank the administration of the University of South Carolina School of Law for the tremendous support and assistance that made this book possible. In particular, I would like to thank Deans Robert M. Wilcox and William C. Hubbard for their incredible support during this process and for their extraordinary efforts in helping to promote this work.

This work was the result of a cumulative effort over the past decade, and the substantial research assistance and administrative help along the way were instrumental to its production. Much of the research and text in this book draw heavily from my prior work:

"The Discrimination Presumption," *Notre Dame Law Review* 94 (2019): 1115–60.

"Platform Pleading: Analyzing Employment Disputes in the Technology Sector," *Washington Law Review* 94 (2019): 1947–86.

"Harassment, Technology, and the Modern Worker," *Employee Rights and Employment Policy Journal* 23 (2019): 85–114.

"A Modern Union for the Modern Economy," *Fordham Law Review* 86 (2018): 1727–84 (with J. Hirsch).

"Tailoring Class Actions to the On-Demand Economy," *Ohio State Law Journal* 78 (2017): 21–72.

"Commonality and the Constitution: A Framework for Federal and State Court Class Actions," *Indiana Law Journal* 91 (2016): 455–92.

"Navigating the Uber Economy," *University of California at Davis Law Review* 49 (2016): 1511–46.

"The Issue Class," *Boston College Law Review* 56 (2015): 121–58.

"Weathering *Wal-Mart*," *Notre Dame Law Review* 89 (2014): 1343–82.

"Plausibility and Disparate Impact," *Hastings Law Journal* 64 (2012): 287–324.

"Plausibility beyond the Complaint," *William & Mary Law Review* 53 (2012): 987–1038.

"After *Iqbal*," *Wake Forest Law Review* 45 (2010): 179–230.

"Pleading Disability," *Boston College Law Review* 51 (2010): 95–150.

"The Trouble with *Twombly*: A Proposed Pleading Standard for Employment Discrimination Cases," *University of Illinois Law Review* 2009 (2009): 1011–60.

A very special thanks to my two coauthors on pieces that are relied upon heavily in this text, Ben Means and Jeff Hirsch, who are both prolific scholars. My work generally, and this book specifically, benefited tremendously from the research and drafting efforts of Megan Clemency, Elliot Condon, Axton Crolley, Chelsea Evans, Arden Lowndes, Elizabeth McCann, Michael Parente, Adair Patterson, Kelsey Poorman, Emily Rummel, Sarah Specter, Christopher Trusk, Colton Tully-Doyle, Matthew Turk, Erin Waldron, Mary Skahan Willis, and Grant Wills. Similarly, the editing and production of this book were greatly enhanced by Rachel Ford, Shannon Palmore, and Carol Young. This book would not have been possible without the tremendous efforts of Vanessa L. McQuinn and Inge Kutt Lewis. The author would also like to acknowledge the generous assistance of The Honorable Mark W. Bennett, Joe Cecil, Miriam Cherry, Lisa Eichhorn, Cynthia Estlund, James Flanagan, Timothy Glynn, Benjamin Gutman, Susan Kuo, Jocelyn Larkin, Jeffrey Pagano, Sanjukta Paul, Thomas Rutledge, Megan Seiner, Charles Sullivan, Suja Thomas, Daniel Vail and the late Michael Zimmer.

Finally, the author would like to specifically thank Cambridge University Press for their assistance in the production of this book. This work also draws heavily from my prior book with Cambridge University Press, *The Supreme Court's New Workplace* (2017).

Thanks to everyone who made this book possible!

1

Introduction

Technological progress has merely provided us with more efficient means for going backwards.

—Aldous Huxley, *Ends and Means*[1]

Workplace law has undergone a complete transformation in light of COVID-19. Forced to move many operations out of traditional brick-and-mortar facilities, many places of business now at least partially rely on workers to perform their job duties at home. Though the onset of the virus accelerated the degree to which many of us are now a part of the virtual workplace, the truth is that this virtual economy was quickly evolving over the last several years, long before the pandemic. Platform-based workers, in particular, have seen a marked increase in employment as a new on-demand economy has emerged. Virtual work and the gig economy are rewriting the employment rules, and the courts and legislatures are struggling to keep up.

From the early concepts of rugged individualism through the industrial revolution in more modern times, the United States was built on a fundamental notion of hard work and personal success and achievement. Since the inception of our country, we have seen tremendous economic growth in widespread areas. From farming to mining to the inception of the automotive industry, different sectors of the economy have grown at different periods in our nation's history. One thing that has remained constant, despite the ebb and flow of particular sectors, has been the concept of work itself.

Working in the traditional sense has until quite recently meant showing up in an office building, working a farm, or transporting goods on the road, among other varied possibilities. The constant of working has typically involved a physical location where an individual arrived each day to accomplish tasks in an assigned place of employment. Obviously, this conceptualization of the workplace is overgeneralized, but the traditional brick-and-mortar facility where individuals spent much of their day has become well-ingrained in our culture. Beyond this, even the traditional working hours – 9 am to 5 pm – have become commonplace. Individuals have always worked at other times and in varying ways, but the basic norm of showing up to the office to work a 9-to-5 job has dominated the traditional definition of what working actually means in our society.

This definition of work has experienced a massive transformation over the last few years. The on-demand economy, as part of the technology sector, has made it far easier for workers to perform their job tasks in a more flexible way and in more varied locations. The unprecedented amount of flexibility in this sector can be seen as an overwhelming benefit to individual workers, providing employment to those who might not otherwise have been able to enter the workforce. Through the use of different platform technologies, workers are now able to work where they want and how often they desire. Workers are free to use these platform-based jobs as a means of full employment or simply to supplement other income.

Take, for example, the often-discussed technology company Uber, a platform-based transportation business that will be at the center of much of the analysis in this book. While thousands of individuals work for Uber around the world, there is not a set physical location that these drivers go to each day to interact. Similarly, individuals now deliver food for services such as DoorDash and GrubHub, and other online apps provide customers access to childcare, lawn services, or help around the house. All of this work is performed without employees interacting with one another, or beginning/ending their day at a brick-and-mortar type facility.

And yet, when most employment laws were established, such varied, flexible working relationships were not anticipated. Indeed, many of the rules and regulations that we identify as forming the basis of employment law were developed in the wake of the Great Depression. At the time, the imbalance of power between businesses and workers was stark, as employees often felt extremely fortunate to have any employment at all. Having a job meant not being destitute, and having the opportunity to provide for the basic needs of self and family. At the time, workers were in no position to bargain with their company for greater benefits, higher pay, or better working conditions.

The federal government stepped in to help balance this power inequality in the working relationship in several different ways. For example, the National Labor Relations Act (NLRA) provided workers with the ability to engage in collective activity. For the first time, under the NLRA, workers could organize and form unions to bargain over better pay and working conditions without fear of reprisal from their employers. Similarly, the Fair Labor Standards Act

(FLSA) was established to provide workers with a basic guaranteed federal minimum hourly wage. The FLSA also established a right to overtime pay that would help spread work out among a greater number of workers. And, the statute put strict regulations on any type of unlawful child labor.

The Civil Rights Movements in the 1960s saw further protections provided to workers. Indeed, Title VII of the Civil Rights Act of 1964 prohibits discrimination in employment on the basis of race, color, sex, national origin, and religion. Subsequent federal laws would also include age and disability as protected classes. And, under the Family and Medical Leave Act, workers would get the right to unpaid leave to take care of themselves, a newborn child, or an immediate family member suffering from an illness or requiring medical care.

The foundations of our employment laws were thus largely established decades ago, and were put in place in a much different social culture and under a much different concept of "work" than what we have today. Brick-and-mortar physical places of work were common, and many laws were often premised on the notion of the male as primary "breadwinner." There has been substantial fluidity over time as to how we have defined work, and diversity in employment has fortunately continued to grow, further redefining our concept of employment.

Image Credit: PeopleImages/Getty Images

The advent of technological advancements and the platform-based economy has presented workers – and the law – with unique challenges. More specifically, and somewhat ironically, the law has struggled with whether platform-based workers even satisfy the definition of being "employees." Without employment status, these workers are not entitled to any of the wage–hour protections, prohibitions against discrimination, or right-to-leave benefits identified above. When these definitions of employment were originally promulgated, the on-demand economy was never even anticipated, and modern technology has pushed the boundaries of what it means to be an employee. There has been a tremendous amount of litigation over this exact question, and the courts have approached the answer in varying ways. This book theorizes a new approach to the question, with a particular emphasis on the issue of flexibility in defining work. This book provides a model that both employers and workers can use to define employment in this new economy, and articulates a clear framework for navigating this threshold inquiry.

Additionally, this text examines some of the complexities involved in pursuing technology-based litigation in the federal courts. This book explores how the Supreme Court has made it increasingly difficult to bring viable employment-based claims in any context. Navigating that case law, along with other precedent in the federal courts, this text explains the best approach to bringing employment-based claims in the platform economy.

Similarly, the Supreme Court has made it far more difficult to aggregate workplace claims. As much of the litigation in this area (e.g., Uber wage/hour claims) centers around workers who perform similar or identical tasks, the technology field is particularly unique in producing claims that seem fitted for class-action status. This text explores a number of the systemic claims that have already been brought in the platform-based economy, and explains the best ways that litigants can situate these claims within the existing case law.

Another area where workers have encountered difficulty in the on-demand economy is in acting collectively. With their employment status in doubt, and without a physical work location in which to gather, platform workers face an uphill battle in having their voices heard within a business. Some companies have explored ways of interacting with technology-based workers (a sort of union-light model), as businesses themselves have a strong interest in understanding the concerns and demands of their workers. This text navigates the NLRA in the context of the on-demand economy, explaining the approaches that can be used for workers to act in a concerted manner.

Finally, the technology sector has seen widespread sex discrimination and issues involving sexual harassment. In the final chapter, this book examines why the technology sector has a strong history of sex discrimination, and looks at some of the recent instances of harassment in this economy. This book addresses different ways that companies and employees can work together to help prevent this type of harassment and minimize the sex discrimination that has been so prevalent in this industry.

This book cannot explore all of the various issues that the evolving technology and platform-based economy will face over the coming years. The new ways in which this industry continues to redefine work will have far-reaching impacts across this economy. By examining some of the more critical and emerging issues facing this industry – defining employment, litigating claims, aggregating cases, and preventing harassment – this book takes on some of the more high-profile instances where the law has not kept pace in this growing area. The book should also serve as a way to spark a more robust debate over the general question of how the law should address working in the evolving technology sector.

NOTE

1 Aldous Huxley, *Ends and Means* (New York: Harper & Brothers Publishers, 1937).

2

Who Is an Employee?

The Machine does not isolate man from the great problems of nature, but plunges him more deeply into them.

—Antoine de Saint-Exupéry[1]

The pandemic has resulted in numerous and varying labor and employment law issues across all industries. Perhaps the most pressing and fundamental issue in technology-based workplace cases is the question of employment status and worker classification. More simply put, who is an "employee" in the eyes of the law, and which technology workers should be afforded statutory-based protections, continues to be a strongly debated issue. In the face of the virus, this categorization of workers has become even more amorphous, as the lines between work and home are more blurred, and it is now increasingly difficult for the law to differentiate between employees and independent contractors. As discussed in greater detail below, the key is for the courts to more fully consider the role of flexibility in making this determination.

In the most notable recent technology case to consider the employment status question, (former) drivers for ride-sharing companies Uber and Lyft brought lawsuits alleging that they were improperly classified as independent contractors and denied employment benefits. The companies countered that they do not employ drivers but instead license access to a platform that matches those who need rides with nearby available drivers.[2]

Image Credit: d3sign/Getty Images

These cases are not only critical for the ride-sharing giants but also for all on-demand workers who offer goods and services as varied as home cleaning, painting, running household errands, personal training, and apartment or home rentals. Employees often cost more than independent contractors because businesses are responsible for, among other things, payroll taxes, workers' compensation insurance, health care, minimum wage, overtime, and the reimbursement of business-related expenses. If burdened with those additional costs, the on-demand business model might not survive, at least not in its current form. At the same time, the importance of adequate protections for workers is not lessened simply because the workers' tasks are coordinated through a technology-based platform.

The current context is new, but the difficulty of classifying workers long predates the platform-based economy. More than seventy-five years ago, the Supreme Court concluded that "[f]ew problems in the law have given greater variety of application and conflict in results than the cases arising in the borderland between what is clearly an employer-employee relationship and what is clearly one of independent entrepreneurial dealing."[3] As "traditional" employment has lessened, borderline cases have increased; gone are the days when a typical worker spent a working lifetime in the employ of a single company. Unfortunately, existing laws fail to provide adequate guidance regarding the distinction between independent contractors and employees, especially when applied to the emerging working arrangements common in a technology-sector economy. Under the Fair Labor Standards Act and analogous state laws, courts consider several factors to assess the "economic reality" of a worker's alleged employment status, yet there is no concrete way to prioritize those factors.

This chapter argues that the classification of workers as independent contractors or employees should be shaped by an overarching question: How much flexibility do individuals have in determining the time, place, price, manner, and frequency of their work? Those who have more control of these variables are more independent than those who must conform to a business owner's schedule. This approach provides an objective basis for resolving classification disputes, particularly those that arise in the context of the technology-based economy. By minimizing legal uncertainty, a focus on worker flexibility would ensure both that workers receive appropriate protections under existing law and that companies are able to innovate without fear of unknown liabilities.

Other scholars have recommended more far-reaching changes to worker classification.[4] However, in light of the politically polarized debate surrounding employment law issues in general, and Uber in particular, a significant advantage of the approach recommended here is that its implementation would not require congressional intervention. Indeed, because worker flexibility clarifies the economic reality of employment arrangements in the platform-based economy, courts should already be required to consider it.

The goal of this chapter is practical: to clarify the framework for resolving worker-classification disputes, thereby saving judicial and litigant resources. It does not engage in generalizations regarding the overall status of workers in a technology-based economy, both because the inquiry is premature and because the law requires that each case be decided on its own merits. In this regard, this chapter recognizes that an individualized and detailed factual analysis is important and that classification disputes cannot be reduced to a single simple formula. Thus this chapter rejects any argument that workers in on-demand businesses are necessarily independent contractors because the businesses are merely technology platforms that take a portion of the transactions they facilitate. Uber and Lyft unquestionably rely on their drivers to generate revenue, and it seems disingenuous to pretend otherwise.

To be clear, when classifying workers, a focus on flexibility does not necessarily guarantee that workers in on-demand businesses will be considered independent contractors. Although greater worker flexibility may be a primary feature of the platform economy, taken as a whole, businesses should not be able to classify their workers as independent contractors unless those workers, in fact, enjoy meaningful flexibility as part of their working experience. For example, if a company such as Uber licenses vehicles to certain of its drivers, and if those drivers must work several hours a day to break even on the lease obligation, there is a strong argument that the drivers' flexibility in scheduling work is actually quite limited – suggesting that worker is an employee.

The chapter proceeds as follows. In Section 2.1, this chapter argues that the employment laws of the twentieth century were based on a fundamental premise: that the flexibility of at-will employment tends to benefit employers, who have the economic power to set terms their employees have little choice other than to accept. From the beginning, then, it has been important to ask whether, as a matter of economic reality, regulation is needed to protect the health, safety, and financial well-being of all workers.

Section 2.2 of this chapter focuses on the obvious threshold issue for application of most employment laws: the existence of an employment relationship itself. Using the FLSA and its broad and influential definition of "employment" as an example, Section 2.2 argues that the factors traditionally used to distinguish employees from independent contractors no longer fit the facts of an emerging economy in which hybrid-type working arrangements are increasingly common. Consequently, decisions in cases involving platform-based companies such as Uber and Lyft can appear arbitrary because the relevant factors conflict and could conceivably – and reasonably – support any result.

Section 2.3 of this chapter argues that a critical, usually overlooked factor for deciding whether a worker is an independent contractor or an employee is the flexibility the worker has in the employment relationship. By using the concept of worker flexibility to make better sense of an incomplete set of balancing factors, the approach suggested here would not only facilitate the resolution of classification disputes but it would also further the broader purposes of labor and employment law. In particular, worker flexibility offers a normatively attractive framework for identifying who is considered an employee in the platform-based economy because it requires us to consider who really benefits from the increased flexibility made possible by technological advances.

2.1 THE FLEXIBLE AND INFLEXIBLE NATURE OF AT-WILL EMPLOYMENT

The common-law principle of at-will employment offers flexibility that benefits both employers and workers. The employment relationship is voluntary and either side can terminate without cause at any time. Thus, in theory, salaries and benefits are generally set according to the supply and demand of the labor market.

This promise of the mutual benefit of flexibility should be immediately recognized by anyone who has followed the development of the platform-based economy. Advocates highlight the potential of technological innovation to relieve workers from the constraints of more traditional employment while, at the same time, promoting economic and corporate growth. However, this theory is premised on a number of assumptions. As this section discusses, it has long been recognized that an unregulated system did not produce mutually beneficial results; in reality, most workers were left with little choice but to accept the terms provided to them by their employers. Thus, this section maintains that the labor and employment laws enacted decades ago are best understood as responses to the problem of worker inflexibility. This background is important because laws from that time, including the FLSA, are critical in present-day disputes between workers and businesses such as Uber and Lyft.

2.1.1 *At-Will Employment and Economic Coercion*

Employment at-will is the overarching principle of the US labor markets, and it is equally intolerant of indentured servitude and entrenched labor rights. As employment is entirely voluntary, either party can terminate the employment relationship at any time, for any reason. At-will employment is, in principle, perfectly symmetrical; the right to terminate is equivalent to the right to leave one's job.

In theory, this symmetrical relationship benefits both capital and labor. For workers, at-will employment guarantees their ownership of their own labor and ensures their ability to sell that labor on the market for its highest value. Employers benefit as well because at-will employment allows them to hire and fire as the economy waxes and wanes, maximizing the economic efficiency of their business.

Although at-will employment has a formal symmetry, substantial inequality of economic power distorts the actual structure of labor markets. In many industries and occupations, workers simply lack any leverage to demand better terms:

> Typically, the worker as an individual has to accept the conditions which the employer offers. [T]he relation between an employer and an isolated employee or worker is typically a relation between a bearer of power and one who is not a bearer of power. In its inception it is an act of submission, in

its operation it is a condition of subordination, however much the submission and the subordination may be concealed by that indispensable figment of the legal mind known as the "contract of employment."[5]

In an at-will employment relationship, employees have no guaranteed job stability, and entire communities can be impacted if mass layoffs occur. Just by virtue of their ability to hire and fire, businesses have tremendous power over their employees. Although the flexibility afforded by at-will employment might seem to be a two-way street, it does not work that way in practicality. The flexibility runs mostly in one direction and, unless constrained by external factors, often produces employment agreements with (both formal and informal) one-sided terms.

2.1.2 At-Will Employment and Regulation

At first, courts refused to recognize a gap between workers' formal rights and the practical conditions affecting the exercise of those rights. Indeed, an early and well-known attempt to limit the number of hours that bakers could work in the state of New York famously found its way to the US Supreme Court in 1905.[6] In *Lochner v. New York*, the Court held that the maximum-hours limitation at issue was unconstitutional as it infringed on the contractual liberty interests of employers and employees.[7] The Court's judgment regarding the constitutionality of the regulation seems to have been influenced by its policy view that paternalism was inferior to contractual bargaining as a method for protecting workers; after all, who better than the workers to decide for themselves what working conditions were desirable? In subsequent years, the Court struck down many attempts at the state and federal levels to provide workers with mandatory wage and hour protections.[8] The so-called *Lochner* era is widely considered to have been a historic low point for many American workers.[9] By 1937, however, the Court had backed down in the face of pressure from President Franklin Roosevelt, including a threat to "pack" the Supreme Court with enough extra justices to uphold his New Deal legislation.[10] With the judicial impediment removed, post-*Lochner* legislation preserved the common-law principle of at-will employment while seeking to protect workers from the vulnerability of their economic circumstances.[11] Such legislation proceeded from the insight that when one party to a contract has far more power than the other, unlimited flexibility to strike any bargain can result in exploitation and oppression.

Federal law now provides mandatory protections for large groups of employees, including anti-discrimination law[12] and wage and benefit guarantees.[13]

Additional worker protections have also been adopted at state and local levels. Thus, society in the United States has determined that in some circumstances there should be limitations on an employer's ability to completely control the structure of the employment relationship.

Enacted in 1938, and amended over the years, the FLSA exemplifies the progressive determination to regulate at-will employment and continues to define many of the wage and hour protections that workers are entitled to receive.[14] The FLSA has three major components: It provides for a guaranteed federal minimum wage,[15] mandates premium pay (overtime) for non-exempt employees working over forty hours per week,[16] and restricts the use of child labor. The content of these protections still remains controversial, and battles are being waged now over the appropriate amount of the minimum wage, with many states and cities greatly departing from the federal standard.[17]

This section's objective is not to defend any particular set of worker protections but to show that such protections were motivated by a perception that employers had almost complete control over the lives of their workers and that workers had little or no practical flexibility, notwithstanding the formal autonomy guaranteed by at-will employment. It is important to appreciate the underlying purpose of labor and employment laws because, as discussed in the next section, the applicability of these provisions usually depends upon whether a worker should be classified as an independent contractor or an employee.

2.2 EMPLOYMENT STATUS DEFINED

Many labor and employment laws apply only to those who are classified as employees.[18] Often, the laws define the employment concept broadly. However, courts must still interpret statutory employment language in light of the preexisting common-law divide between independent contractors and employees. The factors relevant to the common-law analysis generally concerned the principal's vicarious liability for the conduct of agents, instead of the principal's obligations to those agents.

In a premodern economy, and even in common parlance, the meaning of employment would have been obvious in most circumstances:

> In 1848 one simply knew who were the proletarians. One knew because all the criteria – the relation to the means of production, manual character of labor, productive employment, poverty, and degradation – all coincided to provide a consistent image.[19]

The distinction between independent contractors and employees may still have been reasonably clear in the mid-twentieth century when many of today's employment laws were first enacted. However, the more modern context, characterized by multiple classes of skilled labor, unclear boundaries between capital and labor, and a reduction in the importance of the physical workplace, has made classifying workers increasingly difficult. The platform-based economy illustrates this problem because the workers may never even meet their true employers and often use their own capital; for example, the car used to provide rides for Uber or Lyft, or the apartment rented through Airbnb or Vrbo.

This section focuses on the FLSA because its definition of "employee" applies to the overwhelming majority of the American workforce. Section 2.2.1 explains that the factors used by courts to implement the FLSA's definition of employment are intended to determine whether a worker has economic independence or is more under the control of a particular business. Section 2.2.2 argues, however, that those factors are incomplete as stated and do not provide a reliable guide to classification disputes in on-demand businesses.

2.2.1 A *Multifactor Approach to Classifying Workers*

Under the FLSA's somewhat circular definition, an employee is "any individual employed by an employer."[20] The employment relationship covered by the statute is broad – to "[e]mploy includes to suffer or permit to work."[21] That language from the FLSA was drawn from existing state laws and designed to "reach businesses that used middlemen to illegally hire and supervise children."[22] Thus, the broad language of the FLSA suggests that Congress intended to prevent employers from manipulating the form of the working relationship in order to circumvent their responsibilities.

Over the years, the courts have developed a substantial body of law interpreting the FLSA's definition of employment in order to distinguish work done by independent contractors from work done by employees. In *Goldberg v. Whitaker House Cooperative*, the Supreme Court stated that the ultimate basis for classifying workers under the FLSA should be "economic reality" rather than a focus on "technical concepts."[23] The *Goldberg* Court concluded that where workers "are regimented under one organization, [doing] what the organization desires and receiving the compensation the organization dictates,"[24] they are employees under the FLSA. The *Goldberg* Court's characterization of economic reality needs updating; the worker-flexibility approach advocated in this chapter does just that. The more regimented the workplace, the more an individual is likely to be characterized as an employee. The more a worker retains flexibility as to the working relationship itself, the more that worker is likely to be characterized as an independent contractor.

Subsequently, courts have articulated several factors to assist in determining the economic reality of disputed working relationships. Specifically, the courts look to (1) the level of control the employer maintains over the worker; (2) the opportunity for profit or loss maintained by the worker in the business; (3) the amount of capital investment the worker puts into the process; (4) the degree of skill necessary to perform the job; (5) whether performance of the job is integral to the operation of the business; and (6) the permanency of the relationship between the worker and the employer.[25] Under this multifactor, evaluative approach, "employees are those who as a matter of economic reality are dependent upon the business to which they render service."[26] Yet, when the factors conflict, courts need guidelines for deciding which factors highlight the economic reality of the situation.

2.2.2 *Classifying Workers in the Platform-Based Economy*

In typical cases involving on-demand businesses, the traditional factors for assessing economic reality can be analyzed to establish that a worker is an independent contractor or, equally plausibly, that the worker is an employee. On the one hand, a worker may access work assignments via a smartphone app (an instrumentality of the business) and will, as a condition of access, agree to abide by guidelines for how the work should be performed. The work may well be integral to the operation of the business. On the other hand, the working relationship may also be impermanent, involve no in-person interactions, and permit the worker to work whenever she wishes. Often the worker will bring her own equipment to the job: a computer for software development, a car for ride-sharing, or an apartment for vacation rental.

As evidenced by two class-action cases involving Uber and Lyft, respectively, the traditional factors alone cannot resolve classification disputes in the on-demand economy because the factors merely highlight what is already evident – that neither category neatly fits hybrid circumstances. The factors that courts have previously identified are potentially useful, but they lack an organizing framework. What is missing, then, is a higher-level conceptual analysis that would enable courts to adapt existing categories in a manner consistent with the economic reality of a platform-based economy. While the legal battles are still being fought on these questions, and the recent passage of a statewide proposition impacts these workers in California, these court decisions remain quite instructive.

In *O'Connor* v. *Uber Technologies, Inc.*,[27] the court rejected Uber's motion for summary judgment and concluded that whether Uber's drivers are employees or independent contractors under California's Labor Code was a mixed question of law and fact that would have to be decided at trial.[28] Although Uber characterized itself as a "technology company" rather than a "transportation company,"[29] a point strongly contested by the plaintiffs, many of the basic facts were not in dispute. Essentially, Uber matched those who needed rides with available drivers through a smartphone application. The company set the fare for each ride and processed payments from passengers, reserving a percentage for itself. To become an Uber driver, applicants were required to pass a screening process and background check, as well as a "city knowledge test."[30] There was also an interview process, after which successful applicants had to sign a contract with Uber (or a subsidiary) indicating that they were purely independent contractors – there was no employment relationship.

Image Credit: FangXiaNuo/Getty Images

The parties disagreed principally regarding the amount of control Uber has over its drivers. Uber argued that it lacked control because it simply provided a software platform for independent contractors who used their own vehicles, set their own schedules, and operated with very little supervision. The plaintiffs disputed those characterizations and maintained that Uber marketed itself as a transportation company, selected its drivers, monitored their performance (largely through customer ratings), and disciplined individuals who failed to meet company standards.

Under California law at the time, which closely resembled the FLSA, the classification of workers as employees or independent contractors required consideration of several factors.[31] The *O'Connor* court noted the importance of control, but also a number of other factors quite similar to the FLSA test: the types of services performed, whether the work was done at the direction and supervision of the company, the amount of skill required to perform the job, who supplied the instrumentalities of the job, the length of time that the services were rendered, the method of payment, whether the work was a "regular" part of what the company does, and whether the parties intended to create an employment relationship.[32]

While the court was skeptical as to whether those factors ought to control the classification of workers in a modern "sharing economy," it was nevertheless bound to apply existing law and concluded that there was a mixed question of law and fact that could not be resolved before trial.[33] The court rejected Uber's argument that it was merely a "technology company" and held that it was "most certainly a transportation company, albeit a technologically sophisticated one."[34] Thus, the work performed by the drivers was for Uber, and the question of classification could not be avoided. It is thus notable that the federal judge expressed significant doubts about whether that answer to the worker classification question could possibly be satisfactory when premised upon an "outmoded" analysis:

> The application of the traditional test of employment – a test which evolved under an economic model very different from the new "sharing economy" – to Uber's business model creates significant challenges. Arguably, many of the factors in that test appear outmoded in this context. Other factors, which might arguably be reflective of the current economic realities (such as the proportion of revenues generated and shared by the respective parties, their relative bargaining power, and the range of alternatives available to each), are not expressly encompassed by the Borello test. It may be that the legislature or appellate courts may eventually refine or revise that test in the context of the new economy. It is conceivable that the legislature would enact rules particular to the new so-called "sharing economy." Until then, this Court is tasked with applying the traditional multifactor test of Borello.[35]

In *Cotter v. Lyft, Inc.*,[36] issued on the same day as the *O'Connor* decision involving Uber, the court rejected Lyft's motion for summary judgment regarding the classification of its drivers under California law at the time. Like Uber, Lyft uses a smartphone application that matches drivers with individuals in need of transport. The company initially provided a guide for drivers to follow when addressing passengers, which was subsequently replaced by a "frequently asked questions" section placed on its website. The company further reserved the right to investigate workers and ultimately terminate them "at any time, for any or no reason, without explanation."[37] Drivers typically selected their work schedule by either submitting requests in advance with the company or logging onto a website to reserve available hours.

Given these facts, drivers might plausibly be placed in either category. The court observed that "[a]t first glance, Lyft drivers don't seem much like employees," then added, "[b]ut Lyft drivers don't seem much like independent contractors either." The court noted the amount of control exerted by the company over the drivers, including its detailed guidelines concerning how drivers were to perform their job. Also, the company reserved "a broad right to terminate drivers for cause" or for no reason at all.[38] Thus, in some respects, the Lyft drivers appeared to be employees.

Yet, in other respects, the drivers looked like independent contractors. As in *O'Connor*, the drivers provided their own vehicles and chose their own work schedules. Ultimately, although most of the relevant facts were not in serious dispute, the court could not decide as a matter of law which classification was appropriate. Accordingly, just like the court in *O'Connor*, the *Cotter* court decided that the case should proceed to a jury on the question of whether Lyft drivers were employees or independent contractors.[39] However, as the court understood, committing the question for jury determination was simply an admission that the law provides no clear answer:

> As should now be clear, the jury in this case will be handed a square peg and asked to choose between two round holes. The test the California courts have developed over the 20th Century for classifying workers isn't very helpful in addressing this 21st Century problem.... But absent legislative intervention California's outmoded test for classifying workers will apply in cases like this.[40]

These two cases illustrate the need to clarify the basis for distinguishing independent contractors and employees under the law.

And the problems of worker classification are not limited to technology-based businesses. In a case involving the classification of workers who picked cucumbers, Judge Easterbrook authored a separate opinion arguing that it is absurd to decide the economic reality of a worker's classification through a multifactor balancing test: "My colleagues' balancing approach is the prevailing method, which they apply carefully. But it is unsatisfactory both because it offers little guidance for future cases and because any balancing test begs questions about which aspects of 'economic reality' matter, and why."[41]

If the multifactor analysis of worker classification is unpredictable, even when applied to farm workers, it is even more difficult to apply to cases involving on-demand businesses. The essential problem in any context in which the classification question is at issue is that the concept of economic reality has no clear meaning. Assuming that all of the factors identified by the courts are potentially relevant, they still do not all point to the same result. The lack of guidance in the area creates uncertainty and strains judicial resources, creating an expensive litigation process. By leaving open the possibility of punitive damages for misclassifications, pursued through class-action litigation as in the *O'Connor* and *Cotter* cases, the current climate of uncertainty threatens to diminish what has become a vibrant and emerging part of the economy.

Section 2.3 argues that worker flexibility will often be essential to understanding the economic reality of a worker's status and, therefore, the worker's classification as an independent contractor or an employee. In many cases, it may be that workers should be classified as employees to serve the remedial purposes of the current labor and employment laws. However, any such determinations should be based on the specific facts of the case involved.

2.3 THE OVERLOOKED IMPORTANCE OF WORKER FLEXIBILITY

This section argues that, particularly in the platform-based economy, the current approach to examining whether a worker is an independent contractor or an employee has missed a critical, often dispositive question: How much flexibility does the individual have in the working relationship? The more flexible a worker's schedule is – and the more control a worker has over their daily routine – the more likely that individual is an independent contractor. By contrast, if an employer dictates the worker's schedule, the inflexibility of the worker's schedule would suggest an employment relationship.

Unlike many other proposals, the approach of this chapter would not require legislative change, let alone a complete revision of existing practice. The FLSA's definition of employment turns on the economic reality of the working relationship.[42] The factors courts have established to help answer that question "should not be applied in a mechanical fashion, but with an understanding that the factors are indicators of the broader concept of economic dependence."[43] Thus, if the concept of worker flexibility clarifies the economic independence of working relationships in the platform-based economy, courts are already required to consider it.

2.3.1 *The Importance of Worker Flexibility*

An assessment of the economic reality of a specific working relationship must recognize the enormous shift that has taken place from traditional, full-time employment to alternative, contingent work arrangements. According to the US Government Accountability Office, the contingent workforce (which includes part-time employees, self-employed workers, and others who fall outside the category of traditional full-time employment) is increasing and (as of 2010) amounts to over 40 percent of workers.[44] The higher percentage of contingent workers can be explained, in large part, by flexibility sought both by companies and by workers.

However, as was true of the flexibility offered by at-will employment rules, there is no certainty that the flexibility created through technological advances will be enjoyed equally by business and labor. Workers are in many ways more vulnerable and less secure in their income and do not, for those reasons, become more economically independent. If anything, they now have greater need of the protection of employment laws. Just as corporations have always used their ability to fire workers to set advantageous terms, businesses may now use their ability to access labor online, and to substitute workers at low cost, to insist upon more demanding working conditions and to reduce the flexibility that workers have to arrange their own schedules.

To more fully appreciate how flexibility affects the economic reality of a working relationship, it may be helpful to consider the negative impact technology can have. When a company exerts total control over its workers' schedules and uses just-in-time staffing software to deploy workers whenever algorithms suggest demand is likely to be highest, the loss of control workers experience over their own schedules should strongly suggest classifying those workers as employees eligible for all job, wage, and hour protections under the law. Workers who must make real-time adjustments to meet a business's scheduling demands have little or no opportunity to pursue other economic opportunities and may not even be able to manage basic requirements of their own lives.

A *New York Times* piece described the burden placed upon one Starbucks worker, a single parent, who "rarely learned her schedule more than three days before the start of a workweek, plunging her into urgent logistical puzzles."[45] The lack of stability stalled her efforts to pursue a college degree part-time and to thereby achieve greater financial independence.[46] The worker described her situation as a loss of control: "'You're waiting on your job to control your life,' she said, with the scheduling software used by her employer dictating everything from 'how much sleep [my son] will get to what groceries I'll be able to buy this month.'"[47] Starbucks does not contest that its baristas are employees, but the example, more importantly, shows the critical nature of flexibility, or its absence. Not only does Starbucks train and supervise its baristas, its one-sided ability to control the working schedule demonstrates the company's power over the employment relationship.

Thus, worker flexibility is critical to understanding the nature and degree of the employer's control, a key factor under the existing FLSA standard and an important factor in many other tests for employment status. Worker flexibility, properly understood, is a way of evaluating existing factors; it is not a separate standard. For example, to the extent control is the measure of independence, flexibility is often the best evidence of control, particularly in a technology-based working relationship.

This book does not dispute that a worker may be employed regardless of whether she works at an office or from home. Minor flexibility in terms of when and where assigned tasks must be performed may be helpful for workers, but it is not the type of flexibility that should govern the classification analysis of workers in the platform-based economy. Rather, the argument is that when the worker has significant discretion to decide when to work, the worker has, as a matter of economic reality, a greater degree of independence than a worker who must comply with a schedule set by the employer. Whether that flexibility exists in any particular situation will require detailed analysis of the conditions surrounding the relationship, its duration, exclusivity, and the total number of hours worked.

This emphasis on flexibility has three significant policy advantages. First, and appropriate for a standard designed for the benefit of workers, it coincides with the expressed preferences of workers themselves. "Studies suggest that flexibility – no supervisors to answer to, working when you want rather than when the boss wants – is an important part of what attracts workers to companies like Uber."[48] Many employees are now demanding "[f]lexible schedules," a "[s]upportive environment," and "[t]ransparency" on the part of their employers.[49] This new workplace looks nothing like the employment model of the past.[50] Often, on-demand companies advertise flexibility as a benefit for their workers.

Second, a focus on flexibility coincides with a basic understanding of fairness. On the one hand, is a worker who performs tasks on an occasional basis, when and if the worker chooses to do so, really an employee and entitled to the full range of benefits under federal, state, and local law? On the other hand, is a worker who provides full-time services an independent contractor simply because the business formally acts as an intermediary between the worker and a client while taking care not to exert too much control over the work provided? In both cases, the answer should almost certainly be "no." Third, as discussed in Section 2.3.2, because flexibility may vary substantially from business to business and even for workers who operate within a single company, it offers a more nuanced basis for analysis and avoids placing all workers in the on-demand economy into one category or the other.

2.3.2 *Analyzing Worker Flexibility in the Platform-Based Economy*

Although flexibility is a defining characteristic of the platform-based economy, it is important to analyze who benefits from the flexibility. Those who work in this economy, and who may be characterized as independent contractors, may nevertheless function as employees if they lack the flexibility to set their own schedules. Workers who must show up for work when the employer directs them to do so are not, in a very important way, independent. In most cases, on-demand businesses will allege that their workers do have significant flexibility, but courts can and should go beyond these broad generalizations to assure that actual practice matches up with the purported flexibility.

In this regard, consider Amazon's Mechanical Turk platform (MTurk), which matched businesses with "an on-demand, scalable workforce."[51] According to MTurk, "[w]orkers select from thousands of tasks and work whenever it's convenient."[52] To the extent this broad mission statement was accurate, MTurk workers would appear to be independent and not properly classified as its employees. However, despite the apparent flexibility in schedule, one worker maintained that the reality was otherwise. Once an initial match had been made, no further flexibility was permitted:

> "These weren't just people working for five minutes, they were putting in hours and effort," Otey says of his time working for one Amazon Turk user, a company called CrowdFlower. "I didn't have control over the work I did. It was all done on their platform. I couldn't choose my own hours. I had to work when they provided the work. They pretty much controlled all the aspects of the work that was being offered."[53]

MTurk might object that it simply made the match and was not responsible for the hours assigned by the client for whom Otey had agreed to provide services. On the other hand, the FLSA's definition of employment is broad and includes situations where the employer "suffer[s]" or "permit[s]" the employee to work.[54] Given that the original purpose of this language was to capture child labor provided by an intermediary,[55] it seems potentially applicable to employment arrangements established in a platform-based economy. Even if many other people who signed up to provide services using the MTurk site had more control over their own time, consistent with MTurk's own stated emphasis on convenience, and might properly be classified as independent contractors, a fact finder might still properly conclude that Otey was an employee. Thus, a focus on flexibility helps to guide the analysis, helping fact finders to make reasoned judgments in specific cases.

Other platform-based businesses, such as Upwork and TaskRabbit, followed a similar model. Potential clients posted a job request to the website and were matched with workers (whether described as "freelancers" or "taskrabbits") who could handle the job. Upwork, for instance, focused on computer-based projects, including ongoing "mobile programming" and "graphic design."[56]

Upwork's payment system contemplated the processing of hourly fees on a weekly basis or else payments when agreed-upon milestones had been reached.[57] The company established no maximum number of hours or any other limits that would prevent a client from establishing a permanent working relationship, either with an Upwork freelancer or team of freelancers, in which the client assigned tasks and specified when and how they must be completed. Again, the freelance model Upwork established did not preclude a conclusion in a specific case that a freelancer should be characterized as an employee. Rather, that analysis depended on the particular agreement of the client and the freelancer.

The overall flexibility of the workforce supports the conclusion that many workers in the platform-based economy are independent contractors. For example, someone signed up as a driver on the Uber or Lyft platforms may have other full-time employment and drive only limited hours or when the opportunity arises. To the extent Uber and Lyft accommodate drivers' schedules, the flexibility of the relationship should weigh in favor of a finding that the drivers are independent contractors. Indeed, many, if not most, Uber and Lyft drivers may fall in this category. By contrast, FedEx drivers who work regular schedules seem to fall within the employment category, regardless of whether FedEx attempts to create an independent contractor relationship.

Thus, the facts of each case must be closely considered and formal freedom may conceal hidden constraints. Whether Uber's control over its pricing and its communications with drivers infringed upon the drivers' flexibility in the working relationship is a question of fact. Although some drivers may have felt pressure to comply with Uber's requests, Uber may respond that its communications simply reflected market demand and that drivers always remained free to set their own schedule.

Even without a set schedule or other direct indicators of control, the context of the particular situation may support a finding that a worker lacks flexibility in the relationship. For example, drivers who lease vehicles through Uber or one of its partners may need to work steadily just to break even. Although Uber might respond that such a voluntarily assumed obligation is not coercive, the issue is not whether the worker entered the working relationship voluntarily but whether, having done so, the worker retains meaningful flexibility. In this way, a finder of fact might consider total hours worked as a factor in determining whether a particular worker was, as a matter of economic reality, an employee of a business. The more a worker depends on a single employer for her livelihood, the more likely it is that the employer will have the ability to exert significant control over the time, place, price, frequency, and manner of the work.

Without the ability to undertake individualized analysis of work relationships in the platform-based economy, there is a risk that courts will make arbitrary decisions based on factors that could easily support any conclusion. Or, even worse, that decisions will flow from preconceived ideas regarding the on-demand economy as a whole rather than the facts of specific cases. In an apparent example of the latter danger, the California Department of Labor ruled against Uber in a case involving the classification of a driver who alleged she was an employee, not an independent contractor.[58] While legal battles are still being fought in the state, this decision remains instructive. The department's decision properly noted Uber's position that it exerted no control over the hours worked or geographical location of its "Transportation Providers" and that it did not require a minimum number of rides.[59] However, the department's subsequent legal analysis largely ignored Uber's argument.

Instead, the department relied on a factor set forth by the California Supreme Court for distinguishing independent contractors and employees: "Whether the person performing services is engaged in an occupation or business distinct from that of the principal."[60] When the worker's business is not distinct, the worker is more likely to be an employee.[61] (The same is true under the FLSA.[62]) Further, the department found that "Plaintiff's work was integral to Defendants' business. Defendants are in business to provide transportation services to passengers. Plaintiff did the actual transporting of those passengers. Without drivers such as Plaintiff, Defendants' business would not exist."[63] To reinforce its conclusion, the department noted that Uber also exercised control over the relationship by vetting its drivers, setting standards for drivers to follow, and reserving sole power to set the amount of payment for rides.[64]

Whether or not the plaintiff should have been classified as an employee, based upon the particular facts of her dispute with Uber (while legal battles are still being fought, subsequent California state law now largely defines such workers as employees, though the recent passage of a statewide proposition likely changes this), the department's analysis was overbroad and, taken to its logical conclusion, would effectively eliminate independent contractor status in the context of platform-based businesses. A business that uses technology to match supply and demand, whether for car rides, cleaning services, or computer programming, could not exist without people to provide those services. This context should be the starting point for analysis and certainly not the end of the analysis. The general nature of a given platform does not determine whether particular persons who contribute services are independent contractors or employees.

On the other hand, while it might be possible to argue that a platform-based business is nothing more than the creation and implementation of intermediating technology, such a distinction seems highly questionable. Without the contemplated services, whatever they might be, the technology would have no purpose. Moreover, the on-demand business may intervene heavily to structure the supposedly neutral market it facilitates. In order to properly address the classification of workers in the on-demand economy, we should seek to clearly understand how the market actually functions and what role the workers play in specific situations.

2.4 CONCLUSION

This chapter has argued that it would eliminate considerable confusion regarding the classification of workers in the virtual and platform-based economy by recognizing that the central inquiry, at bottom, is quite simple: Were the workers truly free to choose the time, place, price, frequency, and manner of the work? This is an inquiry that can only be answered on a case-by-case basis, but worker flexibility provides an objective basis for deciding classification disputes consistent with the goals that have always engulfed employment law.

Ultimately, though, it may be that clarifying existing law is not sufficient to protect workers in a changing economy in which the distance-bridging possibilities of technology are reducing the role of the firm and of traditional employment. Perhaps laws that regulate at-will employment will need to be rethought in light of technological innovations that provide greater flexibility for those who are able to capture technology's economic potential but threaten to leave vulnerable workers with even less control over their own schedules. Some believe that such worries are overdrawn or at least premature. Other commentators see evidence that a shift has already occurred, arguing that the issue of worker classification is "the most fundamental labor issue of the digital economy: whether those who work for massive digital platforms deserve the protection of employment, or can be treated as mere 'independent contractors' bereft of traditional labor protections."[65] While these issues are beyond the scope of the present book, the worker-flexibility framework discussed in this chapter can be used to evaluate the implications of changes in the structure of the employment market and to design new protections to meet new challenges.[66]

If we have learned anything after the COVID-19 outbreak, it is that we must be flexible in how we conceptualize "employment" in the face of a pandemic. Worker duties, reliance on technology, and the physical location of work all changed overnight. Yet those workers who were employees before the virus outbreak should still keep that same status after. In the same way, we must take a similar, broad, flexible approach to defining and classifying *all* workers in the technology sector.

NOTES

This chapter draws heavily from Benjamin Means and Joseph Seiner, "Navigating the Uber Economy," *University of California Davis Law Review* 49 (2016): 1511–46 and from Joseph A. Seiner, *The Supreme Court's New Workplace* (New York: Cambridge University Press, 2017). A very special thanks to Professor Means for his superb work on the UC Davis piece.

1 Peter Asmus, *Reaping the Wind: How Mechanical Wizards, Visionaries, and Profiteers Helped Shape Our Energy Future* (Washington, DC: Island Press, 2000).

2 *Cotter v. Lyft, Inc.*, 60 F. Supp. 3d 1067, 1070 (N.D. Cal. 2015) (order denying summary judgment); *O'Connor v. Uber Techs., Inc.*, 82 F. Supp. 3d 1133, 1135–38 (N.D. Cal. 2015) (order denying summary judgment).

3 *NLRB v. Hearst Publ'ns, Inc.*, 322 U.S. 111, 121 (1944), *superseded by statute*, Social Security Act of 1948, ch. 468, § 2(a), 62 Stat. 438, 438 (1948), *as recognized in Nationwide Mut. Ins. Co. v. Darden*, 503 U.S. 318 (1992).

4 E.g., Matthew T. Bodie, "Participation as a Theory of Employment," *Notre Dame Law Review* 89 (2013): 665–66, 704–07 (recommending a participation-based analysis); Jeffrey M. Hirsch, "Employee or Entrepreneur?," *Washington and Lee Law Review* 68 (2011): 353, 363–64 (advocating a "fundamental change in the definition of employee" under the National Labor Relations Act while admitting that this amounts to "wishful thinking"); Lewis L. Maltby and David C. Yamada, "Beyond 'Economic Realities': The Case for Amending Federal Employment Discrimination Laws to Include Independent Contractors," *Boston College Law Review* 38 (1997): 239, 242 (arguing that anti-discrimination law should include independent contractors).

5 Marc Linder, *The Employment Relationship in Anglo-American Law* (New York: Greenwood Press, 1989), 18 (quoting Otto Kahn-Freund, *Labor and the Law*, 2nd ed. [London: Stevens & Sons, 1977], 6).

6 *Lochner v. New York*, 198 U.S. 45, 46 (1905), *abrogation recognized in Ferguson v. Skrupa*, 372 U.S. 726 (1963).

7 See ibid., 52–53, 64.

8 See, e.g., *A.L.A. Schechter Poultry Corp. v. United States*, 295 U.S. 495 (1935) (invalidating several provisions of the National Industrial Recovery Act); Michal R. Belknap, "The New Deal and the Emergency Powers Doctrine," *Texas Law Review* 62 (1983): 67, 96–98 (discussing Supreme Court's invalidation of NIRA). Indeed, the Court invalidated many other regulations. See, e.g., *United States v. Butler*, 297 U.S. 1 (1936) (invalidating the AAA); *Panama Refining Corp. v. Ryan*, 293 U.S. 388 (1935) (striking down additional parts of the NIRA).

9 See, e.g., Seymour Moskowitz, "Save the Children: The Legal Abandonment of American Youth in the Workplace," *Akron Law Review* 43 (2010): 107, 132–42.

10 See Bruce Ackerman, *We the People, Vol. 2 Transformation* (Cambridge, MA: Belknap Press of Harvard University Press, 1998), 2:360–61.

11 See National Labor Relations Act, ch. 372, 49 Stat. 449 (1935) (codified as amended at 29 U.S.C. §§ 151–169 [2012]) (establishing the National Labor Relations Board);

Fair Labor Standards Act of 1938, ch. 676, 52 Stat. 1060 (codified as amended at 29 U.S.C. §§ 201–219 [2012]) (setting minimum wage, maximum hours, and minimum ages); William R. Corbett, "Waiting for the Labor Law of the Twenty-First Century: Everything Old Is New Again," *Berkeley Journal of Employment and Labor Law* 23 (2002): 259, 269–70.

12 See generally Joseph A. Seiner, "Weathering Wal-Mart," *Notre Dame Law Review* 89 (2014): 1343 (discussing intersection of employment discrimination and procedural law); Joseph A. Seiner, "Punitive Damages, Due Process, and Employment Discrimination," *Iowa Law Review* 97 (2012): 473 (same).

13 E.g., Fair Labor Standards Act of 1938, 29 U.S.C. § 206(a)(l)(C) (2012); Employee Retirement Income Security Act of 1974 (ERISA), Pub. L. No. 93-406, 88 Stat. 829 (1974). See generally Miriam A. Cherry, "Working for (Virtually) Minimum Wage: Applying the Fair Labor Standards Act in Cyberspace," *Alabama Law Review* 60 (2009): 1077.

14 See generally 29 U.S.C. § 202 (2012) (FLSA declaration of policy).

15 See Kevin J. Miller, Comment, "Welfare and the Minimum Wage: Are Workfare Participants 'Employees' under the Fair Labor Standards Act?," *University of Chicago Law Review* 66 (1999):183, 192–94 (discussing scope of minimum-wage provisions under FLSA).

16 29 U.S.C. § 207(a)(l) (2012).

17 *State Minimum Wage Laws* (Washington, DC: U.S. Department of Labour, 2020), www.dol.gov/agencies/whd/minimum-wage/state; Yuki Noguchi, "More States Raise Minimum Wage, but Debate Continues," *NPR*, January 1, 2015, 10:34 PM ET, www.npr.org/2015/01/01/374406071/more-states-raise-minimum-wage-but-debate-continues.

18 See Steven L. Willborn et al., *Employment Law: Cases and Materials*, 5th ed. (New Providence, NJ: LexisNexis, 2012), § 2(A) (discussing differences in treatment of independent contractors and employees).

19 Linder, *The Employment Relationship*, 19 (quoting Adam Przeworski, *Capitalism and Social Democracy* [Cambridge: Cambridge University Press, 1985], 56).

20 29 U.S.C. § 203(e)(1) (2012).

21 Ibid., § 203(g) (internal quotation marks omitted).

22 *Antenor v. D & S Farms*, 88 F.3d 925,929 n.5 (11th Cir. 1996).

23 *Goldberg v. Whitaker House Coop.*, 366 U.S. 28, 33 (1961) (internal quotation marks omitted).

24 Ibid., 32–33.

25 See *Sec'y of Labor v. Lauritzen*, 835 F.2d 1529, 1534–35 (7th Cir. 1987); see also *Rutherford Food Corp. v. McComb*, 331 U.S. 722, 730 (1947) (approving a factors-based approach). Other jurisdictions have developed alternate formulations. See, e.g., *Irizarry v. Catsimatidis*, 722 F.3d 99, 104–05 (2d Cir. 2013).

26 *Bartels v. Birmingham*, 332 U.S. 126, 130 (1947), *superseded by statute*, Act of June 14, 1948, ch. 468, § 2(a), 62 Stat. 438, 438. See generally Bodie, *Participation*, 684–88 (discussing economic realities test).

27 82 F. Supp. 3d 1133 (N.D. Cal. 2015) (order denying summary judgment).

28 Ibid., 1135.

29 Ibid., 1137 (internal quotation marks omitted).

30 Ibid., 1136–44 (internal quotation marks omitted).

31 See, e.g., CAL. LAB. CODE § 2750.5 (2016).

32 O'Connor, 82 F. Supp. 3d 1139 (citing S.G. Borello & Sons, Inc. v. Dep't of Indus. Relations [Borello], 769 P.2d 399, 404 [Cal. 1989] [en banc]).

33 O'Connor, 82 F. Supp. 3d 1153 (internal quotation marks omitted).

34 Ibid., 1140–45 (internal quotation marks omitted).

35 Ibid., 1153.

36 60 F. Supp. 3d 1067 (N.D. Cal. 2015) (order denying summary judgment).

37 Ibid., 1070–73 (internal quotation marks omitted).

38 Ibid., 1069, 1078–79.

39 Ibid., 1070.

40 Ibid., 1081–82.

41 Sec'y of Labor v. Lauritzen, 835 F.2d 1529, 1539 (7th Cir. 1987) (Easterbrook, J., concurring)

42 Goldberg v. Whitaker House Coop., 366 U.S. 28, 33 (1961).

43 Administrator's Interpretation No. 2015-1, 2.

44 Contingent Workforce: Size, Characteristics, Earnings, and Benefits (Washington, DC: US Government Accountability Office, GA0–15-168R, 2015), 1, 4, www.gao.gov/assets/670/669899.pdf. Lauren Weber, "New Data Spotlights Changes in the U.S. Workforce," Wall Street Journal, May 28, 2015, 10:56 AM ET, http://blogs.wsj.com/atwork/2015/05/28/new-data-spotlights-changes-in-the-u-s-workforce.

45 See Jodi Kantor, "Working Anything but 9 to 5," New York Times, August 13, 2014, www.nytimes.com/interactive/2014/08/13/us/starbucks-workers-scheduling-hours.html.

46 Ibid. (noting that the barista's "degree was on indefinite pause because her shifting hours left her unable to commit to classes").

47 Ibid.

48 James Surowiecki, "Gigs with Benefits," New Yorker, July 6, 2015.

49 See Jeanne Sahadi, "How Companies Are Changing Old Ways to Attract Young Workers," CNN Money, July 23, 2015, 3:45 PM ET, http://money.cnn.com/2015/07/23/pf/companies-millennial-workers.

50 See ibid.

51 "Mechanical Turk Is a Marketplace for Work," Amazon Mechanical Turk, www.mturk.com/mturk/welcome.

52 Ibid.

53 Sarah Kessler, "The Gig Economy Won't Last Because It's Being Sued to Death," Fast Company, February 17, 2015, 6:00 AM, www.fastcompany.com/3042248/the-gig-economy-wont-last-because-its-being-sued-to-death.

54 Fair Labor Standards Act, 29 U.S.C. § 203(g) (2012) ("'Employ' includes to suffer or permit to work"); see also Administrator's Interpretation No. 2015-1, 1–2.

55 See Antenor v. D & S Farms, 88 F.3d 925, 929 n.5 (11th Cir. 1996).

56 "Get the Job Done Right," *Upwork,* www.upwork.com/i/howitworks/client. TaskRabbit has a similar scheme. See "Become a Tasker," *Taskrabbit,* www.taskrabbit.com/become-a-tasker.

57 "Get the Job Done Right."

58 *Berwick v. Uber Techs., Inc.,* No. 11-46739 EK, 2015 WL 4153765, *6 (Cal. Dep't Labor June 3, 2015).

59 Ibid., *3.

60 Ibid., *4–6 (citing *S.G. Borello & Sons, Inc. v. Dep't of Indus. Relations (Borello),* 769 P.2d 399 [Cal. 1989] [en banc]).

61 Ibid., *5 (citing *Yellow Cab Coop. v. Workers' Comp. Appeals Bd.,* 277 Cal. Rptr. 434 [1991]).

62 See, e.g., *Lauritzen,* 835 F.2d 1537–38; *Donovan v. DialAmerica Mktg., Inc.,* 757 F.2d 1376, 1385 (3d Cir. 1985).

63 *Berwick,* 2015 WL 4153765, *6.

64 Ibid.

65 Trebor Scholz and Frank Pasquale, "Serfing the Web: On-Demand Workers Deserve a Place at the Table," *Nation,* July 16, 2015, www.thenation.com/article/serfing-the-web-on-demand-workers-deserve-a-place-at-the-table.

66 This chapter also benefited greatly from the scholarship and work of numerous other authors. See Bibliography.

3

Pleading Standards and the Technology Sector

Even the technology that promises to unite us, divides us. Each of us is now electronically connected to the globe, yet we feel utterly alone.
— Dan Brown, *Angels & Demons*[1]

Technology workers during the pandemic may have experienced discrimination on the basis of a protected characteristic such as race, color, national origin, sex, religion, age, or disability. As companies were forced to furlough – and sometimes terminate – workers in record numbers, it is entirely possible, if not likely, that some of these decisions were made pursuant to an unlawful basis. These aggrieved workers (just like technology workers before COVID-19) must successfully prove such claims to be entitled to relief and must carefully navigate our court system when attempting to do so.

Access to the courts remains a tremendous hurdle for all workplace plaintiffs. Given the complexities of platform-based employment, gig-sector workers face additional hurdles to bringing these claims. This chapter addresses how relatively recent Supreme Court case law has negatively impacted *all* workplace plaintiffs. It further addresses how the technology-sector worker can successfully address the obstacles identified here. Thus, this chapter sets the stage for pleading all employment discrimination claims, then moves on to specifically examine claims brought in the technology sector.

The plausibility standard created by the Supreme Court has established perhaps the most daunting pleading requirement for aggrieved workers. The Court's decision in *Ashcroft* v. *Iqbal*[2] extends the controversial holding of *Bell Atlantic Corp.* v. *Twombly*[3] – that a plaintiff's allegations must state a *plausible* claim to avoid dismissal – to *all* civil cases, including "antitrust and discrimination suits alike."[4] The *Iqbal* decision thus resolves the debate as to whether the *Twombly* plausibility standard is limited to the antitrust context where it arose, making clear that the standard applies to all civil matters, including employment-discrimination cases.[5] Indeed, recent research suggests that the plausibility test is already being used by some lower courts to dismiss workplace claims.[6]

The plausibility standard announced in *Twombly* and confirmed by *Iqbal* replaces the more relaxed test from *Conley* v. *Gibson*[7] that a complaint should not be dismissed "unless it appears beyond doubt that the plaintiff can prove no set of facts in support of his claim which would entitle him to relief."[8] This "no set of facts" language from *Conley* governed federal pleading for fifty years until the recent Supreme Court cases abrogated the decision and required plaintiffs to plead sufficient facts to state a *plausible* claim.[9] While *Twombly* and *Iqbal* significantly changed the pleading rules for all civil cases, these decisions provide little guidance regarding what must be alleged to sufficiently state a claim of employment discrimination brought pursuant to Title VII of the Civil Rights Act of 1964 (Title VII).[10]

Nevertheless, *Iqbal* does help clarify *Twombly* on the question of *intent* and explains that discriminatory intent cannot be alleged "generally" but must instead be alleged in the proper factual context. Similarly, *Iqbal* warns against making conclusory statements when attempting to allege that the defendant's discriminatory intent is plausible. *Iqbal* provides that plausibility "is not akin to a *probability* requirement, but it asks for more than a sheer *possibility* that a defendant has acted unlawfully."[11] This book attempts to pinpoint exactly where plausibility falls in that gray area between *possible* and *probable* when alleging discriminatory intent in an employment case brought pursuant to Title VII.

This chapter begins by explaining the pleading requirements of the Federal Rules of Civil Procedure. Next, this chapter explores how Supreme Court case law has shaped those rules, emphasizing the Court's recent decisions in *Twombly* and *Iqbal*. Then, this chapter outlines the results of numerous research studies that examine the current state of employment discrimination in our society. Building on this research, this book proposes a unified analytical framework for pleading intent in employment-discrimination claims brought under Title VII. The chapter then explains how the proposed pleading model comports with the federal rules, as interpreted by *Twombly* and *Iqbal*. The chapter further explores the best approach to pleading claims arising in the technology-sector context.

3.1 FEDERAL RULES OF CIVIL PROCEDURE

The pleading standards in federal employment-discrimination cases are governed by the same Federal Rules of Civil Procedure (FRCP) that apply to other civil causes of action. FRCP 12(b)(6) allows a defendant to move for the dismissal of a complaint for "failure to state a claim upon which relief can be granted."[12] To state a sufficient claim and avoid a 12(b)(6) dismissal, an employment-discrimination plaintiff must satisfy FRCP 8(a)(2), which requires a complaint to include "a short and plain statement of the claim showing that the pleader is entitled to relief."[13]

The sample pleading forms attached to the federal rules help clarify the pleading requirements by providing an example of a sufficient complaint. Form 11 thus provides the following example of an adequate allegation of negligence:

> On date, at place, *the defendant negligently drove a motor vehicle against the plaintiff.*[14]

These rules are therefore relatively straightforward. Pursuant to Rule 8, a complaint must provide a "short and plain statement of the claim."[15] According to the sample pleading form, this short and plain statement would include the date, place, and nature of the alleged violation, as well as the actor(s) involved.[16] If the complaint fails to allege these minimum requirements, the case is subject to dismissal.[17] Though the federal pleading rules are simple on their face, recent Supreme Court decisions have taken some of the certainty out of these seemingly clear-cut requirements.

3.2 SUPREME COURT CASES

3.2.1 *The History of Pleading and the Complaint*

Put simply, the pleading requirements of the FRCP establish a minimum threshold for what a litigant must allege to proceed with a civil claim. These rules thus set the bar for what a plaintiff must assert in a case if it is allowed to go forward. While the rules have established this threshold, the courts have interpreted the meaning of these rules. And the Supreme Court's view has changed over time.

Indeed, the pleading rules used in this country evolved over hundreds of years,[18] and borrowed heavily from English law.[19] While this book is not a historical text, it can be useful to examine the change in case law that brought the law to where it is today. Perhaps the most well-known Supreme Court pleading decision came in *Conley* v. *Gibson*, an opinion issued in 1957.[20]

Image Credit: benoitb/Getty Images

3.2.2 Conley v. Gibson

One of the earliest cases addressing the federal pleading requirements, *Conley* v. *Gibson*,[21] provided a straightforward standard for litigants to follow. In *Conley*, the Supreme Court addressed the sufficiency of a complaint alleging a civil rights violation. The Court noted that when considering a plaintiff's allegations, a court should apply "the accepted rule that a complaint should not be dismissed for failure to state a claim unless it appears beyond doubt that the plaintiff can prove *no set of facts* in support of his claim which would entitle him to relief."[22] In announcing this test, the Court emphasized that navigating the federal pleading rules was not meant to be "a game of skill in which one misstep by counsel may be decisive to the outcome" and that "the purpose of pleading is to facilitate a proper decision on the merits."[23]

Over the next five decades, the *Conley* "no set of facts" language became the relevant inquiry of any federal court addressing a 12(b)(6) motion to dismiss. During that time, a plaintiff's civil complaint was not subject to dismissal unless it was "beyond doubt" that the plaintiff would be unable to produce sufficient facts to support the viable allegations in the complaint.[24] This so-called notice-pleading standard placed a very minimal requirement on plaintiffs, who were only required to give the defendant basic notice of the claim.[25] This would all change, however, when the Supreme Court reassessed this standard fifty years later in *Bell Atlantic Corp. v. Twombly*.[26]

3.2.3 Swierkiewicz *v.* Sorema N.A.

Although it was decided prior to *Twombly*, *Swierkiewicz v. Sorema N.A.* provided the Supreme Court's best explanation of the pleading standards for employment-discrimination cases.[27] In *Swierkiewicz*, the Court considered a claim brought by a fifty-three-year-old native of Hungary who alleged that his employer had terminated him because of his race and age in violation of Title VII and the Age Discrimination in Employment Act of 1967 (ADEA). In upholding the plaintiff's complaint in the case, the Court concluded that an employment-discrimination litigant need not plead a prima facie case of discrimination to survive a motion to dismiss.[28] Under *McDonnell Douglas Corp. v. Green*,[29] a prima facie case of employment discrimination is established by showing that the plaintiff is part of a protected class, that the plaintiff is qualified for the position, that the plaintiff suffered an adverse employment action, and that there is other evidence giving rise to an inference of discrimination.[30] The Court emphasized that the *McDonnell Douglas* test is only "an evidentiary standard" and does not represent a "pleading requirement."[31]

The *Swierkiewicz* Court stated that under the notice-pleading framework of the federal rules, it is too burdensome to require a plaintiff to plead all of the facts establishing a *McDonnell Douglas* prima facie case, particularly when the *McDonnell Douglas* test is not even applicable to every case involving discrimination.[32] And, as discovery often "unearth[s] relevant facts and evidence," the prima facie case should be flexible and "not . . . transposed into a rigid pleading standard for discrimination cases."[33] The Court emphasized that under *Conley*, the plaintiff need only give the opposing party "fair notice of what the plaintiff's claim is and the grounds upon which it rests."[34] The Court further pointed out that under a notice-pleading framework, "liberal discovery rules and summary judgment motions" must be used "to define disputed facts and issues and to dispose of unmeritorious claims."[35] This system allows the parties to "focus litigation on the merits of a claim," and vague or unmeritorious claims can be addressed by the defendant through a motion for a definite statement or a motion for summary judgment.[36] Thus, *Swierkiewicz* emphasized that the liberal pleading standard set forth in *Conley* applies to employment-discrimination claims and that such suits are not subject to a "heightened pleading standard."[37]

3.2.4 Bell Atlantic Corp. v. Twombly

In *Bell Atlantic Corp. v. Twombly*, the Court reassessed the federal pleading requirements in a complex antitrust case brought under section 1 of the Sherman Act.[38] In *Twombly*, the plaintiffs alleged that several regional telephone companies had "conspired to restrain trade," which resulted in "inflat[ed] charges for local telephone and high-speed Internet services."[39] The purported conspiracy between the phone companies allegedly consisted of both improper "parallel conduct," which prohibited the development of potential competitors, and improper agreements by the companies not to compete with each other.

In addressing the plaintiffs' allegations, the Court noted that the "no set of facts" standard from *Conley* had often "been questioned, criticized, and explained away." Thus, as this language had been "puzzling the profession for 50 years, this famous observation has earned its retirement."[40] The *Conley* "no set of facts" language should therefore be "forgotten."[41] In place of the *Conley* standard, the Court imposed a "plausibility" requirement for pleading a federal claim.[42]

According to the Court, a plausible claim does "not require heightened fact pleading of specifics."[43] However, the plausibility standard "requires more than labels and conclusions, and a formulaic recitation of the elements of a cause of action will not do."[44] Therefore, to survive a motion to dismiss, the plaintiff must allege "enough facts to state a claim to relief that is plausible on its face."[45] In this regard, there must be sufficient facts set forth in the complaint "to raise a right to relief above the speculative level ... on the assumption that all the allegations in the complaint are true (even if doubtful in fact)."[46] In the case at issue, the plaintiffs had not sufficiently "nudged their claims across the line from conceivable to plausible," and the Court therefore dismissed the complaint.[47]

In *Twombly*, then, the Court moved away from the notice-pleading paradigm of *Conley* where the plaintiff was only required to give the defendant basic notice of the claim. In its place, the Court now specifically requires plaintiffs to *plead facts* in their complaints. Plaintiffs must set forth sufficient facts to state a plausible claim or face dismissal of the case.

Studies have already suggested that the *Twombly* plausibility standard has had a substantial impact in the civil rights and employment settings.[48] A higher percentage of federal district court opinions relying on *Twombly* have granted a motion to dismiss in the employment-discrimination context than those earlier decisions that relied on *Conley*.[49] This is true for cases brought under Title VII, which prohibits discrimination on the basis of race, color, religion, sex, or national origin,[50] as well as the Americans with Disabilities Act of 1990 (ADA), which prohibits disability discrimination.[51]

At one time, there was considerable debate as to whether the lower courts should even apply the *Twombly* standard to cases outside the antitrust setting where the case arose.[52] In *Ashcroft* v. *Iqbal*, the Supreme Court definitively resolved this debate and refused to limit the *Twombly* plausibility standard to Sherman Act cases.

3.2.5 Ashcroft v. Iqbal

In *Iqbal*, the Supreme Court reassessed the breadth of the plausibility standard that it had announced two years earlier in *Twombly*.[53] In the *Iqbal* case, Javaid Iqbal, a Muslim and Pakistani citizen, was arrested in the United States after September 11, 2001, on immigration-related charges. Because he was deemed to be "of high interest" to the ongoing investigation of the events of September 11th, Iqbal was housed in a maximum-security environment where he was held in lockdown for twenty-three hours a day. After pleading guilty to various criminal charges, Iqbal spent time in prison and was subsequently sent to Pakistan. In light of perceived constitutional violations during his confinement, Iqbal filed a *Bivens* action in federal court against various officials, including former Attorney General John Ashcroft and Robert Mueller, the director of the FBI. Iqbal alleged that Ashcroft and Mueller "adopted an unconstitutional policy" on the basis of race, religion, or national origin, which resulted in his being subjected to poor prison conditions. Specifically, the complaint alleged

> that petitioners designated respondent a person of high interest on account of his race, religion, or national origin, in contravention of the First and Fifth Amendments to the Constitution.... [T]he [FBI], under the direction of Defendant Mueller, arrested and detained thousands of Arab Muslim men ... as part of its investigation of the events of September 11.... [T]he policy of holding post-September-11th detainees in highly restrictive conditions of confinement until they were "cleared" by the FBI was approved by Defendants Ashcroft and Mueller in discussions in the weeks after September 11, 2001.... [P]etitioners "each knew of, condoned, and willfully and maliciously agreed to subject" respondent to harsh conditions of confinement "as a matter of policy, solely on account of [his] religion, race, and/or national origin and for no legitimate penological interest."[54]

Quoting *Conley*'s "no set of facts" language, the federal district court denied the defendants' motion to dismiss the case for failure to state a claim. While an appeal was pending, the Supreme Court issued its opinion in *Twombly* abrogating the *Conley* standard. Applying *Twombly*'s plausibility standard, the US Court of Appeals for the Second Circuit upheld the district court decision, finding that Iqbal's complaint sufficiently set forth the defendants' "personal involvement in discriminatory decisions which, if true, violated clearly established constitutional law."[55]

In considering the case, the Supreme Court initially determined that the district court properly had jurisdiction to consider the matter. The Court then discussed the elements of a successful *Bivens* claim, which, under the First and Fifth Amendments, requires the plaintiff to plead "that the defendant acted with discriminatory purpose."[56] Thus, Iqbal had to establish that the defendants put the questioned policies in place "not for a neutral, investigative reason but for the purpose of discriminating on account of race, religion or national origin."[57] Citing *Twombly*, the Court noted that the federal rules do not mandate "detailed factual allegations," but they do require "more than an unadorned, the-defendant-unlawfully-harmed-me accusation."[58] Therefore, a complaint will be held inadequate where it relies on "naked assertion[s]" that are "devoid of further factual enhancement."[59] The Court also reiterated the plausibility standard announced in *Twombly*, noting that a complaint is plausible where it includes sufficient facts to permit the court to make a "reasonable inference" that the defendant is responsible for the unlawful conduct.

In applying the *Twombly* standard to the case, the Court concluded that Iqbal's allegations had "'not nudged [his] claims' of invidious discrimination 'across the line from conceivable to plausible.'"[60] In particular, Iqbal's assertions regarding Mueller and Ashcroft's alleged involvement in the discriminatory policy were too "conclusory."[61] Thus, "the conclusory nature of respondent's allegations, rather than their extravagantly fanciful nature ... disentitles them to the presumption of truth."[62] Additionally, as the Court found that there was a nondiscriminatory explanation for the government's policies that were put in place after September 11th that was "more likely" than Iqbal's assertions, the plaintiff failed to plausibly state a claim for discrimination. In this regard, the arrests that the FBI director supervised were probably permissible and "justified by his nondiscriminatory intent to detain aliens who were illegally present in the United States and who had potential connections to those who committed terrorist acts."[63] The Court further concluded that there was nothing in the complaint that established that the defendants "housed detainees ... due to their race, religion, or national origin."[64] Rather, all the complaint suggested was that high-ranking officials, "in the aftermath of a devastating terrorist attack," attempted to house "suspected terrorists in the most secure conditions available."[65] Due to the inadequate and conclusory nature of his allegations, then, Iqbal's complaint failed to plausibly state a claim for discrimination and was rejected by the Court.

After rejecting the sufficiency of Iqbal's factual assertions in the complaint, the Court also addressed – and rejected – Iqbal's legal arguments. First, the Court refused to restrict the *Twombly* plausibility standard to antitrust claims. Rather, the Court concluded that this standard should apply to "all civil actions," including "antitrust and discrimination suits alike."[66] This significant holding firmly resolved considerable controversy over the issue of the breadth of the *Twombly* standard, and it is now clear that the plausibility test should apply to all civil claims.

Second, the Court rejected the plaintiff's argument that the FRCP 8 motion-to-dismiss standard should be "tempered" by a "careful case-management approach" to discovery utilized by the lower courts.[67] Thus, the plausibility standard should not be relaxed even where the lower courts assure the litigants "minimally intrusive discovery."[68] The Court found this particularly true in litigation involving government officials, as such officials must be able "to devote time to [their] duties," and litigation would present a "substantial diversion" from these efforts.[69]

Finally, the Court rejected Iqbal's argument that discriminatory intent can be alleged "generally."[70] The Court therefore found no merit in the argument that a complaint that alleges that a defendant discriminated against the plaintiff "on account of [his] religion, race, and/or national origin" is sufficient to survive a motion to dismiss.[71] In rejecting this argument, the Court noted that "the Federal Rules do not require courts to credit a complaint's conclusory statements without reference to its factual context."[72] The Court thus concluded that the FRCP did not permit Iqbal to allege the "bare elements" of his claim and still survive dismissal.[73] In sum, the Court rejected Iqbal's assertions that his complaint satisfied the pleading requirements of the federal rules, as it "fail[ed] to plead sufficient facts to state a claim for purposeful and unlawful discrimination."[74]

Justice Souter – joined by justices Stevens, Ginsburg, and Breyer – dissented from the majority opinion.[75] The dissent noted that at this early stage of the litigation, the allegations in the complaint must be taken as true, regardless of whether the allegations make the Court "skeptical." The dissent argued that if the allegations in the complaint were true, the defendants were at least "aware of the discriminatory policy being implemented and deliberately indifferent to it." And, because Iqbal's complaint contained several "allegations linking Ashcroft and Mueller to the discriminatory practices of their subordinates," the complaint satisfied the *Twombly* standard. The dissent therefore would have upheld the sufficiency of Iqbal's complaint, and these Justices found "no principled basis for the majority's disregard of the allegations linking Ashcroft and Mueller to their subordinates' discrimination."[76]

3.3 LESSONS FROM SUPREME COURT DECISIONS

The Supreme Court's decisions in *Twombly* and *Iqbal* have left the requirements for pleading intentional employment-discrimination claims in disarray, and the proposed pleading framework outlined in this book attempts to provide some clarity to this area of the law. The recent Supreme Court decisions took the clear, straightforward pleading standard set forth in *Conley* and replaced it with a much more amorphous plausibility requirement.[77] Despite the lack of clarity in its decisions, the Court's cases do provide some guidance that can be imported to employment-discrimination claims and the proposed pleading framework discussed in this book.

3.3.1 *Guidance from Decisions*

From *Swierkiewicz*, we know that an employment-discrimination plaintiff need not plead all of the elements of a prima facie case of discrimination. Thus, the plaintiff need not assert all of the components of the *McDonnell Douglas* framework in the complaint to sufficiently allege a claim of employment discrimination. Therefore, if *Swierkiewicz* is still good law, *something less* than a prima facie case of discrimination can be set forth in a Title VII complaint and still satisfy FRCP 8(a). *Twombly* provides some clarity on what that "something less" is; specifically, a plaintiff must set forth sufficient facts in the complaint to state a *plausible* claim of discrimination. Plausibility does not "require heightened fact pleading of specifics"; however, there must be sufficient facts set forth in a Title VII complaint to make it more than simply "speculative."[78] Thus, *Twombly* teaches us that an employment-discrimination plaintiff cannot rely on a conclusory, "formulaic recitation" of the basic components of a Title VII case.[79]

Twombly makes clear that a Title VII plaintiff must allege sufficient facts to state a plausible claim, and *Iqbal* confirms this standard. Indeed, *Iqbal* resolves any doubt that the plausibility standard extends beyond Sherman Act cases, as the standard is applicable to "all civil actions," including "antitrust and discrimination suits alike."[80] *Iqbal* provides that conclusory, "naked assertion [s]" and "unadorned, the-defendant-unlawfully-harmed-me accusation[s]" must fail.[81] And, perhaps most importantly, *Iqbal* offers some guidance on pleading discriminatory intent, which cannot be alleged "generally."[82] Thus, conclusory statements regarding intent will not suffice, and an allegation of discriminatory intent must be considered with "reference to its factual context."[83] In sum, *Iqbal* confirms the validity of the plausibility standard announced in *Twombly*, clarifies that this standard applies to all civil cases, and explains what is necessary to allege discriminatory intent.[84]

3.3.2 *The Fate of* Swierkiewicz

It is worth considering that there may be serious concern following *Iqbal* as to the validity of the *Swierkiewicz* decision.[85] After all, *Swierkiewicz* cites to *Conley* three times and notes that "conclusory allegations of discrimination" can be permitted to proceed in an employment case.[86] *Iqbal*, which confirms the abrogation of the *Conley* standard, specifically rejects the argument that "mere conclusory statements" may be used to support a complaint.[87] And, the *Iqbal* decision does not cite to *Swierkiewicz* a single time.[88] Thus, a strong argument can be made that *Iqbal* runs counter to (and implicitly overrules) *Swierkiewicz*,[89] and the lower courts have already taken varying approaches to this issue.[90]

While there may be some legitimate concern about the validity of *Swierkiewicz* generally, the decision should be considered good law at least as to cases brought under Title VII.[91] The decision plainly states the standard for pleading employment-discrimination cases and makes clear that a plaintiff need not allege a prima facie case to sufficiently state a Title VII claim. And while *Iqbal* does not endorse the *Swierkiewicz* decision, it does not expressly overrule it – nor does it express any opinion about the decision whatsoever. Moreover, even the recent *Twombly* decision cites to *Swierkiewicz* with approval. Notably, the *Twombly* Court explains how its decision is distinguishable from *Swierkiewicz* rather than choosing to overrule the decision. Thus, it is somewhat premature to forecast the demise of *Swierkiewicz*, whose holding should continue to apply to Title VII cases. This is particularly true given the unique role of summary judgment in employment-discrimination matters, which is discussed in greater detail below. Nonetheless, *Swierkiewicz* must now be viewed under the more restrictive lens of *Twombly* and *Iqbal*, and plaintiffs must make sure to plead sufficient (and plausible) facts to satisfy all three decisions.

3.4 PLEADING DISCRIMINATORY INTENT AFTER *IQBAL*

Swierkiewicz, *Twombly*, and *Iqbal* have clouded the pleading requirements for employment-discrimination claims. In my previous analyses, I have argued for a unified pleading standard for cases brought under Title VII and the ADA. Such a unified standard would provide clarity to this area of the law and help litigants and the courts in assessing the validity of their cases. The *Iqbal* decision has muddied the waters, however, on the question of what a Title VII plaintiff must allege to *plausibly* plead intent in an employment-discrimination case. Notably, after *Iqbal*, intent cannot be alleged "generally" or with conclusory statements, and an allegation of discriminatory intent must be considered with "reference to its factual context."[92]

Proving intent in an employment-discrimination case is certainly a tricky endeavor, and pleading intent after *Iqbal* may be even trickier. What it means to plausibly plead discriminatory intent under Title VII remains an open question and will likely be a matter for the courts to resolve. This chapter attempts to define what facts are necessary to plausibly plead discriminatory intent pursuant to Title VII through a proposed analytical framework. Before undertaking this analysis, however, it is important to understand how establishing intent in a Title VII case is different from other areas of the law.

In particular, the facts of a typical employment-discrimination matter are quite distinct from those of either *Twombly* or *Iqbal*. Employment discrimination is an everyday occurrence in our society, with the Equal Employment Opportunity Commission (EEOC) receiving tens of thousands of discrimination charges each year.[93] Over the past decade, the EEOC has found reasonable cause to believe that discrimination has occurred in thousands of charges brought pursuant to Title VII.[94] It is therefore much more plausible on its face that employment discrimination has occurred than that a high-level governmental conspiracy has been perpetrated or that a complex antitrust violation has been carried out.

3.5 DIFFERENT FACTUAL PLEADING REQUIREMENT FOR TITLE VII CLAIMS

The factual pleading requirement for Title VII cases should be significantly different from the requirements faced by the plaintiffs in *Twombly* and *Iqbal*.

3.5.1 *Distinction between Title VII Claims and Claims Like Those in* Twombly *and* Iqbal

A strong argument can be made that an allegation of discriminatory intent in the employment context is on its face *plausible*. While *Iqbal* warns against making conclusory allegations about discriminatory intent without the proper factual support, the decision (like *Twombly*) arises miles from the employment setting, where discrimination is a frequent occurrence. Indeed, both *Twombly* and *Iqbal* involve allegations that on their face seem somewhat extraordinary. Alleging that the FBI director and the attorney general of the United States undertook a policy to violate the civil rights of a particular group or that major telephone companies engaged in a complex and unlawful conspiracy to prevent entry into the market are somewhat fantastic claims. This did not mean that these allegations were untrue – but on their face the claims certainly raised doubts, and there were "obvious alternative [and lawful] explanation[s]" for the alleged conduct involved.[95] These conclusory allegations – without some factual detail supporting the claims – seemed hollow, unsubstantiated, and implausible.

Comparatively speaking, then, it is far more plausible to believe that an employer has intended to discriminate against one of its workers than it is to believe the unlikely factual scenarios presented by *Twombly* and *Iqbal*. Employment discrimination (which is likely to occur on a fairly regular basis) can easily be contrasted with these recent Supreme Court pleading decisions, especially considering that the Court specifically noted the possible factual alternatives that are "more likely" than the facts alleged by the *Twombly* and *Iqbal* plaintiffs.

This is not to say that a simple conclusory allegation of discriminatory intent in an employment case will sufficiently state a plausible claim. Indeed, *Iqbal* expressly states that this cannot be the case. Rather, as *Iqbal* requires, a claim alleging improper discriminatory intent in the workplace *must be made in the proper factual context.* However, the required factual support for an employment-discrimination claim, which often has merit, should be significantly different than it is for a complex antitrust or high-level governmental-conspiracy claim. Allegations of discriminatory intent in the employment setting must be sufficiently supported with necessary facts, but this requirement should be considered a *somewhat lower* factual threshold than it was for the more unlikely scenarios presented by the plaintiffs in *Twombly* and *Iqbal*.

A basic allegation of negligent driving, which occurs on a fairly routine basis, is expressly endorsed as acceptable by the sample forms attached to the federal rules.[96] Similarly, a basic allegation of employment discrimination, which also occurs on a regular basis, should also satisfy the federal pleading requirements when made with the proper factual support. This chapter helps define the proper factual setting for a plausible Title VII claim and sets forth a proposed factual pleading framework that would support any individual case of intentional employment discrimination.

3.5.2 *Unique Role of Summary Judgment in Title VII Cases*

The Supreme Court's decision in *Swierkiewicz* v. *Sorema* N.A. further supports the argument that there should be a different factual threshold for pleading employment-discrimination claims.[97] In *Swierkiewicz,* the Court held that an employment-discrimination litigant need *not* plead a *McDonnell Douglas* prima facie case of discrimination to survive a motion to dismiss. To establish a prima facie case of employment discrimination, a plaintiffs must show that they are part of a protected class, that they are qualified, that they suffered an adverse employment action, and that there is other evidence giving rise to an inference of discrimination.[98] Thus, a plausible employment-discrimination allegation, which falls between the possible and probable thresholds, requires a lower factual showing than this traditional prima facie case.

In holding that a Title VII plaintiff need not plead a prima facie case, the *Swierkiewicz* Court emphasized the unique function of summary judgment in employment-discrimination cases, noting that "liberal discovery rules and summary judgment motions" must be used "to define disputed facts and issues and to dispose of unmeritorious claims."[99] This approach permits the parties to address vague or unmeritorious claims through a motion for summary judgment, which in turn allows the parties to "focus litigation on the merits of a claim."[100]

Indeed, summary judgment performs a distinctive role in Title VII cases. The sufficiency of the *McDonnell Douglas* prima facie case is typically evaluated at the summary-judgment stage of the proceedings. Once the plaintiff makes the prima facie showing, the employer must assert a legitimate nondiscriminatory reason for the alleged unlawful employment action. If this showing is sufficiently made, the plaintiff maintains the burden of production and persuasion of establishing that the employer's stated reason is pretext for discrimination. Thus, at summary judgment, an employee must *refute* the employer's stated reason for taking the adverse action.

In *Iqbal,* the Court found it problematic that there was a nondiscriminatory explanation for the government's policies that were put in place after September 11th that was "more likely" than the plaintiff's assertions of discrimination – a desire by high-ranking officials to prevent terrorism.[101] Because he had not refuted this explanation, Iqbal's complaint failed to state a plausible claim. By contrast, in employment cases a mechanism has long existed to refute the employer's explanation for taking an adverse action against the employee. As set forth above, during summary judgment the plaintiff must show that the employer's explanation is a mere pretext for discrimination. This unique function of summary judgment in employment-discrimination matters – refuting the employer's explanation for the adverse action – helps explain why a somewhat lower factual showing must be made at the complaint stage of the proceedings in Title VII cases and why *Swierkiewicz* is still good law as to these specific claims.

After *Iqbal* and *Twombly*, then, most civil litigants should refute any obvious alternative explanations for the alleged unlawful conduct set forth in the complaint. Employment-discrimination plaintiffs, however, are not expected to make this showing until summary judgment, and *Swierkiewicz* is clear that a heightened pleading standard must not be applied to workplace-discrimination claims. Thus, the *Swierkiewicz* Court's emphasis on a relaxed pleading standard and liberal discovery is a direct result of the distinct function of summary judgment in Title VII cases and distinguishes these cases from other civil claims.

In employment-discrimination matters, summary judgment often acts as a broad filter in rejecting workplace claims that lack merit. In *Swierkiewicz*, the Supreme Court made clear that this filtering process should not take place at the earlier motion-to-dismiss stage of the proceedings in Title VII matters. And *Twombly* and *Iqbal* do not abrogate the basic holding of *Swierkiewicz* as applied to employment-discrimination cases; indeed, *Twombly* even cites to *Swierkiewicz* with approval.

In summary, as a general matter it is far more plausible to believe that an employer has discriminated against one of its workers than it is to believe the somewhat doubtful factual allegations set forth in *Twombly* or *Iqbal*. Discrimination in employment continues to be a serious problem. An allegation of discrimination made pursuant to Title VII is therefore distinct from (and far more plausible than) the assertions found in these recent Supreme Court decisions. The research on this issue, combined with the unique role of summary judgment in employment-discrimination cases, strongly suggests that there is a different (and somewhat lower) factual pleading requirement for Title VII claims. Unfortunately, however, *Twombly* and *Iqbal* fail to provide any substantive guidance as to what facts are necessary to sufficiently plead a plausible employment-discrimination claim.

In Section 3.6, I propose a new analytical framework for alleging discriminatory intent in Title VII cases. This three-part pleading model attempts to provide a framework for determining what facts are necessary to put discriminatory intent in the proper context and to sufficiently allege a plausible Title VII claim.

3.6 NEW ANALYTICAL FRAMEWORK FOR ALLEGING DISCRIMINATORY INTENT

While *Twombly* and *Iqbal* have significantly changed the pleading rules for civil cases, these recent Supreme Court decisions provide little guidance on what must be alleged to sufficiently state discriminatory intent in a Title VII case. We do know from these cases that the overall allegation of employment discrimination must be plausible on its face. Similarly, we learned from *Iqbal* that discriminatory intent cannot be alleged "generally" and must be made in the proper factual context. Finally, from *Swierkiewicz*, we know that this proper factual context is something less than a prima facie showing for Title VII allegations. As I have argued above, *Swierkiewicz* is still good law as to Title VII cases, and the lower factual threshold required by this decision is well supported by various studies demonstrating the inherent plausibility of employment-discrimination allegations.

Though *Twombly* and *Iqbal* require a civil claim to be plausible on its face, the decisions do not define what plausibility actually means or what factual components would comprise a plausible claim. The common dictionary definition of "plausible" provides that a plausible argument is one that "appear[s] worthy of belief."[102] And this definition seems to be how the Supreme Court generally uses the term. In *Iqbal*, for example, the Court provided that plausibility "is not akin to a '*probability* requirement,' but it asks for more than a sheer *possibility* that a defendant has acted unlawfully."[103] So the plausibility line falls somewhere in the gray area between possible and probable. As many employment-discrimination claims *at least* rise to the level of being possible and/or probable, it is reasonable to expect that these allegations – with the proper factual support – should often survive the dismissal stage of the proceedings.

I have attempted to formulate an analytical framework that answers the difficult question of what factual context must be asserted to sufficiently plead discriminatory intent in all individual cases of intentional discrimination brought under Title VII. This three-part framework pinpoints exactly where plausibility falls in the gray area between *possible* and *probable* that is discussed in the recent Supreme Court decisions. It also provides the precise factual context that must be alleged for Title VII claims and establishes a clear road map for litigants to follow when asserting an employment-discrimination claim, and it navigates the *Twombly* and *Iqbal* decisions and clearly satisfies the pleading requirements of the federal rules. If adopted, this framework would streamline the pleading process in employment-discrimination cases and simplify this area of the law. The analytical model advocated in this book also comports with – and is patterned after – the pleading framework I have proposed previously for Title VII claims.[104] In light of *Iqbal*, the framework set forth in this book emphasizes adequately pleading discriminatory intent.

The pleading model proposed by this book is thus intended to satisfy the Supreme Court's standard for alleging discriminatory intent as articulated in *Iqbal*. As a practical matter, however, pleading discriminatory intent and alleging an actual claim of Title VII discrimination cannot be easily separated out for analytical purposes. Thus, the proposed model, which emphasizes adequately asserting intent in a Title VII case, also provides a basic framework for alleging an overall employment-discrimination claim. To sufficiently plead discriminatory intent pursuant to Title VII (and to adequately state an overall Title VII claim), a plaintiff should thus allege the following three elements.

3.6.1 *Factual Context*

As the *Iqbal* Court noted, discriminatory intent must be alleged in the proper "factual context."[105] For Title VII claims, that factual context must be sufficient to support an allegation of employment discrimination on the basis of race, color, religion, sex, or national origin.[106] The statute prohibits an employer from taking an adverse action against an employee on the basis of any one of these protected characteristics.

Thus, to state the proper factual context for a Title VII claim, the plaintiff must first assert the identity of the victim of the discrimination. That is, the plaintiff should simply identify who it is that has suffered the adverse action in the employment setting. In most cases, this will be easily accomplished by indicating that "*I* suffered an adverse employment action," though in some cases the government, rather than the aggrieved individual, will be bringing the suit. Asserting the identity of the victim is the easiest and most straightforward fact that must be alleged in the complaint to provide the proper context for establishing discriminatory intent.

Next, the plaintiff should allege the protected characteristic that formed the basis of the employer's discriminatory intent and resulting unlawful actions. As noted above, Title VII protects employees from being discriminated against on the basis of "race, color, religion, sex, or national origin."[107] The plaintiff should indicate in the complaint on which of these bases the employer has discriminated. Certainly, the employee can allege that she was discriminated against on the basis of multiple protected characteristics, if applicable to the situation (for example, "I was fired because I am an African-American and because I am a female"). If, during the course of discovery, the plaintiff learns that the defendant discriminated against her on the basis of an additional protected characteristic not set forth in the complaint, the court should liberally consider allowing the plaintiff to amend the complaint to reflect this additional allegation.

To place the employer's discriminatory intent in the proper factual context, the plaintiff must further allege the adverse action suffered by the victim. Thus, the employee must assert what negative consequence she suffered as a result of the employer's discriminatory intent. Title VII specifically states that an employer may not "fail or refuse to hire or to discharge any individual, or otherwise . . . discriminate against any individual" on the basis of a protected characteristic.[108] Failing to hire and firing an employee on the basis of a protected characteristic are therefore statutorily enumerated "adverse acts."[109] It is also likely, based on Supreme Court precedent, that failure to promote and reassignment with substantially different work duties also amount to adverse acts. Aside from these clear adverse actions, whether a particular employment action rises to the level of being sufficiently adverse is often a question of jurisdiction, and the courts have applied varying tests. Some jurisdictions impose a somewhat stringent standard for qualifying adverse acts, while other courts have a more relaxed requirement. The plaintiff should therefore make sure to properly assert the adverse action she suffered based on the relevant case law, as failure to do so would subject the complaint to dismissal.

Finally, the plaintiff must allege the approximate timing of the adverse action. The plaintiff should thus assert her best estimate of when the specific negative action took place. By providing the employer with the timing of the purported discrimination, it can much more easily begin an investigation into the allegations. For discrete acts, such as failure to hire or termination, identifying this date should be relatively simple. For acts that are not as clear-cut, or for continuing violations (such as claims of sexual harassment), identifying the timing of the discrimination can be a more onerous task. The courts should take a flexible approach in permitting plaintiffs to amend a complaint in these circumstances, particularly where discovery has further clarified the exact timing of the discrimination involved. The timing of the adverse action, then, helps clarify the nature of the discrimination asserted and provides a more developed factual context for the allegations in the complaint.

In summary, to provide a sufficient factual context for the allegations of discriminatory intent contained in a Title VII complaint, the plaintiff must set forth the victim of the discrimination, the protected characteristic that caused the employer to discriminate, the adverse action that the employee suffered, and the approximate time that the adverse action occurred. By asserting these essential facts, the employee puts the discriminatory intent in the proper setting and gives the employer sufficient notice of the claim. All Title VII litigants should have this basic information at their disposal, and it should not be difficult to include these factual elements in the complaint. By providing this factual context, the employee avoids making the *general* or *conclusory* allegation of discriminatory intent against which *Iqbal* so strongly advises.

3.6.2 *Discriminatory Intent*

In addition to pleading the factual elements discussed above, the employee must also allege causation to properly assert discriminatory intent. The plaintiff must allege that the adverse action was taken by the employer *because of* the employee's protected characteristic. By making this assertion, the plaintiff satisfies the discriminatory-intent requirement of Title VII, which prohibits the employer from taking an unlawful action "*because of* such individual's race, color, religion, sex, or national origin."[110] The assertion of discriminatory intent therefore provides the causal link between the employer's prohibited actions and the characteristics protected by the statute.[111]

Thus, by asserting that the discrimination suffered was because of the individual's protected characteristic, the plaintiff has satisfied the discriminatory-intent requirement for all Title VII intentional-discrimination claims. This allegation of discriminatory intent, made alongside the critical facts of the claim – which assert the victim's identity, the relevant protected characteristic, the adverse action, and the timing of the unlawful act – sufficiently states a claim of employment discrimination. And this allegation of discriminatory intent easily complies with the federal rules.

The sufficiency of the factual allegations required by this proposed framework is best illustrated by the sample pleading form attached to the Federal Rules of Civil Procedure.[112] This form provides that an adequate allegation of negligence would state that "[o]n *date*, at *place*, the defendant negligently drove a motor vehicle against the plaintiff."[113] Thus, an adequate allegation of a violation of federal civil law includes the timing and nature of the act as well as an assertion of causation (in the above example, negligent driving). The proposed analytical framework for pleading Title VII claims easily satisfies these requirements, as it provides the basic factual components of the employment-discrimination claim coupled with an assertion of the causal link between the unlawful acts and the protected characteristic of the victim. Just as an assertion of negligence, with the proper factual support, establishes a sufficient claim under the federal rules, so too does an allegation of discriminatory intent made in the appropriate factual context.

And, as already discussed, negligent driving and employment discrimination both occur on a fairly regular basis in our society. As both claims are fairly common, they are distinguishable from the more complex (and unlikely) allegations set forth in *Twombly* and *Iqbal*. The more routine nature of employment discrimination and negligent driving further explains why Form 11 and the *Swierkiewicz* decision were cited with approval by the *Twombly* Court, and why a lower factual threshold likely applies to these specific claims.[114]

3.6.3 *Plaintiff's Rebuttal of Employer's Reason for Adverse Action*

In *Iqbal*, the Court found it problematic that there was an easily identifiable explanation for the allegedly unlawful policies that were put in place after September 11th that was "more likely" than Iqbal's assertions of discrimination – a desire by high-ranking officials to prevent terrorism. For the Court, Iqbal's failure to refute this explanation seemed to undermine any argument that the plaintiff had plausibly stated a claim for discrimination. As previously discussed, Title VII intentional-discrimination claims already have a mechanism for rebutting the employer's asserted "more likely" explanation for taking the adverse action. Under the framework set forth by the Supreme Court in *McDonnell Douglas*, the plaintiff must refute the employer's stated reason for taking the adverse action at summary judgment. The *McDonnell Douglas* test, combined with the Supreme Court's holding in *Swierkiewicz*, suggests that a Title VII plaintiff is not required to rebut any "more likely" explanations for the employer's adverse action in the context of the complaint. Indeed, it may even be the case that the employee is unaware of the employer's rationale for taking the adverse employment action at the time the complaint is filed. This is particularly true in the hiring context, where the prospective employee may simply fail to hear anything after submitting an employment application to a potential employer.

Nonetheless, employers often do provide employees with a reason for taking a particular adverse action. When an employee is terminated, for example, that worker is typically given a reason for the discharge – such as poor performance, insubordination, or company cutbacks. When the employee learns of the employer's purported rationale for the adverse action prior to trial, the employee should strongly consider rebutting the employer's explanation in the complaint. As already noted, an employee's opportunity to rebut the employer's legitimate nondiscriminatory reason for the adverse action usually occurs at summary judgment, rather than at the pleading stage of the proceedings. Thus, rebutting the employer's stated reason in the complaint would be an *optional* component of the proposed analytical framework.

However, by including in the complaint an explanation as to why the employer's stated rationale is pretext for discrimination, the plaintiff bolsters her claim and strengthens the allegations. This pleading strategy also gives the plaintiff the first word as to the true reason for the adverse action and undercuts the defendant's subsequent response. With *Iqbal* in mind, then, it would benefit an employee to rebut the employer's rationale for taking the disputed employment action, if the employee is aware of that rationale. Rebutting the employer's reasoning should be relatively simple and straightforward. However, as an optional component of the framework, this rebuttal would only enhance the plaintiff's claim and should certainly never be *required* by a court.

3.6.4 *Summary of Proposed Title VII Pleading Framework*

In summary, the proposed analytical pleading framework for alleging discriminatory intent (and properly pleading a Title VII claim in general) includes providing the overall factual context of the claim, the causal link between the adverse action and the protected characteristic, and an optional statement rebutting the employer's rationale for its actions. This three-part pleading framework for intentional claims of employment discrimination brought pursuant to Title VII is summarized below:

(1) Plaintiff asserts the victim of the discrimination, the protected characteristic of the individual, the adverse action that was taken by the employer, and the timing of the purported unlawful act;

(2) Plaintiff alleges a causal link between the adverse action and the protected characteristic; and

(3) If applicable, plaintiff may rebut the employer's stated reason for taking the adverse action.

The following example provides an illustration of a sufficient allegation of Title VII employment discrimination. This example easily comports with the above three-part analytical framework:

> On January 1, 2021, my employer failed to promote me to a position that I applied for because I am African-American. Despite my employer's assertion that I am not qualified for this position, I have the requisite background and experience for the job.

This example demonstrates the straightforward nature of the proposed framework and the ease with which it can be satisfied. The above example clearly provides the victim ("I" or the individual signing the complaint), the protected characteristic (African-American), the purported adverse action (failure to promote), the timing of the alleged violation (January 1, 2021), and the causal connection (promotion denied *because* of protected status). Additionally, this sample fact pattern further rebuts the employer's stated reason for taking the adverse action. Such an allegation, though simple, states a sufficient Title VII claim and clearly establishes discriminatory intent.

Thus, the proposed pleading framework outlined above includes the critical components of any individual claim of intentional discrimination brought under Title VII. As already noted, this model framework is consistent with the federal rules, and it complies with the sample pleading form attached to the rules.[115] Similarly, the proposed framework adheres to both *Twombly* and *Iqbal*. Indeed, a Title VII plaintiff complying with this framework will have stated the factual nature of the discrimination suffered and provided a causal link between the adverse act and the protected characteristic, thereby stating a *plausible* claim for relief. And, by providing the factual background of the discrimination in the first step of the model framework, the plaintiff will have avoided making a general and conclusory allegation of discriminatory intent. Finally, in many instances (as in the above example), the plaintiff will also have rebutted the employer's stated reason for taking the adverse action, leaving little doubt that she has complied with *Iqbal*.

The sufficiency of the proposed model framework can best be seen in Judge Easterbrook's statement in a Title VII case that "[b]ecause racial discrimination in employment is a claim upon which relief can be granted . . . '*I was turned down for a job because of my race*' is all a complaint has to say."[116] Though Judge Easterbrook's pleading standard predates both *Twombly* and *Iqbal*, it demonstrates the relative ease with which a Title VII plaintiff can satisfy the federal rules. The analytical pleading framework set forth above requires slightly more than Judge Easterbrook in light of the recent Supreme Court decisions, but the proposed model is still straightforward and can be easily satisfied by plaintiffs.

Furthermore, the ease and simplicity of the proposed analytical pleading framework for Title VII claims is well supported by the *Swierkiewicz* holding that an employment-discrimination litigant need *not* plead a prima facie case of discrimination to survive a motion to dismiss. Thus, the above framework does not require that a plaintiff plead a prima facie Title VII case, but it does call for the plaintiff to assert the essential factual elements of the claim. And the studies set forth in this book leave little doubt that employment discrimination continues to pervade our society, an allegation of discriminatory intent – combined with the factual elements required in the proposed framework – clearly establishes a *plausible* Title VII claim. Indeed, when put in the proper factual context outlined above, a claim of discrimination is far more plausible than the somewhat questionable factual allegations set forth in *Twombly* and *Iqbal*. Unlike the plaintiffs in these recent Supreme Court decisions, a plaintiff alleging all of the facts required by the proposed pleading framework will have provided the defendant with fair notice of the charges made against it, thereby allowing the employer to begin looking into the allegations.

Finally, it should also be noted that in addition to setting forth the facts required by the proposed pleading framework, a Title VII plaintiff should make certain that she has also complied with the rules and case law of her particular jurisdiction. It is not unusual for the case law and procedural rules to vary among courts, and a prudent plaintiff will make sure to satisfy any nuances in the local law.

3.6.5 *Limitations of the Proposed Framework*

The unified pleading framework proposed above provides a valuable tool for litigants and the courts in assessing whether a plaintiff has adequately stated a Title VII claim for relief. The proposed framework provides a straightforward, simple model for evaluating employment-discrimination claims. Nonetheless, like any framework, the proposed model does have certain limitations that are worth addressing.

Initially, it should be noted that the proposed model is intended to address the *substantive* elements of a Title VII claim (with an emphasis on adequately pleading discriminatory intent) and does not address any jurisdictional requirements or prerequisites to filing suit. Thus, for example, a plaintiff will likely want to establish that the employer has the requisite number of employees to be covered by the statute,[117] though such an allegation is beyond the scope of this book.

Additionally, the proposed framework applies primarily to *individual* claims of intentional employment discrimination. Thus, the model was not intended for systemic or class-action discrimination claims, which would require a more complex analysis of the pleadings. Similarly, as the elements of a cause of action for harassment or retaliation in the employment context are substantially different from traditional Title VII disparate-treatment cases, these claims are also beyond the scope of this chapter. Moreover, the proposed model set forth above is intended for intentional-discrimination claims and would not apply to a cause of action alleging a disparate-impact (unintentional) violation of Title VII. And as the model addresses Title VII claims exclusively, it is not meant to apply to workplace claims brought under the ADA[118] or the ADEA.[119]

Finally, it is worth noting that the proposed framework applies a *minimum* standard to Title VII pleading. Thus, navigating *Twombly* and *Iqbal*, the proposed model examines the essential components of a plausible Title VII claim. Keeping this minimum standard in mind, however, there is nothing preventing a plaintiff from alleging additional facts or legal arguments that are above and beyond the scope of the proposed framework. Indeed, in certain circumstances and jurisdictions, alleging additional facts may enhance the plaintiff's overall Title VII case. Nonetheless, plaintiffs should still be careful not to *over* allege facts that might lead to the dismissal of their claims. As Judge Posner has warned in a Title VII case, a litigant "who files a long and detailed complaint may plead himself out of court by including factual allegations which if true show that his legal rights were not invaded."[120]

3.6.6 *The* Swierkiewicz *Safe Harbor*

The proposed pleading framework set forth in this book provides a minimum pleading standard for Title VII plaintiffs. Navigating *Twombly* and *Iqbal* – *and* relying on research demonstrating the continued prevalence of discrimination – the proposed model establishes which factual elements are critical for alleging discriminatory intent when asserting a workplace claim. As already noted, however, plaintiffs are free to assert additional facts not required by this framework, and there may be some advantages to doing so.

In this regard, it should be noted that the *Swierkiewicz* decision likely provides a safe harbor for employment-discrimination plaintiffs. As discussed earlier, *Swierkiewicz* holds that a Title VII plaintiff need *not* plead a prima facie case of discrimination to survive a motion to dismiss. If this decision remains good law as applied to Title VII cases (and I have argued throughout this book that the decision is still viable), it follows that a plaintiff who does successfully plead the prima facie elements of an employment-discrimination claim should inherently survive a motion to dismiss. Under the reasoning of *Swierkiewicz*, any court that requires more than these prima facie elements at the motion-to-dismiss stage of the proceedings would be inappropriately applying a "heightened pleading standard" to the case.

Under the *McDonnell Douglas* test discussed earlier, a Title VII plaintiff establishes a prima facie case of discrimination by showing that the plaintiff is part of a protected class, that the plaintiff is qualified, that the plaintiff suffered an adverse employment action, and that there is other evidence giving rise to an inference of discrimination. A plaintiff sufficiently asserting all of these prima facie elements has alleged more than what is required by *Swierkiewicz* (or by the proposed pleading model established in this book), and that plaintiff's complaint should not be dismissed.

Swierkiewicz, therefore, creates a safe harbor for Title VII litigants by providing a pleading floor for workplace claims. Plaintiffs who allege a prima facie case of employment discrimination have surpassed this floor and should be permitted to proceed with their case. Courts should not require plaintiffs to satisfy all of these prima facie elements, but those plaintiffs that do allege all of these factors should not find their claims subject to dismissal.

3.6.7 *Pleading and the Platform Economy*

Beyond Title VII, workers in the technology sector have experienced substantial difficulty pleading their claims. Given the unique and individualized nature of platform-based work, these workers face an uphill battle in conforming their modern claims to an outdated set of established employment rules. In the virtual workplace, then, bringing viable claims of workplace discrimination can be extraordinarily difficult.

At a minimum, the plausibility standard has generated substantial confusion in the lower courts. And, some courts have applied the plausibility test in a way that has heightened the pleading requirements for plaintiffs, though there is certainly debate on this question and empirical studies are far from conclusive.[121] Nonetheless, as discussed above, some studies suggest that there has been an overall negative impact for civil rights plaintiffs.[122] The creation and development of the plausibility standard also coincides with the expanding platform economy[123] over the past several years.[124] As discussed in greater detail below, the courts have had difficulty applying this standard,[125] and, more specifically, defining "employment" with respect to technology workers.[126]

Courts across the country have recently addressed the difficulty of applying the plausibility standard to technology-sector cases. The standard itself is in flux, as it is still in its early stages and being more fully discussed in the courts and academic literature. Applying this developing standard to a developing economy thus presents unique challenges.[127] Indeed, the facts necessary to "sufficiently allege employment"[128] for technology workers are unclear at best. And, as gig-sector cases are now brought in courts across the country, jurisdictional differences are beginning to appear.

In the workplace context, the contours of the employment relationship are perhaps the most critical issue currently being developed in the lower courts. Regardless of how the courts have approached this question, there is always a focus on the issue of control. To be considered an "employee" in the courts, employers must exert a sufficient amount of control over the worker. The resolution of the question of a worker's employment status is a threshold issue, and a worker failing to be considered an employee will be protected by few, if any, of the state or federal employment laws. Where enough facts are alleged to suggest an employment relationship exists, however, the case will typically be permitted to proceed, absent any other potential shortcomings.

The question of employment status is unquestionably specific to individual jurisdictions and factual scenarios. Nonetheless, the Supreme Court has provided some overarching guidance on how to approach this issue, emphasizing the element of control. In the seminal case of *Nationwide Mutual Insurance Co. v. Darden*,[129] the Court outlined the elements to be considered for control, noting that the lower courts should apply common-law agency principles as part of the analysis.

The *Darden* Court listed twelve discrete common-law agency factors. As noted by the *Darden* Court, these agency factors include the following:

> the skill required [for the job]; the source of the instrumentalities and tools; the location of the work; the duration of the relationship between the parties; whether the hiring party has the right to assign additional projects to the hired party; the extent of the hired party's discretion over when and how long to work; the method of payment; the hired party's role in hiring and paying assistants; whether the work is part of the regular business of the hiring party; whether the hiring party is in business; the provision of employee benefits; and the tax treatment of the hired party.[130]

These control factors set out in *Darden* have been applied in varying ways by the lower courts – dependent upon the facts of the case and the jurisdiction where the claim is brought.[131] Moreover, the *Darden* test was developed at a time when brick-and-mortar companies were far more common than we see today. The technology sector has forced employers and the courts to reconceptualize what the employment relationship means, and nontraditional type relationships are now far more common.[132]

The question of who is an employee in the technology sector is relatively new to the academic literature, and there has been little research synthesizing the law on this question. Indeed, only in recent years have we begun to see the cases emerge on this question in the federal courts and the analysis has largely been at the district court level. This chapter surveys much of this law, bringing together the many federal district court decisions on this question. This chapter thus examines how the courts have ruled at the pleading stage of a case on the question of who an employee in the technology sector is. This chapter synthesizes those decisions, evaluating how the courts have approached this question. Ultimately, this chapter seeks to navigate these cases, providing guidance on the information that must be pled to survive dismissal of an employment claim in the technology sector.

After reviewing the cases in this area, this chapter concludes that the federal district courts tend to address dismissal motions in platform-based employment cases in one of three different ways. This is a broad generalization, but one that is helpful in understanding how the courts have approached this new and complex question.

Thus, by examining the courts' recent decisions in gig-sector employment disputes at the motion-to-dismiss stage, this chapter concludes that the courts have responded (1) by finding the case to include insufficient facts and thus granting dismissal; (2) by concluding that the complaint contains sufficient factual allegations and thus allowing the matter to proceed; or (3) by sidestepping the question at this early stage of the analysis. This chapter first examines cases where the courts have found the complaint to contain insufficient facts to properly allege an employment relationship. It then examines claims where the courts have concluded that workers have properly pled employment within the platform economy. Finally, it examines cases in which courts have simply avoided the issue of sufficient technology-sector pleading.

The most high-profile decisions in this area have arisen in the ride-sharing context. To be sure, there have been numerous gig-sector cases in other areas of the on-demand economy, but decisions involving Uber and Lyft have attracted the most headlines.[133] To simplify the discussion in this area, this chapter will look primarily at how the courts have approached this particular subset of technology-sector cases, given that those cases have driven the law in this area. Nonetheless, this chapter seeks to be broad in scope, and to examine the more general question of the type of elements necessary to successfully plead any workplace case in the platform-based sector – regardless of the exact nature of the technology employer involved.

3.6.7.1 Insufficient Pleadings

The courts, generally, have been reluctant to dismiss platform-based cases early in the proceedings. Where the courts have rejected these claims, they have looked to contradictory statements, overly generalized allegations, and insufficient factual detail in the complaint to explain the dismissal.

For example, in *Carter v. Rasier-CA, LLC,*[134] the District Court for the Northern District of California granted ride-sharing company Uber's motion to dismiss with leave to amend in a case involving a driver because the court found that the plaintiff had not pled sufficient factual detail to support his employment status. The court rejected the complaint, holding that it was "insufficient, even at the motion to dismiss stage." In dismissing the complaint, the court emphasized the lack of factual support in the pleadings:

> Plaintiff asserts that Defendants "employed Plaintiff as an employee," . . . but offers minimal factual allegations to support this conclusion. He states that Uber sets the fare model and collects fares from users and . . . direct[s] drivers where to drive. . . . Plaintiff further alleges that Uber may terminate drivers or require them to take additional training if their "rating" falls below a certain level. . . . The Court finds this is insufficient, even at the motion to dismiss stage.[135]

The court focused on the question of control, holding that conclusory statements were insufficient to establish this element of employment. The court further required "more factual detail" from the plaintiff to show how control was actually evidenced by the employer to establish a plausible claim.[136] The court thus required that any amended complaint "clearly set forth each legal claim and the facts supporting such claims, including each Defendant's specific conduct, if he can do so truthfully."[137]

In *Alatraqchi v. Uber Technologies, Inc.,*[138] the District Court for the Northern District of California similarly granted the defendant's dismissal motion (with leave to amend) because of the plaintiff's failure to sufficiently plead his employment status. The court specifically found that the Uber driver in the case had not "adequately allege[d] an employment relationship with [the company]"[139] and similarly concluded that the facts did not support this relationship, and that the plaintiff's statements were inconsistent on this issue.

The court emphasized the plaintiff's "inconsistent allegations" – i.e., that he was both an employee and also engaged in a "business relationship" with Uber.[140] The court also raised concerns about the worker's "several references to his 'business arrangement,' 'business relationship,' and/or 'partnership' with [the company]."[141] The court did grant leave to amend, but noted that at the present time it could not "supply essential elements of the claim that were not initially pled."[142]

These cases demonstrate the approach of certain courts on the issue of what must be pled to establish an employment relationship in the technology sector. As seen here, these courts have tended to require a high level of specificity in pleading these facts, rejecting conclusory (or conflicting) allegations. Indeed, as these cases illustrate, technology cases will not be allowed to proceed where the allegations fail to include detailed facts about the working relationship between employer and employee. And, by rigidly adhering to the *Iqbal* requirements, these courts have rejected generalized statements about whether an employment relationship has been established. Failure to sufficiently plead these facts, or to make consistent statements throughout the complaint, will result in dismissal of the claim.

The early case law has thus suggested that platform-based pleadings should be consistent, specific, and detailed to survive dismissal. Plaintiffs bringing claims in the technology sector should make sure to satisfy this standard if they want to move their cases into discovery.

3.6.7.2 Sufficient Pleadings

Unlike the courts in *Carter* and *Alatraqchi*, several other courts have denied motions to dismiss in platform pleading cases.[143] A close examination of these cases – where the courts have allowed the matters to proceed – will help to better illustrate the pleading requirements in this area. Generally speaking, these federal courts have applied a much more relaxed pleading standard from *Iqbal* and *Twombly*, forgoing the more rigid standard used by many other courts.

For example, in *Doe v. Uber Technologies, Inc.*,[144] the District Court for the Northern District of California found that the Uber drivers in the case had "alleged sufficient facts to claim plausibly that an employment relationship exist[ed]."[145] In reaching that result, the court noted that the allegations were sufficient to show that Uber sets the price of rides, controls driver routes, controls customer contact data, and maintains the power to fine drivers.[146] The company further employs workers with no specialized skills on a frequent basis.[147] The complaint also established that Uber controls the appearance of drivers, as well as the overall atmosphere experienced by the worker.[148] In analyzing the case, the court fully considered the factors weighing both in favor of and against the creation of an employment relationship in the matter.[149]

The court also looked to prior decisions on the employee/independent contractor issue involving Uber and Lyft.[150] Considering the allegations and prior case law, the court held that even if there are facts "that disprove plaintiffs' allegations or that tilt the scales toward a finding that Uber drivers are independent contractors[,] ... plaintiffs have alleged sufficient facts that an employment relationship may plausibly exist."[151]

In a similar case, the District Court for the District of Columbia held that an assault victim of an Uber driver sufficiently alleged the worker's employment status with the business when "a reasonable factfinder could conclude that Uber exercised control over [him] in a manner evincing an employer-employee relationship."[152] The court examined each element of the District of Columbia's five-factor test. In reaching its result, the court thus looked to a multifactor control test that is utilized in the jurisdiction. The court here – just like in *Doe* – found the allegations sufficient to show that the defendant exerts control over fares, wages, and other terms of employment.[153] And, like in *Doe*, the court also held that the allegation of these elements in the case was sufficient to survive dismissal.[154] The court further noted that the company here controlled the day-to-day operation of workers,[155] thus further creating a factual dispute in the case as to employment status.[156]

In yet another jurisdiction to address the issue, the District Court for the Eastern District of Pennsylvania found an Uber driver's complaint sufficient to establish an employment relationship because it articulated "several well-pleaded allegations."[157] The court in this case again looked to the critical element of control, stating that the defendants

> "control the number of fares each driver receives," "have authority to suspend or terminate a driver's access to the App," "are not permitted to ask for gratuity," and "are subject to suspension or termination if they receive an unfavorable customer rating." ... [I]n order to serve as Drivers, "drivers must undergo [...] training, testing, examination, a criminal background check and driving history check."[158]

The court also noted that there was factual support to demonstrate that Uber drivers are financially dependent on the company.[159]

The court therefore outlined the specific facts plaintiffs had alleged that supported employment status under federal law. And, the court emphasized the drivers' assertion that they were "dependent upon the business to which they render service," looking to prior case law.[160] Thus, the court concluded that, pursuant to federal law and prior precedent, the plaintiffs had sufficiently pled their employment status.

In sum, federal courts have favored technology-sector complaints brought in the employment context that have included detailed factual allegations supporting an employment relationship with the company. The courts have tended to allow these cases to proceed where the facts and allegations presented are more than generalizations. Where permitted to proceed, technology-sector employment cases also avoid inconsistent allegations. And, the courts that have been willing to entertain these cases have taken a more liberal approach to the pleading standards than those courts discussed in the prior section.

Overall, then, federal courts have accepted complaints in the technology sector that factually support allegations of an employment relationship, avoid contradictory statements, and provide more than legal and factual generalizations.

3.6.7.3 Avoiding the Plausibility Standard

A third approach worth noting – of those courts that have addressed employment questions arising in the technology sector – has been for those courts to simply avoid the plausibility issue altogether. These courts have tended either to conclude that the question of the sufficiency of the allegations is premature or to find that the case should be permitted to proceed without further analysis. Some courts, then, have simply avoided applying the plausibility standard completely, showing that clear guidance in this area is badly needed.

For example, in *Bekele* v. *Lyft*,[161] the District Court for the District of Massachusetts concluded that the Lyft drivers bringing the allegations were employees when considering the company's motions to compel and dismiss. The court stated that while Lyft "classifies its drivers in Massachusetts as independent contractors," "the complaint alleges" differently and the "Court will assume that [the plaintiff] is an employee for purposes of this motion."[162] The court looked further to prior precedent to find an employment relationship with the company, noting other ride-sharing cases that had allowed complaints to survive dismissal. The court thus simply sidestepped the issue by deferring to the analysis and results of other courts in this area.

Similarly, the District Court for the District of Massachusetts also noted the "litigated position of Uber" in considering the sufficiency of an employment complaint brought against the company.[163] The court pointed to cases in California, New York, and Pennsylvania to support this result.[164] The court concluded that, "[b]ased on the litigated position of Uber, then, plaintiffs have stated a plausible claim."[165]

The District Court for the Western District of Oklahoma also sidestepped the question of the existence of an employment relationship for workers at Uber.[166] The court stated that it "does not address this dispute because even assuming defendant is John Doe's employer, for the reasons set forth below, plaintiff has still failed to assert a cause of action that survives defendant's motion to dismiss."[167] Like the other cases discussed here, this federal court also avoided squarely addressing the worker misclassification issue.

In a similar state court decision, the Superior Court of Massachusetts concluded that a ride-sharing driver had sufficiently alleged an employment relationship under the Massachusetts Wage Act. The court stated that "in the light most favorable to [the plaintiff], the complaint [did] not fail to state a claim."[168] The court did note that, under Massachusetts law, "it is [Uber's] burden to prove that [plaintiff] meets all three prongs of the independent contractor test; it is not [plaintiff's] burden to plead that he does not."[169]

In sum, a third approach used by the courts when analyzing whether technology-sector workers have been misclassified has been to sidestep the issue altogether. This is not a surprising approach, given the complex allegations often involved as well as the confusion surrounding the *Twombly* and *Iqbal* decisions, and the plausibility standard itself. Several courts have thus decided not to address the issue at all. As detailed below, this chapter sets forth a proposed pleading standard for technology-sector employment cases. By creating more certainty in the type of allegations and facts that would typically be expected in a technology-sector employment case, this chapter provides more clarity in this area. With a greater level of certainty, the courts may be more willing to address these issues directly when they arise. Nonetheless, at the current time, many courts are simply choosing to avoid wading into the issue at all. The popularity of this approach illustrates the need for clear guidance in this area.

3.6.8 *Drafting the Complaint: A Proposed Pleading Standard*

Image Credit: t_kimura/Getty Images

After surveying the recent complaints and case law in this area, it is now appropriate to provide suggestions for drafting a complaint that plausibly pleads an employment relationship with a technology-sector business. Given the confusion noted above – and even the willingness of some courts to completely avoid the issue altogether – a model pleading standard is needed to assist the courts and parties in analyzing this issue.

A successful pleading model should closely consider the existing case law where plaintiffs have been successful in establishing an employment relationship with a technology-sector business. Looking to the *Carter* and *Alatraqchi* cases discussed above, we learn that technology-sector workers must carefully articulate their factual allegations of employment status. Plaintiffs should avoid any reference to a "partnership," or "business relationship," or "independent worker" status. Instead, plaintiffs should identify themselves as "workers" or preferably as "employees." And plaintiffs must do more than simply allege conclusory terms, and should include specific facts supporting their employment status with the company.

There can be no magic "template" to establish a satisfactory hypothetical complaint in this or any other area, but there are a number of general guideposts to use to enhance the likelihood of success of a particular claim in this sector. This chapter proposes a basic framework to help evaluate employment claims brought in the technology sector.

The test set forth here is not meant to be exhaustive. Indeed, it is more of a descriptive summary of the factors the federal courts have already relied upon before letting a particular platform-type case proceed. Thus, the framework suggested below must be considered flexible, and each case must be evaluated on its own merits.

Plaintiffs should thus strongly consider pleading the following elements of the proposed model:[170]

- when individual works;
- where individual works;
- how often work occurs;
- manner of work performed;
- pricing/cost information; and
- any other factors related to control.

Adequately pleading these six factors should sufficiently articulate an employment relationship that is sufficient to survive a motion to dismiss. To the extent any details can be provided for each of these factors, they should be set out in the complaint itself. While the pleadings need not be lengthy, they should be sufficient to overcome the plausibility standard of *Twombly* and *Iqbal*. It is important to note that no single factor will be dispositive in this test. Nor is any factor necessarily weighed more heavily than another. Rather, the court will look to the totality of these factors to determine whether an employment relationship exists. This test aims for simplicity, as well as effectiveness in practice. An outline more fully developing each of these factors is discussed below as well as an excellent example of a complaint in this area.

3.6.8.1 When Work Performed

The plaintiff should allege any facts supporting when the work was performed. The exact timing of the performance of one's job goes directly to the factors discussed by the Supreme Court in *Darden*.[171] When the performance of work occurs can greatly impact the nature of the job. When one's work is performed also raises the question of the level of control in the employment relationship.[172] Independent contractors tend to set their own hours, whereas employees work when required by the business. The platform economy has put this question into flux, however, as employers may encourage workers to perform their tasks during certain peak periods, though not necessarily require the work to be performed during this time.[173]

3.6.8.2 Where Work Performed

The plaintiff should also allege any facts related to where the work was performed. The exact location where one performs the job can substantially impact the nature of the work. Whether one performs one's work primarily in an office building, in a car, or in a customer's home, the exact location of where the work duties are performed will go directly to the question of control.[174] Where an employer has more oversight over a worker, and exercises more supervision over day-to-day activities, the more likely it is that an employment relationship will be created. Supervision can occur in many ways, however, and a supervisor need not physically oversee a worker to exercise control over a particular relationship.[175]

3.6.8.3 How Often Work Occurs

The plaintiff should further assert in the complaint how often the work occurs. This is a critical inquiry in the technology sector. Many workers in the platform economy will use the particular job as a way to supplement their primary income from another source. It is thus important to allege whether the employment is part-time in nature or whether it should be considered more of a full-time job. Where a worker spends fifty to sixty hours a week working for a particular employer, that employer will have far more control over that particular relationship. And such an employee would be far more likely to satisfy the control test articulated by the Supreme Court in *Darden*.[176]

3.6.8.4 Manner of Work

The plaintiff should further set forth clearly in the complaint the manner in which work is being performed in the technology sector. This is critical as this emerging industry presents many opportunities for employment that have never before existed. Some federal courts may be unfamiliar with certain jobs that exist in the platform economy, and a concise and accurate description of the type of work being performed is critical for the complaint. The manner of the work performed goes specifically to the control question as well. How the job is done, including the specific requirements imposed by the company, demonstrates how much supervision is involved in the worker's day-to-day activities.

3.6.8.5 Pricing/Cost Information

The pricing model is an often-forgotten – yet critical – aspect of the employment relationship. How the pricing is set reveals much about whether a worker is seen as an employee. Independent contractors set their own pricing (and often their own hours). Employees, however, rely on the business to establish what rate customers will pay.[177] Again, these are general guidelines developed over time. A house contractor will typically provide a quote to a customer based on their own experience and skill set, whereas an employee at McDonald's will allow the business to establish the prices paid for particular menu items. These examples are obviously at the extremes, however, and again the platform economy creates some uncertainty in this area.[178] Nonetheless, pricing is an important factor to examine and often reveals where the true control exists in the working relationship between the business and individual performing the job.

3.6.8.6 Any Other Factors Related to Control

As clearly discussed throughout this chapter, the platform-based economy is new, still emerging, and evolving in many ways. The industry itself places a high value on new ideas and different ways to reach customers and potential clients. It is impossible to fashion a test here that would be directly applicable to every company in the technology industry, as well as one that would capture future businesses in this area. Indeed, there can be little doubt that the sector will look far different in five years from how it appears today. Thus, the factors set forth here are important guidelines for establishing where control lies in the working relationship,[179] but the proposed model does not purport to be an all-inclusive test. It is therefore important to have some type of catch-all provision that would allow plaintiffs to assert certain other facts specific to their employment relationship that are suggestive of control. These factors could represent any information that would further help a court to determine whether a worker is an employee or an independent contractor.

Perhaps more importantly, this final factor is a reminder to plaintiffs to take a step back and look more holistically at the facts of the case to determine if there are any other elements that should be alleged. In the face of *Twombly* and *Iqbal*, plaintiffs must look beyond conclusory allegations to more broadly represent early on the nature of the employment relationship and any supporting facts. Thus, as no test is all inclusive, plaintiffs should consider alleging other facts and should be encouraged to assert any information in the case that suggests that the employer has more control in the working relationship.

In summary, plaintiffs should plead as many supporting facts as possible in a technology-sector complaint. They should outline facts specific to their working experience that help support the business's control over the working relationship. They should be as concise as possible, avoiding any "contradictory" statements in establishing the claim.

3.6.8.7 The Bradshaw Complaint: An Illustrative Example

The model proposed here may be a bit abstract, and it can be helpful to examine an actual technology-sector pleading that implicates a worker's employment status. In *Bradshaw v. Uber Technologies, Inc.*, the ride-sharing company did not argue that the plaintiffs had insufficiently pled their employment relationship with the business.[180] The federal district court noted that

> [i]n the motion for judgment on the pleadings, Defendants do not take issue with Plaintiff's pleading sufficient facts to establish that they were his employer for purposes of [federal wage/hour law]. Defendants contend, however, that Plaintiff failed to plead sufficient facts to support his contention that he was paid less than the statutory minimum wage or that he was entitled to overtime pay.[181]

The detailed nature of this complaint helped the worker in this case to establish an employment relationship with Uber. Thus, the *Bradshaw* complaint includes highly detailed factual allegations that are set forth in Appendix at the end of this book. This detailed complaint alleges general facts supporting the workers' employment status and specific facts setting forth the plaintiff's individual experience with Uber.

Technology-sector workers should examine the *Bradshaw* complaint when drafting their own pleadings in a similar case. The ideal allegations would not only plead general facts concerning the business's relationship with workers but further state facts supporting the individual's relationship with the company. Additionally, the ideal complaint would frame these facts in the context of the proposed framework set forth in this chapter, using the elements set forth as a guide to including all of the relevant facts. While the *Bradshaw* complaint does not perfectly model the approach suggested here, it is nonetheless an excellent example of the type of detailed pleadings sufficient to allege an employment relationship in the technology sector. While not perfect, then, the attached complaint is currently the best attempt by a plaintiff to demonstrate that such a working relationship exists in a platform-based business. It thus provides a nice template – combined with the proposed framework set forth here – for technology-sector workers to consider when preparing a complaint in this area.

3.6.9 *Evaluating the Proposed Standard*

This chapter has examined many of the current cases in the federal courts analyzing who is an employee in technology-based cases. Synthesizing this case law, this chapter proposes an analytical framework for pleading these technology sector claims. As noted throughout this chapter, this approach is not intended to be exhaustive and should serve merely as a guideline for approaching these types of claims. As with any framework, there are a number of benefits and drawbacks to analyzing cases under a more fixed approach. It is worth highlighting some of those implications here, but it is also important to note that this test should never be applied in an overly rigid way. Indeed, the test itself specifically incorporates flexibility into the factors enumerated. And, as seen in the *Bradshaw* complaint attached here, there may be many ways to successfully plead a case outside of (or in conjunction with) the proposed model.

Perhaps the greatest benefit of the framework proposed here is the ability it provides the courts to better understand whether there are any shortfalls in a particular claim. As demonstrated in the cases above, the courts have taken highly varied approaches with respect to analyzing these types of technology-sector cases. The courts have been openly frustrated with the lack of guidance they have been given in this area, struggling to fit the square peg of the evolving modern economy into the round hole of existing – and outdated – case law and legislation.[182] The approach suggested here gives the courts a template from which to work and to examine the types of factors necessary to establish an employment relationship in a platform-based claim. The courts can thus compare the facts of the case before them against the framework proposed here in determining whether a complaint is sufficient to proceed. The approach proposed here specifically incorporates and navigates the Supreme Court plausibility case law, and further considers the recent platform-based decisions of the federal district courts. Thus, this framework provides an updated examination of the pleading requirements necessary for litigants to be permitted to proceed in the technology field. The courts, while understandably confused when considering these claims, will now have better guidance when undertaking this endeavor.

Similarly, this test assists both defendants and plaintiffs to better understand, evaluate, and frame litigation in this area. Plaintiffs will have a template to use to help explore what facts to highlight in their claims. The test proposed here thus allows plaintiffs to work from a framework in setting forth the necessary elements for creating an employment relationship in the technology sector. Previously, plaintiffs were left with the general guidance provided in the Supreme Court's *Darden* decision of control and its many possible elements. This framework has simply not been updated to reflect the evolving modern economy. The test proposed here attempts to do just that, incorporating the reality of platform-based work with the traditional test for control and common-law agency principles.

In the same way, defendants can determine if there are any shortfalls in the case, and the proposed factors quickly establish what arguments can be made with respect to the lack of any employment relationship. Defendants can thus use the framework to quickly determine whether the workers involved in a platform-based claim are employees or independent contractors. Where an employment relationship does not appear to have been created, defendants can move to dismiss the claim.

The test proposed here would also bring greater certainty to this area of the law. Given the confusion that currently exists, some general guidelines are long overdue. Through more certainty in this area, the likelihood that technology-based cases will settle is greatly enhanced.[183] This has the additional benefit of reducing the amount of litigation in the area, benefiting both parties as well as the judiciary. More certainty and more settled law in a particular field inherently leads to greater settlement numbers.[184] Reduced litigation financially benefits all parties and allows the courts to focus more closely on those claims where true legal disputes exist.

Working from a common framework, this model also allows plaintiffs to better streamline their allegations. Rather than throwing everything at a complaint to see what sticks, plaintiffs will have a standard model to help better focus their claims. More streamlined, straightforward complaints will allow cases to move forward much more quickly and more readily provide notice to defendants of the allegations against them. And, through this analytical framework, plaintiffs will much more easily be able to identify and assert the factors necessary to establish the existence of an employment relationship.

Though the model suggested here would lead to many efficiencies for plaintiffs, defendants, and the courts, there are nonetheless certain drawbacks. Perhaps the greatest concern raised by the use of this test would be that the courts would apply it too rigidly. As seen in the federal court decisions issued shortly after the creation of the plausibility standard in *Twombly*, many federal courts – particularly in the civil rights context – used the new standard to heighten the pleading bar and dismiss otherwise legitimate claims. With any test, then, the possibility exists for the courts to use a given standard as a reason to dismiss a particular claim. Some courts may thus consider the proposed standard to create a heightened bar and not apply it with the flexibility that was intended. Though the concern certainly exists that the courts would apply the proposed framework too rigidly, the same courts would likely find other reasons to dismiss the case even in the absence of the standard suggested here.

3.6.10 Conclusion

As this chapter demonstrates, there is widespread confusion and conflicting federal court opinions on the question of worker classification in the technology sector. The courts have always struggled with defining the employment relationship, and the new platform-based jobs in the modern economy have only complicated this inquiry. As this chapter shows, federal courts have issued varied opinions on the issue of worker classification in the platform economy. The need for guidance in this area has never been greater, particularly as we are likely to see a surge in COVID-19-related claims in the technology sector, and this chapter attempts to provide some fundamental ground rules for litigating in this field. The *virtual workplace* is only expanding, and the courts must act quickly to provide some clear boundaries and definitions to this changing field.

No model is perfect, and no framework can capture every factual scenario in this evolving industry. The guidance proposed here, however, provides some clarity to an otherwise confused area of the law. The law must adapt and evolve with the changing economy, and new rules are needed to define employment outside of the traditional brick-and-mortar working relationship. Looking to the realities of technology-sector work, this chapter attempts to provide this new definition. Hopefully, this chapter will spark a dialogue as to how employment should be characterized in this new economy and how we can help better secure the federal and state workplace protections that are now at risk for many workers in this emerging industry. As we begin to see those workplace claims related to the pandemic enter the court system in increasing numbers, we must take a new look at how we litigate these cases, particularly where the allegations are based on virtual employment.

NOTES

This chapter draws heavily from Joseph A. Seiner, "The Trouble with *Twombly*: A Proposed Pleading Standard for Employment Discrimination Cases," *University of Illinois Law Review* 2009 (2009): 1011–60; Joseph A. Seiner, "After *Iqbal*," *Wake Forest Law Review* 45 (2010): 179–229; Joseph A. Seiner, "The Discrimination Presumption," *Notre Dame Law Review* 94 (2019): 1115–60; Joseph A. Seiner, "Platform Pleading: Analyzing Employment Disputes in the Technology Sector," *Washington Law Review* 94 (2019): 1947–86; Joseph A. Seiner, *The Supreme Court's New Workplace* (New York: Cambridge University Press, 2017); and Joseph A. Seiner, "Pleading Disability," *Boston College Law Review* 51 (2010): 95–149.

1 Dan Brown, *Angels & Demons* (Washington Square Press, 2006), 319.

2 129 S. Ct. 1937 (2009).

3 550 U.S. 544 (2007).

4 *Iqbal*, 129 S. Ct. 1953.

5 See Kendall W. Hannon, Note, "Much Ado about *Twombly*? A Study on the Impact of *Bell Atlantic Corp.* v. *Twombly* on 12(b)(6) Motions," *Notre Dame Law Review* 83 (2008): 1811, 1814–15.

6 Joseph A. Seiner, "The Trouble with *Twombly*," 1011, 1014, 1035–38.

7 355 U.S. 41 (1957), *abrogated by Twombly*, 550 U.S. 544.

8 Ibid., 45–46.

9 See, e.g., *Iqbal*, 129 S. Ct. 1949; *Twombly*, 550 U.S. 557; Scott Dodson, "Pleading Standards after *Bell Atlantic Corp.* v. *Twombly*," *Virginia Law Review in Brief* 93 (2007): 135, www.virginialawreview.org/inbrief.php?s=inbrief&p=2007/07/09/Dodson.

10 42 U.S.C. §§ 2000e to e-17 (2006).

11 *Iqbal*, 129 S. Ct. 1949 (emphasis added) (internal quotation marks omitted) (citing *Twombly*, 550 U.S. 556).

12 Fed. R. Civ. P. 12(b)(6).

13 Ibid., 8(a)(2).

14 Ibid. It is worth noting that *Twombly* discusses the sample negligence form with approval (in its previous Form 9 version). See *Bell Atl. Corp.* v. *Twombly*, 550 U.S. 544, 565 n.10 (2007).

15 Fed. R. Civ. P. 8(a)(2).

16 Ibid. Form 11.

17 Ibid. r. 12(b)(6).

18 See Victor E. Schwartz and Christopher E. Appel, "Rational Pleading in the Modern World of Civil Litigation: The Lessons and Public Policy Benefits of *Twombly* and *Iqbal*," *Harvard Journal of Law and Public Policy* 33 (2010): 1107, 1111.

19 Ibid., 1116. See generally Seiner, "The Discrimination Presumption," 1115.

20 Schwartz and Appel, "Rational Pleading," 1120.

21 355 U.S. 41 (1957), abrogated by *Twombly*, 550 U.S. 544.

22 Ibid., 45–46 (emphasis added).

23 Ibid., 48.

24 *Conley*, 355 U.S. 45–46; Paul Stancil, "Balancing the Pleading Equation," *Baylor Law Review* 61 (2009): 90, 111.

25 See A. Benjamin Spencer, "Plausibility Pleading," *Boston College Law Review* 49 (2008): 431, 435.

26 550 U.S. 544, 554–63 (2007).

27 *Swierkiewicz v. Sorema N.A.*, 534 U.S. 506 (2002).

28 Ibid., 510–11.

29 411 U.S. 792 (1973).

30 Ibid., 802.

31 *Swierkiewicz*, 534 U.S. 510.

32 Ibid., 511.

33 Ibid., 512.

34 Ibid. (citing *Conley v. Gibson*, 355 U.S. 41, 47 [1957]).

35 Ibid.

36 Ibid.

37 Ibid., 514–15.

38 *Bell Atl. Corp. v. Twombly*, 550 U.S. 544 (2007).

39 Ibid., 550.

40 Ibid., 563.

41 Ibid.

42 Ibid., 557.

43 Ibid., 570.

44 Ibid., 555.

45 Ibid., 570.

46 Ibid.

47 Ibid.

48 See Hannon, "Much Ado about *Twombly*?," 1815; Seiner, "The Trouble with *Twombly*," 1014, 1027–38; see also Suja A. Thomas, "Why the Motion to Dismiss Is Now Unconstitutional," *Minnesota Law Review* 92 (2008): 1851, 1853. See generally Patricia W. Hatamyar, "The Tao of Pleading: Do *Twombly* and *Iqbal* Matter Empirically?," *American University Law Review* 59 (2010): 553–633.

49 See Seiner, "The Trouble with *Twombly*," 1014, 1027–38; Seiner, "Pleading Disability," 117–26. Both motion-to-dismiss studies compared district court opinions issued the year before *Twombly* that relied on *Conley* to district court opinions issued the year following *Twombly* that relied on *Twombly*.

50 42 U.S.C. § 2000e-2(a)(l) (2006).

51 See Seiner, "Pleading Disability," 117–26; Seiner, "The Trouble with *Twombly*," 1014.

52 See Hannon, "Much Ado about *Twombly*?," 1814–15; see also Seiner, "Pleading Disability," 101 n.54, 121–22; Seiner, "The Trouble with *Twombly*," 1014.

53 *Ashcroft v. Iqbal*, 129 S. Ct. 1937, 1953 (2009).

54 Ibid., 1942–44 (quoting Complaint at ¶ 96).

55 Ibid.

56 Ibid., 1948–49.

57 Ibid.

58 Ibid., 1949 (citing *Bell Atl. Corp. v. Twombly*, 550 U.S. 544, 555 [2007]).

59 Ibid. (quoting *Twombly*, 550 U.S. 557).

60 Ibid., 1951 (quoting *Twombly*, 550 U.S. 570).

61 Ibid.

62 Ibid.

63 Ibid.

64 Ibid., 1952.

65 Ibid.

66 Ibid.

67 *Iqbal*, 129 S. Ct. 1953.

68 Ibid., 1953–54.

69 Ibid., 1953.

70 Ibid., 1954.

71 Ibid.

72 Ibid.

73 Ibid.

74 Ibid.

75 Ibid. (Souter, J., dissenting).

76 Ibid., 1959–61.

77 Benjamin Spencer, "Pleading Civil Rights Claims in the Post-*Conley* Era," *Howard Law Journal* 52 (2008): 160 (referencing *Twombly*'s "amorphous concept of 'plausibility'").

78 *Twombly*, 550 U.S. 555, 570.

79 Ibid., 555.

80 *Iqbal*, 129 S. Ct. 1953.

81 Ibid., 1949.

82 Ibid., 1954.

83 Ibid.

84 Ibid.

85 See, e.g., Scott Dodson, "Beyond *Twombly*," *Civil Procedure & Federal Courts Blog*, May 18, 2019, https://lawprofessors.typepad.com/civpro/2009/05/beyond-twombly-by-prof-scott-dodson.html; Seiner, "Pleading Disability," 103–104; Seiner, "The Trouble with *Twombly*."

86 *Swierkiewicz v. Sorema N.A.*, 534 U.S. 506, 512, 514–15 (2002).

87 *Iqbal*, 129 S. Ct. 1940, 1944, 1949.

88 See ibid., 1937; Dodson, "Beyond *Twombly*."

89 See Suja A. Thomas, "The New Summary Judgment Motion: The Motion to Dismiss under *Iqbal* and *Twombly*" (Ill. Pub. L. Research Paper No. 09-16), http://ssrn.com/abstract=1494683; cf. A. Benjamin Spencer, "Understanding Pleading Doctrine," *Michigan Law Review* 108 (2009): 1, 4.

90 Compare, e.g., *al-Kidd v. Ashcroft*, 580 F.3d 949 (9th Cir. 2009) ("In *Twombly*, the Supreme Court ... reaffirmed the holding of *Swierkiewicz* ... rejecting a fact pleading requirement for Title VII employment discrimination"), with *Fowler v. UPMC Shadyside*, 578 F.3d 203, 211 (3d Cir. 2009) ("We have to conclude, therefore, that because *Conley* has been specifically repudiated by both *Twombly* and *Iqbal*, so too has *Swierkiewicz*, at least insofar as it concerns pleading requirements and relies on *Conley*.").

91 See Adam N. Steinman, "The Pleading Problem," *Stanford Law Review* 62 (2010): 1293–360.

92 *Ashcroft v. Iqbal*, 129 S. Ct. 1937, 1954 (2009).

93 "U.S. Equal Employment Opportunity Comm'n, Charge Statistics," EEOC, www.eeoc.gov/enforcement/charge-statistics-charges-filed-eeoc-fy-1997-through-fy-2019.

94 "U.S. Equal Employment Opportunity Comm'n, Title VII of the Civil Rights Act of 1964 Charges," EEOC, www.eeoc.gov/enforcement/title-vii-civil-rights-act-1964-charges-charges-filed-eeoc-includes-concurrent-charges.

95 *Iqbal*, 129 S. Ct. 1951. As the *Iqbal* Court suggested, "the arrests Mueller oversaw were likely lawful and justified by his nondiscriminatory intent to detain aliens who were illegally present in the United States and who had potential connections to those who committed terrorist acts." Ibid.

96 Fed. R. Civ. P. Form 11 (providing the following as a sufficient negligence allegation: "On *date*, at *place*, the defendant negligently drove a motor vehicle against the plaintiff."). It should also be noted that Form 11 (previously Form 9) is discussed with approval in the *Twombly* decision. *Twombly*, 550 U.S. 565 n.10 ("A defendant wishing to prepare an answer in the simple fact pattern laid out in Form 9 would know what to answer; a defendant seeking to respond to plaintiffs' conclusory allegations in the § 1 context would have little idea where to begin.").

97 *Swierkiewicz v. Sorema N.A.*, 534 U.S. 506, 510–11 (2002).

98 See *McDonnell Douglas Corp. v. Green*, 411 U.S. 792, 802 (1973). The fourth element of the prima facie case is often established by showing that "similarly situated employees outside of the protected class received more favorable treatment." *Lucas v. PyraMax Bank, FSB*, 539 F.3d 661, 666 (7th Cir. 2008).

99 Ibid., *Swierkiewicz*, 534 U.S. 512.

100 Ibid., 514.

101 *Ashcroft v. Iqbal*, 129 S. Ct. 1937, 1951 (2009).

102 *Merriam-Webster's Online Dictionary*, www.merriam-webster.com/dictionary/plaus
    ible; see also *The Oxford American Dictionary of Current English* (New York: Oxford
    University Press, 1999), 602 (defining plausible as "seeming reasonable or probable").

103 *Iqbal*, 129 S. Ct. 1949 (citing *Bell Atl. Corp.* v. *Twombly*, 550 U.S. 544, 556 [2007]
    [emphasis added]).

104 See Seiner, "Pleading Disability" (proposing a pleading standard for ADA cases);
    Seiner, "The Trouble with *Twombly*" (suggesting a unified model for alleging
    Title VII claims). See generally Seiner, *The Supreme Court's New Workplace*.

105 Ibid., 1954.

106 42 U.S.C. § 2000e-2(a) (2006).

107 42 U.S.C. § 2000e-2(a)(1) (2006).

108 42 U.S.C. § 2000e-2(a)(1).

109 Ibid. § 2000e-2(a).

110 42 U.S.C. § 2000e-2(a)(1) (2006) (emphasis added).

111 Ibid.

112 Fed. R. Civ. P. Form 11.

113 Ibid.

114 *Bell Atl. Corp.* v. *Twombly*, 550 U.S. 544, 563, 565 n.10, 569 n.14, 570 (2007).
    Twombly discusses the sample negligence form (Fed. R. Civ. P. Form 11) with
    approval in its previous Form 9 version. Ibid., 565 n.10.

115 Fed. R. Civ. P. Form 11.

116 *Bennett* v. *Schmidt*, 153 F.3d 516, 518 (7th Cir. 1998) (Easterbrook, J.) (emphasis
    added).

117 See 42 U.S.C. § 2000e(b) (2006) ("The term 'employer' means a person engaged in
    an industry affecting commerce who has fifteen or more employees for each
    working day in each of twenty or more calendar weeks in the current or preceding
    calendar year, and any agent of such a person.").

118 42 U.S.C. § 12111 (2006).

119 29 U.S.C. § 621 (2006).

120 *Am. Nurses' Ass'n* v. *Illinois*, 783 F.2d 716, 724 (7th Cir. 1986).

121 See generally William H. J. Hubbard, "The Empirical Effects of *Twombly* and
    Iqbal" (Coase-Sandor Inst. for Law and Econ., Working Paper No. 773, 2016),
    https://chicagounbound.uchicago.edu/cgi/viewcontent.cgi?article=2479andcon
    text=law_and_economics [https://perma.cc/6588-DCJ2] (summarizing studies).

122 Suzette M. Malveaux, "The Jury (or More Accurately the Judge) Is Still Out for
    Civil Rights and Employment Cases Post-Iqbal," *New York Law School Law
    Review*, 57 (2012–13): 719, 728–31; see also Raymond H. Brescia, "The *Iqbal*
    Effect: The Impact of New Pleading Standards in Employment and Housing
    Discrimination Litigation," *Kentucky Law Journal* 100 (2011): 235 (discussing
    housing cases); Edward A. Hartnett, "Taming *Twombly*, Even after *Iqbal*,"
    University of Pennsylvania Law Review 158 (2010): 473; Suzette M. Malveaux,
    "Clearing Civil Procedure Hurdles in the Quest for Justice," *Ohio Northern*

University Law Review 37 (2011): 621, 623–31; Suzette M. Malveaux, "Front Loading and Heavy Lifting: How Pre-Dismissal Discovery Can Address the Detrimental Effect of Iqbal on Civil Rights Cases," *Lewis and Clark Law Review* 14 (2010): 65.

123 See generally Lawrence F. Katz and Alan B. Krueger, "The Rise and Nature of Alternative Work Arrangements in the United States, 1995–2015" (Nat'l Bureau of Econ. Research, Working Paper No. 22667, 2016), www.nber.org/papers/w22667.pdf [https://perma.cc/LV9L-Z5BY]; cf. Diana Farrell and Fiona Greig, "The Online Platform Economy: Has Growth Peaked?," *J.P. Morgan Chase and Co. Institute*, November 2016, www.jpmorganchase.com/corporate/institute/document/jpmc-institute-online-platform-econ-brief.pdf [https://perma.cc/57CJ-T8NZ].

124 See generally Ryan Calo and Alex Rosenblat, "The Taking Economy: Uber, Information, and Power," *Columbia Law Review* 117 (2017): 1623, 1635; Orly Lobel, "The Law of the Platform," *Minnesota Law Review* 101 (2016): 87, 94.

125 See Colleen McNamara, "*Iqbal* as Judicial Rorschach Test: An Empirical Study of District Court Interpretations of *Ashcroft v. Iqbal*," *Northwestern University Law Review* 105 (2011): 401, 424–25; Steinman, "The Pleading Problem," 1293, 1299, 1311–13; see generally *Swanson v. Citibank, N.A.*, 614 F.3d 400, 403 (7th Cir. 2010); Lonny Hoffman, "Plausible Theory, Implausible Conclusions," *University of Chicago Law Review Online* 83 (2016): 143.

126 See generally Nancy Leong and Aaron Belzer, "The New Public Accommodations: Race Discrimination in the Platform Economy," *Georgetown Law Journal* 105 (2017): 1271, 1311; Brishen Rogers, "Employment Rights in the Platform Economy: Getting Back to Basics," *Harvard Law and Policy Review* 10 (2016): 479, 482; E. Gary Spitko, "A Structural-Purposive Interpretation of 'Employment' in the Platform Economy," *Florida Law Review* 70 (2018): 409, 427.

127 See David Weil, "Lots of Employees Get Misclassified as Contractors. Here's Why It Matters," *Harvard Business Review*, July 5, 2017, https://hbr.org/2017/07/lots-of-employees-get-misclassified-as-contractors-heres-why-it-matters [https://perma.cc/6CBK-3VU7]. See generally *Brookhaven Baptist Church v. Workers' Comp. Appeal Bd. (Halvorson)*, 912 A.2d 770, 777 (Pa. 2006); Dan Eaton, "Gig Economy Creates Legal Puzzles for the Courts," *San Diego Union-Tribune*, September 3, 2017, www.sandiegouniontribune .com/business/technology/sd-fi-labor-eaton-column-20170807-story.html# [https:// perma.cc/3KTH-VE4B].

128 *Dejesus v. HF Mgmt. Servs., LLC*, 726 F.3d 85, 91 (2d Cir. 2013).

129 503 U.S. 318, 323 (1992).

130 Ibid., 323–24 (quoting *Cmty. for Creative Non-Violence v. Reid*, 490 U.S. 730, 751–52 [1989]).

131 Cf. Richard R. Carlson, "Why the Law Still Can't Tell an Employee When It Sees One and How It Ought to Stop Trying," *Berkeley Journal of Employment and Labor Law* 22 (2001): 338–39 ("Employer control over the details of the work has been the factor most courts place at the heart of any test of worker status . . . Indeed,

one could argue that nearly all the other factors listed by courts are merely different ways of evidencing the employer's means of control.").

132 See Abha Bhattarai, "Now Hiring, for a One-Day Job: The Gig Economy Hits Retail," *Washington Post*, May 4, 2018, www.washingtonpost.com/business/econ omy/now-hiring-for-a-one-day-job-the-gig-economy-hits-retail/2018/05/04/ 2bebdd3c-4257-11e8-ad8f-27a8c409298b_story.html?noredirect=onandutm_term= .e653cb6902c1 [https://perma.cc/Q5JX-TN6C].

133 See generally Tracey Lien, "California Lawsuits Accuse Uber and Lyft of Discriminating against Wheelchair Users," *Los Angeles Times*, March 15, 2018, www.latimes.com/ business/technology/la-fi-tn-uber-lyft-wheelchair-20180315-story.html [https://perma.cc/ 6RWL-QUHZ]; "Judge Approves $27 Million Settlement in Lyft Driver Lawsuit," *CNBC*, March 17, 2017, 7:01 AM, www.cnbc.com/2017/03/17/judge-approves-27-mil lion-driver-settlement-in-lyft-lawsuit.html [https://perma.cc/4KM8-898K].

134 No. 17-cv-00003-HSG, 2017 WL 4098858, *5 (N.D. Cal. September 15, 2017).

135 Ibid., *2.

136 Ibid., *2.

137 Ibid., *5.

138 No. C-13-03156 JSC, 2013 WL 4517756 (N.D. Cal. August 22, 2013).

139 Ibid., *4.

140 Ibid., *5, *89 (internal quotations omitted).

141 *Alatraqchi*, 2013 WL 4517756, *5. See also "Uber Driving Partner – A Great Part Time Opportunity," *Uber*, 2019, https://get.uber.com/p/part-time-driving-partner [https://perma.cc/SN7Y-MR7V].

142 *Alatraqchi*, 2013 WL 4517756, *4 (internal quotations omitted).

143 See, e.g., *Phillips v. Uber Techs., Inc.*, 16 Civ. 295 (DAB), 2017 WL 2782036, *5 (S.D.N.Y. June 14, 2017) (finding it "premature at this point to make a finding based [on] the limited record before it," but stating allegations "insufficient alone legally to establish control indicative of an employment relationship").

144 184 F. Supp. 3d 774, 782 (N.D. Cal. 2016).

145 Ibid.

146 "In support of this assertion, plaintiffs have alleged that Uber sets fare prices without driver input and that drivers may not negotiate fares. If a driver takes a circuitous route, Uber may modify the charges to the customer. Uber retains control over customer contact information." Ibid., 782 (citations omitted) (citing Amended Complaint at ¶¶ 39, 40, 42, *Doe*, 184 F. Supp. 3d 774 [No. 3:15-cv-4670-SI]).

147 "Uber's business model depends upon having a large pool of non-professional drivers. There are no apparent specialized skills needed to drive for Uber. Uber retains the right to terminate drivers at will." Ibid. (citations omitted) (citing Amended Complaint at ¶¶ 25, 36–38, 53–66, 43, *Doe*, 184 F. Supp. 3d 774 [No. 3:15-cv-4670-SI]).

148 "Uber also controls various aspects of the manner and means by which drivers may offer rides through the Uber App. Among these, plaintiffs have alleged that Uber requires drivers to accept all ride requests when logged into the App or face

potential discipline ... Uber requires drivers to: dress professionally; send the customer who has ordered a ride a text message when the driver is 1–2 minutes away from the pickup location; keep their radios either off or on 'soft jazz or NPR'; open the door for the customer; and pick up the customer on the correct side of the street where the customer is standing." Ibid. (citations omitted) (citing Amended Complaint at ¶¶ 44, 45, *Doe*, 184 F. Supp. 3d 774 [No. 3:15-cv-4670-SI]).

149 "Certain factors, as alleged, support Uber's assertion that drivers are independent contractors, though not enough to convert the question into a matter of law. These include that the drivers generally do not receive a salary but are paid by the ride and that the drivers supply their own cars and car insurance. Even these factors, however, are not necessarily dispositive. It matters not whether Uber's licensing agreements label drivers as independent contractors, if their conduct suggests otherwise." Ibid., 782–83 (citations omitted) (first citing *S.G. Borello and Sons, Inc. v. Dep't of Indus. Relations*, 769 P.2d 399 (Cal. 1989); then citing Amended Complaint at ¶¶ 40, 50–51, Doe, 184 F. Supp. 3d 774 (No. 3:15-cv-4670-SI); then citing *Estrada v. FedEx Ground Package System, Inc.*, 154 Cal. App 4th 1, 5 (2007) ("finding drivers for FedEx to be employees even where drivers supplied their own trucks and maintained their own car insurance"); then citing Amended Complaint at ¶¶ 47–48, *Doe*, 184 F. Supp. 3d 774 (No. 3:15-cv-4670-SI) ("[A]lleging that in certain cities Uber drivers may receive a guaranteed minimum rate, 'tantamount to a salary,' and that in January 2016 Uber announced that drivers will have guaranteed earnings, thereby – in plaintiffs' view – giving 'Uber drivers everywhere ... essentially guaranteed salaries ...'"); then citing *Estrada*, 154 Cal. App. 4th 10–11; and then citing Motion to Dismiss at 6–7, Doe, 184 F. Supp. 3d 774 [No. 15-cv-04670 SI]).

150 *Doe*, 184 F. Supp. 3d 783.

151 Ibid.

152 *Search v. Uber Techs., Inc.*, 128 F. Supp. 3d 222, 233 (D.D.C. 2015).

153 "Uber screens new drivers, dictates the fares they may charge, and pays such drivers weekly. [Plaintiff] claims that '[u]pon threat of termination, Uber subjects its drivers to a host of specific requirements,' including, *inter alia*, the use of the Uber app, standards for the cleanliness and mechanical functioning of their cars, rules regarding tipping, minimum timeframes and acceptance rates for ride requests, and display of the Uber logo. According to Plaintiff, these facts establish the first four factors of the aforementioned test. Search maintains that the fifth factor, whether Deresse's work is part of Uber's regular business, is satisfied by his allegation that 'Uber is a car service' for which Deresse was a driver." See ibid., 232 (citations omitted) (first citing Amended Complaint at ¶¶ 7–12, 15, *Search*, 128 F. Supp. 3d 222 (No. 1:15-cv-00257); then citing Opposition to Motion to Dismiss at 12–13, Search, 128 F. Supp. 3d 222 (No. 1:15-cv-00257 [JEB]); and then citing Amended Complaint at ¶ 6, *Search*, Inc., 128 F. Supp. 3d 222 [No. 1:15-cv-00257]).

154 "The Court agrees, for the most part. The Amended Complaint sets forth facts illustrating Uber's involvement in the selection process of new drivers (by way of its

screening procedures); payment of wages (by paying drivers weekly rather than permitting them to collect payment or tips directly from passengers); and termination of employees (by enjoying broad latitude to terminate employees who fail to comply with the company's standards). As to the question whether driving is Uber's regular business, Defendant simply disagrees with Plaintiff's factual allegation that the company is a 'car service.' It does not argue – for good reason – that even if Uber is a car service, as alleged, Deresse's driving is not its regular work." Ibid., 232.

155 "Here, Plaintiff has alleged that Uber controls the rate of refusal of ride requests, the timeliness of the drivers' responses to requests, the display on vehicles of its logo, the frequency with which drivers may contact passengers, the drivers' interactions with passengers (including how they accept tips and collect fares), and the quality of drivers via its rating system." Ibid., 233 (citations omitted) (citing Amended Complaint at ¶¶ 15, 8, *Search*, 128 F. Supp. 3d 222 [No. 1:15-cv-00257]).

156 "Taking these allegations as true, a reasonable factfinder could conclude that Uber exercised control over Deresse in a manner evincing an employer–employee relationship ... in sum, the Court cannot determine as a matter of law that [the driver] was an independent contractor." Ibid.

157 *Razak v. Uber Techs., Inc.*, No. 16-573, 2016 WL 5874822, *4 (E.D. Pa. October 7, 2016).

158 Ibid.

159 "Plaintiffs also specifically allege that they are 'dependent upon the business to which they render service.'" Ibid., *4 (citations omitted) (citing Complaint at ¶ 157, *Razak*, No. 16-573, 2016 WL 5874822 (No. 2:16-CV-00573) ("Plaintiffs and Class members are financially dependent on the fare provided to them by Defendants."); and then citing *Donovan v. DialAmerica Mktg., Inc.*, 757 F.2d 1376, 1383 [3d Cir. 1985]); see also *Razak*, 2016 WL 7241795, *5.

160 *Razak*, 2016 WL 5874822, *4.

161 199 F. Supp. 3d 284, 303 (D. Mass. 2016).

162 Ibid.

163 *Malden Transp., Inc. v. Uber Techs., Inc.*, 286 F. Supp. 3d 264, 281 (D. Mass. 2017).

164 Ibid. Many courts have not been persuaded by Uber's claim that it lacks the control necessary over its drivers necessary to create an employment relationship. See generally *Mumin v. Uber Techs., Inc.*, 239 F. Supp. 3d 507, 532 (E.D.N.Y. 2017); *Razak v. Uber Techs., Inc.*, 2016 WL 5874822, *5 (E.D. Pa. October 7, 2016); *O'Connor*, 82 F. Supp. 3d 1135.

165 *Malden Transp.*, 286 F. Supp. 3d 281.

166 *Mazaheri v. Doe*, No. CIV-14-225-M, 2014 WL 2155049, *3 n.2 (W.D. Okla. May 22, 2014).

167 Ibid.

168 *Lavitman v. Uber Techs., Inc.*, No. SUCV201204490, 2015 WL 728187, *5–6 (Mass. Super. Ct. January 26, 2015).

169 Ibid.

170 This model is based on the factors of the test for establishing the employment relationship suggested in Means and Seiner, "Navigating the Uber Economy."

171 See *Nationwide Mut. Ins. Co. v. Darden*, 503 U.S. 318, 323–24 (1992).

172 See ibid., 323 (including "the extent of the hired party's discretion over when and how long to work" as elements suggesting control).

173 See Maya Kosoff, "Stop Complaining about Uber's Surge Pricing," *Business Insider*, November 1, 2015, www.businessinsider.com/uber-surge-pricing-on-new-years-eve-2015-10 [https://perma.cc/QG4R-7CMN].

174 See *Darden*, 503 U.S. 323–24 (including "the location of the work" as a consideration in the control test).

175 Cf. Carlson, "Why the Law Still Can't Tell," 340–41.

176 See ibid., 299, 340–41 (including "how long" an individual works as a consideration of control).

177 Means and Seiner, "Navigating the Uber Economy" (discussing the importance of pricing models in evaluating employment status in the on-demand economy).

178 See Heather Somerville, "True Price of an Uber Ride in Question as Investors Assess Firm's Value," *New York Daily News*, August 23, 2017, www.nydailynews.com/newswires/news/business/true-price-uber-ride-question-investors-assess-firm-article-1.3435439 [https://perma.cc/8JFB-4NLZ].

179 See Carlson, "Why the Law Still Can't Tell," 339.

180 *Bradshaw v. Uber Technologies Inc.*, No. CIV-16-388-R, 2017 WL 2455151, *8 (W.D. Okla. June 6, 2017).

181 Ibid.

182 *Cotter v. Lyft, Inc.*, 60 F. Supp. 3d 1067, 1081 (N.D. Cal. 2015).

183 Richard B. Stewart, "The Discontents of Legalism: Interest Group Relations in Administrative Regulation," *Wisconsin Law Review* (1985): 655, 662 ("The more certain the law – the less variance in expected outcomes – the more likely the parties will predict the same outcome from litigation, and the less likely litigation will occur because of differences in predicted outcomes.").

184 See ibid., 662.

4

Aggregating Claims

Better never means better for everyone.
— The Commander, *The Handmaid's Tale*[1]

The recent spread of the coronavirus has impacted a large swath of the workforce. Indeed, there is almost no part of the economy that has been left untouched by COVID-19. There can be little doubt that in the wake of this pandemic many workers will feel victimized and will attempt to vindicate their labor and employment rights in court. While these workers will always be permitted to bring individual claims, there may be instances where aggregating claims and pursuing class actions will have a more powerful impact. Indeed, the way in which employers respond to the pandemic may create individual classes of workers who have seen their rights violated in a similar way. Many of these workers will be part of the virtual economy, and a large portion may even be platform-based workers. As explained below, workers in the virtual economy, irrespective of COVID-19, are particularly likely to see their claims appropriate for class aggregation.

In the technology sector, Uber and Lyft have provided substantive examples of what this type of systemic litigation would look like that is brought against platform-based companies. These companies – which provide a technological platform that allows just about anyone to drive for hire – represent an emerging (and certainly controversial) modern economy.[2] This growing industry faces enormous legal challenges, and these new technologies are not always "better for everyone."[3] The class action litigation brought in *O'Connor v. Uber Technologies, Inc.* – and certified by a California federal court in late 2015 – alleges that the company has been misclassifying its workers since its inception.[4] As discussed previously in this book, these workers maintain that they should be considered employees, rather than independent contractors, which would entitle them to a higher rate of pay and additional benefits – putting the business at risk for additional liability.[5] The issue continues to make headlines as more technology companies join the growing number of companies involved in this type of litigation.[6] Worker misclassification suits have even found their way to the on-demand food industry as class action cases have been brought against GrubHub and DoorDash, businesses that have seen particular demand as more individuals stayed at home after the COVID-19 outbreak.[7]

Individual claims brought against these emerging companies are certainly appropriate. But the class action mechanism – the aggregation of each of the individual claims into a single case – should only be permitted after much more careful scrutiny. Class action litigation on the independent contractor/employee issue in cases that involve modern technologies is often self-defeating because it asks a "one-size-fits-all" question.[8] There is often no single answer to this question for the extraordinarily varied workers who are typically involved.

To some extent, we are beginning to see a piling-on effect with these cases. Many of these businesses in the gig economy are highly successful and represent an irresistible target.[9] While the question of whether the workers are employees or independent contractors in these cases is a fair one to ask, there is frequently no single, broad-based answer to the question. The issue that we are seeing is not new. Over seven decades ago, US Supreme Court Justice Wiley Blount Rutledge wrote, "Few problems in the law have given greater variety of application and conflict in results than the cases arising in the borderland between what is clearly an employer-employee relationship and what is clearly one of independent, entrepreneurial dealing."[10] This problem persists today, and we must be careful to handle it in a way that does not undermine job growth, technological advancement, or worker flexibility.

This chapter seeks to provide much-needed clarity to this confused area by addressing the nuances of the platform-based economy and situating them within the context of the class action mechanism. Navigating this area of the law – as well as the Supreme Court's decision on class action litigation in *Wal-Mart Stores, Inc. v. Dukes*,[11] this chapter proposes a framework for analyzing whether systemic litigation is appropriate for technology cases on the employee/independent contractor question.

Through an extensive review of the case law, federal statutes, and platform-based economy, this chapter provides a model for the courts and litigants to follow when evaluating whether there is sufficient *commonality* under recent Supreme Court precedent to proceed in a class action case. The proposed framework helps determine whether systemic litigation should be pursued in these technology-sector cases by setting forth five critical components of the working relationship – the time, place, frequency, and manner of the work performed, as well as the pricing model of the business involved – and exploring their importance. These elements are similar to those examined in Chapter 3 and must be considered specifically in the context of class action litigation. This chapter synthesizes the cases, regulations, and statutes to bring clarity to this area. Where these cases are permitted to proceed, the framework discussed here further provides helpful guidance on the appropriate size and scope of the class involved.[12]

This chapter also applies the framework to the class action in *O'Connor v. Uber*.[13] It examines how the framework would apply in that particular context, outlining the importance of each of the elements in the test. The problem here is much broader than *O'Connor* and involves the entire technology sector. Given the high-profile nature of this class certification decision, as well as its likely influence on other cases, however, *O'Connor* provides a helpful example for explaining how the model outlined here should be applied.[14]

This is not to say that the suggested framework is exhaustive; indeed, the five factors are meant only to provide general, straightforward guidelines for the courts to consider to focus the inquiry in this area. As cases continue to emerge, and as other scholars begin to weigh in on the topic, the parameters of the test proposed here can be further refined. Similarly, the weight given to the factors identified in this chapter will vary depending upon the facts of the particular case. This chapter does not examine the well-traveled question of *how* the independent contractor/employee test should be analyzed. Instead, it addresses the more expansive issue of how to shape the proper scope of the class often involved in this type of litigation.

This chapter proceeds in several parts. First, this chapter sets forth the guidelines for systemic litigation under the Federal Rules of Civil Procedure. This section further examines the Supreme Court's litigation in *Wal-Mart Stores, Inc. v. Dukes*, explaining how the Court has redefined the standard for commonality under the Federal Rules. Next, this chapter examines one of the most important statutes for worker classification issues – the Fair Labor Standards Act (FLSA) – which creates the federal requirements for wage/hour claims. This chapter then examines the federal district court decision in *O'Connor v. Uber*, which permitted the aggregation of a class on the worker classification issue. This chapter further examines the potential harm of the *O'Connor* analysis, the need for more clarity in this area, and other systemic litigation in the technology sector. This chapter proposes a framework for analyzing whether class action claims should be permitted to proceed in technology-based cases, and applies the analysis to the *O'Connor* decision. Finally, this chapter explores how Federal Rule of Civil Procedure 23(c)(4) – issue class certification – can impact the analysis of class action cases in the on-demand economy.

4.1 CLASS ACTIONS GENERALLY

Class action litigation is complex and has evolved over time. This section examines the basic rules of systemic litigation and explores how the Supreme Court has refined those rules.

4.1.1 *The Rules and Benefits of Class Action Litigation*

The class action mechanism has had a controversial history over the years. The benefits of the class action model are numerous, as it provides the ability to resolve hundreds or thousands of legal claims as part of a single piece of litigation, thus substantially streamlining the judicial process.[15] Through aggregation, the parties can achieve judicial economies that translate into substantial savings of time and money. By resolving a question only once, the entire process becomes far more efficient and much less cumbersome.

At the same time, aggregating claims into a single lawsuit presents possible drawbacks. There is a concern that this type of litigation will strip some potential plaintiffs of their day in court. The Supreme Court has held that – if done properly – class action litigation can still protect the rights of aggrieved persons that are foregoing the opportunity for individual litigation.[16] Rule 23 of the Federal Rules of Civil Procedure was put in place to help effectuate the many benefits of the class action mechanism while still preserving these rights of individuals.[17] Under Rule 23(a), a proposed class must satisfy a number of specific elements to be permitted to proceed. Specifically, the purported class must demonstrate sufficient numerosity, typicality, commonality, and adequacy of representation.[18] In recent years, the Supreme Court has taken a much more narrow view of systemic litigation involving workplace claims. In particular, in *Wal-Mart Stores, Inc. v. Dukes*,[19] the Court expressed reluctance to permit these claims where there was not well-defined evidence to support the commonality requirement of the test.[20]

4.1.2 *The* Wal-Mart *Standard*

The Supreme Court has narrowly interpreted class action employment claims in recent years.[21] The centerpiece of the Court's jurisprudence in this area is

Wal-Mart Stores, Inc. v. *Dukes.*[22] Much has already been written on this case, so this chapter only briefly summarizes the relevant facts and holdings here.

In *Wal-Mart*, the Court considered whether a class of over a million current and former female employees should be certified where the workers alleged discrimination on pay and promotion issues. The case, "one of the most expansive class actions ever,"[23] was brought against Wal-Mart, the country's largest private employer. The plaintiffs in the matter maintained that there was a unified "corporate culture" at the company that was biased against women and subsequently led to discriminatory decisions.[24] The plaintiffs further argued that the discretion given to management-level employees to evaluate pay and promotion issues was being exercised consistently in a way that negatively impacted female workers. In light of these facts, the plaintiffs alleged a violation of Title VII of the Civil Rights Act of 1964, which protects workers on the basis of several characteristics, including gender.

The federal district court certified the class, and the appellate court largely affirmed the lower court ruling. The Supreme Court granted certiorari to determine whether class certification was appropriate under Federal Rule of Civil Procedure 23(a). Specifically, the Supreme Court addressed whether the claimants satisfied the *commonality* requirement of the rule. Under Rule 23(a)(2), plaintiffs must demonstrate sufficient "questions of law or fact" that are "common to the class."[25] According to the Court, this "common contention" in the case "must be of such a nature that it is capable of classwide resolution."[26] The question presented must therefore "resolve an issue that is central to the validity of each one of the claims in one stroke."

Applying this standard to the facts of the case, the Supreme Court found no *commonality* in the million-plus claims asserted. The plaintiffs failed to establish that the discretion exercised by management was performed in a common way that discriminated against female employees. Indeed, there was no showing of "a common mode of exercising discretion that pervades the entire company."[27] Given the "size and geographical scope" of Wal-Mart, the Court found it "quite unbelievable that all managers would exercise their discretion in a common way without some common direction."[28] The plaintiffs had only put forth a "bare existence of delegated discretion," failing to establish a "specific employment practice" that "tie[d] all their 1.5 million claims together."[29] In sum, the Court concluded that there was no commonality established in the case, noting that the plaintiffs were attempting "to sue about literally millions of employment decisions at once. Without some glue holding the alleged *reasons* for all those decisions together, it will be impossible to say that examination of all the class members' claims for relief will produce a common answer to the crucial question *why was I disfavored*."[30]

In sum, allowing management discretion in making pay and promotion decisions is – in and of itself – insufficient to support a class action Title VII claim. This is not to say that discrimination did not occur in each of the cases or that the individual class members were not treated disparately when it came to pay and promotion decisions. Indeed, each individual class member would still be allowed to pursue claims against Wal-Mart (assuming that administrative and procedural requirements had otherwise been satisfied). The Court's holding, then, stands for the proposition that, while discrimination may have occurred in individual instances, there was no "glue" holding all of the claims together. In this instance, individual, rather than aggregate, litigation was appropriate, at least in the view of the court.

Image Credit: KAREN BLEIER/Staff/Getty Images

More recent case law in *Tyson Foods, Inc. v. Bouaphakeo* may call into question the way the commonality standard should be applied to certain workplace cases.[31] Still, the *Wal-Mart* case makes clear that this commonality requirement will now be applied much more rigidly in most class action cases.

4.2 CLASSIFICATION AND THE FLSA

The commonality question in *Wal-Mart* arose in the workplace context, and much has been written on the extent to which the case provides a more rigid standard for employment class action cases.[32] In technology-sector claims, the common employment law question, which the courts continue to face, is the issue of whether workers are employees or independent contractors.[33] Under federal law, if a business misclassifies a worker as an independent contractor, it can be subjected to back pay and liquidated damages.[34] And, more potentially damaging to the companies involved, these types of claims often raise the potential for systemic litigation. Where an employer misclassifies one worker, it may misclassify others as well. After *Wal-Mart*, then, it is helpful to examine what factors these misclassified workers might share that would satisfy the more rigid commonality requirement for class certification. A discussion of wage/hour law in this area helps to situate this analysis more clearly.

The FLSA is a federal employment law that provides three primary areas of protection.[35] First, it establishes a minimum wage, which is currently set at $7.25 per hour. Second, it mandates premium pay (time and a half) for any work over forty hours in a given week. Finally, it makes unlawful the oppressive work of children, establishing extensive child labor restrictions. Coverage under the FLSA is quite broad, and almost all businesses must abide by the provisions of this federal law.[36] Thus, most businesses easily satisfy the requirement of being "employers" under the law.[37] A more difficult inquiry, however, is whether a particular worker is an "employee" under the statute. Only *employees* are protected by the FLSA, and independent contractors have no avenue of recourse under this statute.[38] As discussed earlier in this book, the independent contractor/employee distinction has caused substantial confusion over the decades since the FLSA was passed, and the problems of interpreting the statute still persist. Under the statute, to "[e]mploy" means "to suffer or permit to work."[39] This broad, circular definition provides little help when establishing the proper standard for coverage in many cases.[40] To help resolve this ambiguity, the courts have developed numerous tests on the question to better analyze the issue. There is variation on the exact parameters of these tests, but the courts frequently consider

(1) the level of control the employer maintains over the worker;

(2) the opportunity for profit or loss maintained by the worker in the business;

(3) the amount of capital investment the worker puts into the process;

(4) the degree of skill necessary to perform the job;

(5) whether performance of the job is integral to the operation of the business; and

(6) the permanency of the relationship between the worker and the employer.[41]

The major consideration in this test is *control.* Arguably, all of the other factors stated above play into the amount of control exerted by either the company or the worker. The more control a *business* has in the working relationship, the more the worker is likely to be considered an employee. The more control the *worker* has, the more likely it is that that individual will be characterized as an independent contractor. The exact amount of control required, and how that control is analyzed, varies in the courts. There has been a steady development in the case law on the question of what it takes for an individual worker to satisfy the "employee" test. While the courts have taken varying approaches to the issue – sometimes with conflicting results – the parameters of the test have been roughly defined over time. The cases arising in the modern economy and technology sector, however, have pushed the boundaries of the "employee" definition and created widespread uncertainty in this area of the law. Technology-sector cases have transformed the question of employment under the law, as these workers look far different from those employed in traditional brick-and-mortar facilities. The platform-based economy has only further placed this area into flux. Workers now perform services at home, on the road, on a part-time or full-time basis, and in many ways never before considered possible.[42]

The courts have taken the now long-established definition of "employee" in the FLSA and attempted to apply it to this modern workforce. As previously noted, one federal court best characterized the situation as being "handed a square peg and asked to choose between two round holes."[43] This text has already explored the difficulty of applying a test created decades ago to cases arising in the technology sector, highlighting the importance of flexibility in the analysis.[44] This chapter looks at a more expansive issue – the scope of the class action mechanism used to litigate these claims.

This chapter does not revisit the well-considered ground of how the independent contractor/employee test should be analyzed, which was already discussed in this book. Instead, in those growing number of technology-sector cases where the test is at issue, this chapter examines whether the class action model can be helpful in resolving the question. Given the individualized nature of these questions, this book argues for a more limited, narrowly tailored class-based approach.

As noted earlier, class action cases are particularly prevalent in the technology sector. The question most frequently addressed in these cases is whether the worker is an employee or an independent contractor. In greater detail below, this chapter provides the parameters that should be considered to help answer this question, as well as a model for analyzing the appropriate scope of the class. It is difficult to conceptualize this question in the abstract, however, and it is thus helpful to address the issue in the context of more concrete litigation when evaluating the proposed framework discussed below.

4.3 THE O'CONNOR CASE

The Supreme Court's reluctance to allow class action litigation impacts all areas of the law. And, Supreme Court decisions have cut back on the ability of plaintiffs to bring systemic arbitration claims[45] as well as antitrust litigation.[46] In the face of this trend, it is interesting to see the federal district court decision in *O'Connor* permit class certification on the worker misclassification issue. Indeed, this lower court decision may conflict with the Supreme Court's precedent in this area. The Court has clearly expressed its view that commonality must be narrowly construed in employment cases, and that class action litigation should only proceed where all of the requirements of the Federal Rules of Civil Procedure have been satisfied. This is not to say that the Supreme Court was correct in its decision to establish a heightened commonality standard. Given the *Wal-Mart* test for commonality, however, it is difficult to reconcile the reasoning in *O'Connor* with the Supreme Court's heightened standard.

As noted earlier, the number of technology companies involved in systemic litigation on the worker misclassification issue is only growing. A sampling of these cases (discussed in greater detail below) include systemic litigation against GrubHub, DoorDash, Handy, CrowdFlower, Yelp, and Amazon. In terms of high-profile cases, however, there is no comparison with the class action litigation brought against Uber, which has captured headlines across the nation. The case may change the very way that the workplace is structured, and how we interpret the employment relationship. This text has already looked at the worker classification issue in the ride-sharing industry; this chapter delves more deeply into the question of whether and how these particular claims should be aggregated.

The district court in *O'Connor* struggled with the commonality requirement under Rule 23(a)(2). In examining this issue, the court noted the restrictive commonality standard enunciated in the *Wal-Mart* decision. The court concluded that this "rigorous" standard had been satisfied.[47] In reaching this decision, the court found that the jury's resolution of the classification question could be outcome determinative, noting that if the "jury determine[s] that the class members here are not Uber's employees, this class action will have reached its end."[48] On the other hand, if the trier of fact reaches the opposite conclusion, then the drivers "are likely to be entitled to relief as a class."[49] With respect to commonality, the court further determined that the "worker classification claim presents a common issue capable of classwide adjudication because all (or nearly all) of the individual elements of the ... test themselves raise common questions which will have common answers."[50]

In the thirty-seven-page opinion, the court gave very limited attention to the Supreme Court's Wal-Mart decision. Indeed, the district court's citations to this case are primarily for the basic propositions that class actions represent an exception for similarly situated litigants to the general rule of individual litigation in civil cases, and that there must be at least one common claim for a class action to proceed. The district court does not fully address anywhere in its opinion the restrictive commonality standard that was articulated by the Wal-Mart case.[51]

4.4 A CLOSER LOOK AT O'CONNOR AND THE CLASS ACTION MODEL

4.4.1 Another Look at the O'Connor Decision

As discussed in O'Connor, the federal district court essentially allowed a class action to proceed against Uber that included 160,000 litigants. The judge's analysis did not properly consider the importance of the revised and more rigorous commonality developed in the Supreme Court's Wal-Mart decision. The O'Connor case creates important precedent, as other class action litigation is pending on the same question in similar cases brought against other businesses in the technology sector across the nation. The analysis used in O'Connor should be reconsidered, as it provides little guidance and affords insufficient weight to the Wal-Mart commonality standard. While it is only federal district court precedent, the case threatens to create an unworkable model for systemic cases in the technology sector, given the attention the litigation received and the high-profile nature of the issues involved.[52]

The analysis used by the court basically concluded that there was sufficient commonality because the resolution of the issue would help resolve the case. While it is true that if the classification issue were decided, it would greatly streamline – and potentially resolve – the matter, this is not the appropriate question to be asking when evaluating commonality under the Federal Rules after Wal-Mart. There are many issues a jury could weigh in on that would help clear the court's docket, but this does not mean that these issues are appropriate for class certification. The commonality test articulated in Wal-Mart demands a far more detailed and rigorous analysis than what the district court was willing to give in this case, as demonstrated by the court's limited citation to the Supreme Court's decision. The district court acknowledged the restrictive nature of the commonality test articulated by the Supreme Court, but it did not apply this more restrictive standard.

A more appropriate inquiry into the commonality test would have examined the *Wal-Mart* Court's analysis of Rule 23(a)(2) and whether the plaintiffs sufficiently demonstrated "questions of law or fact" that are "common to the class."[53] According to the Supreme Court, this "common contention" in the case "must be of such a nature that it is capable of classwide resolution."[54] The question presented must, therefore, "resolve an issue that is central to the validity of each one of the claims in one stroke."[55] Here, the district court certified the issue of whether Uber drivers are employees or independent contractors. This question cannot be answered in a single way on a classwide basis, at least not with the enormous 160,000 worker class presented by the *O'Connor* case. Instead, a more individualized analysis is necessary. The flexibility and diversity of individuals who pursue employment in this industry result in key differentiating factors within this group. Trying to aggregate all of these workers as part of a single class in this industry is difficult, if not impossible, across such a broad range of individuals.

As required by the Supreme Court in *Wal-Mart*, there must be "some glue holding" the case together.[56] That bond does not seem to exist here for all 160,000 individuals, as these workers differ in a number of critical ways, including with respect to their hours, rate of pay, work schedules, and other important elements of employment. This is not to say that a class could not proceed as to certain groups of workers with similar employment-related characteristics. Or, as will be addressed in greater detail below, an "issue class" could be pursued as to certain questions in the case. But aggregating a class of 160,000 workers who each possess such individualized employment characteristics should not be permitted under the more rigorous *Wal-Mart* analysis.

This is not to say that the *Wal-Mart* Court got the analysis right. But in light of *Wal-Mart*, we must more carefully look at how – and when – technology-sector claims should be aggregated.

4.4.2 *The Harm of the* O'Connor *Analysis*

It may seem that there is little harm in treating workers on an aggregate basis in technology cases. While it is true that Uber is a multi-billion dollar company that can likely withstand substantial litigation costs, such cases do create potentially large and sometimes crippling business expenses for certain employers. With the risk of this possible litigation, existing employers may become more cautious about expanding operations or creating new employment opportunities, and prospective businesses may even think twice about incorporating.

Obviously, litigation costs should be borne where appropriate, and labor/employment laws are certainly not unnecessarily hindering business. Rather, the concern created by cases such as *O'Connor* is the cost and uncertainty that is generated by potentially inappropriate aggregate litigation, at least as defined by the Supreme Court. These costs can directly impact how the entire technology sector operates, as well as the growth of this particular industry. The threat of enormous class action cases like we see in *O'Connor* will have to be considered when structuring a business model in this sector, and employment (and economic growth) will likely be impacted as well. As already noted, although this book takes no view on the validity of the *Wal-Mart* commonality standard, a more careful consideration of class action cases in the technology sector is nonetheless necessary in light of that standard.

Some have argued that this type of case will be disastrous for the technology sector – restricting flexibility and imposing an outdated, rigid employment model on this newly emerging industry.[57] Such predictions are premature, and sometimes overstated. But these arguments do demonstrate the existing conflict between the emerging modern economy and the older, brick-and-mortar employment model that has existed for years. Until the law evolves further, and the legal standards are clarified, it will be impossible to understand the precise effect cases such as *O'Connor* will have on the larger employment landscape, and on the technology sector more broadly.

This chapter, then, does not maintain that all class action litigation is inappropriate in the technology sector. Rather, such systemic litigation should be allowed to proceed in many technology-sector cases. A more clear standard is necessary to assist the courts in better understanding when such aggregate litigation should be allowed to proceed.

4.4.3 *Grubhub, DoorDash, Amazon, and More*

Though this chapter examines the existing litigation against Uber, the case really represents part of a much bigger picture. There is substantial other litigation that has recently been brought against businesses throughout the technology-based economy. Several of these cases involve the question of worker classification and are worth brief exploration. These cases underscore the prevalence of this issue, and the increasing importance of finding a way to address systemic litigation in the technology sector.

For example, it can be instructive to look at one area that has grown in light of the recent pandemic – food delivery services. In the face of the COVID-19 outbreak, this particular segment of the platform-based economy saw an uptick in growth as individuals began to place more mobile orders. This was the result of a number of different factors, including state and local laws imposing lockdown orders, businesses that were not permitted to offer in-room dining services, as well as the general public feeling uncomfortable taking advantage of such in-room dining services even where they were lawfully provided.

Image Credit: Cindy Ord/Staff/Getty Images

In particular, GrubHub and DoorDash are leaders in this segment, providing on-demand food delivery services and allowing customers to order from local businesses and restaurants through online and mobile applications.[58] It can be helpful to look at litigation brought against both companies. On September 23, 2015, delivery drivers for GrubHub brought a class action in California state court maintaining that they were misclassified as independent contractors, when they should have been considered as employees for purposes of wage payment law.[59] The drivers for GrubHub receive a flat fee for each delivery as well as any tip that is added by the customer.[60] The drivers alleged that they were employees because they signed up for shifts in advance.[61] GrubHub controls the drivers' work by instructing them where to report, how to dress, where to pick up deliveries, and how to handle the food (as well as the timeliness of the deliveries themselves).[62] However, GrubHub required the drivers to bear the expenses associated with their vehicle, gas, parking, and phone data.[63] A similar complaint was also filed against DoorDash for the alleged misclassification of workers as independent contractors in California state court.[64]

Similarly, Instacart is an on-demand "grocery delivery service."[65] The company hires workers to purchase and deliver grocery orders to Instacart's customers.[66] The company has been quite successful and boasted an impressive

$2 billion dollar valuation in 2015.[67] However, Instacart has been immersed in litigation over the classification of its workers.[68] In February 2015, several workers initiated a class action lawsuit in California's state courts – later removed to the Northern District of California – claiming that Instacart misclassified the workers as independent contractors.[69] The plaintiffs claimed that they were entitled to a minimum wage, overtime pay, and employment-related expenses such as automobile maintenance, fuel, and insurance.[70] The plaintiffs further argued that Instacart asserted extensive control over its workers as evidenced by the company's control over "when and where [workers] were to collect and deliver groceries," the manner by which workers interfaced with customers, and the requirement that workers dress in clothing displaying the Instacart logo.[71] Furthermore, Instacart fired workers at will,[72] determined workers' wages[73] and the prices charged to customers,[74] required workers to work in shifts,[75] and frequently monitored workers' actions.[76] The courts consistently granted Instacart's motions to compel arbitration.[77]

Other segments of the virtual economy have similarly seen class-action efforts. Amazon Prime Now provided a benefit to users of Amazon Prime that allowed the members to place orders for same-day delivery in select zip codes through the use of a mobile application. The drivers of Amazon Prime Now filed a class-action suit in California state court on October 27, 2015, alleging their misclassification as independent contractors and failure to pay minimum wage.[78] The drivers stated that they worked regular shifts for hourly pay in order to deliver only the packages that Amazon Prime specifically assigned to them, while wearing an Amazon uniform.[79] Amazon provided the drivers with a smartphone to use for the deliveries, but drivers had to provide their own vehicle and fuel.[80] The drivers worked fixed shifts in which they checked in with the dispatcher to receive their package assignments.[81] They could neither reject assignments nor request to work in a particular geographic location.[82] Amazon determined the sequence of their deliveries as well as the routes and could track the drivers while they were out on delivery routes.[83] The drivers did not have the opportunity to negotiate any aspect of their compensation.[84]

Similarly, in yet another area of the virtual economy, Yelp was founded as a means of connecting customers with local businesses.[85] Through the Yelp platform, consumers can find local businesses and leave reviews for the companies that they have visited or services they have used.[86] Business managers can set up accounts to post photos of their business and message customers.[87] Yelp reviewers filed a class action suit in federal district court against the company arguing that the reviewers should be considered employees.[88] However, the court granted Yelp's motion to dismiss for failure to state a claim on August 13, 2015.[89] The court emphasized that the language used by the plaintiffs to assert that they were "hired" by Yelp should reasonably be inferred to refer to a process by which any individual can sign up on Yelp and submit reviews.[90]

The household services segment of the platform-based economy has also seen class-action efforts. Handy, previously Handybook, was an online platform that connected individuals looking for household jobs, such as cleaning or handy services, with independent professionals.[91] Cleaning professionals booked their work through the list of available jobs provided by the application.[92] Handy retained control over the cleaning professionals through its ability to terminate at will and through its control over the location of the job and amount charged to the customer.[93] These independent professionals filed a class action suit alleging that Handy was misclassifying its employees as independent contractors and failed to pay the workers the appropriate overtime compensation.[94] The complaint was filed on October 30, 2014.[95] The court granted the cleaning service's motion to compel arbitration.[96]

And yet another class-action attempt included Postmates, a delivery service that "connects customers with local couriers who can deliver anything from any store or restaurant in minutes."[97] The couriers filed several class-action lawsuits against Postmates for worker misclassification.[98] A class-action complaint filed in the Northern District of California alleged that Postmates misclassified its couriers as independent contractors and failed to properly pay a minimum wage, overtime, and various expenses that an employer should incur.[99] The complaint further alleged that couriers "are required to follow detailed requirements imposed on them by Postmates, and they are graded, and are subject to termination, based on Postmates' discretion and/or their failure to adhere to these requirements (such as rules regarding their conduct with customers, their timeliness in picking up items and delivering them to customers, the accurateness of their orders, etc.)."[100] Couriers alleged responsibility for many of their job-related expenses, such as transportation and phone costs.[101]

And still another area, crowdsourcing, has seen litigation. CrowdFlower is a company that provides data enrichment, data mining, and crowdsourcing.[102] Customers could upload their data onto the CrowdFlower website and set up instructions to create their job.[103] After the job had been created, people would task on the job until it had been completed.[104] Individuals that had performed some of these tasks for CrowdFlower brought a class action suit against the company, arguing that they were misclassified as independent contractors and paid less than the legal minimum wage.[105] The parties entered a settlement agreement in the case in which defendants agreed to pay $585,507 to be distributed among the plaintiffs and plaintiffs' counsel.[106]

The settlement was approved on July 2, 2015, though there is additional procedural history in the case.[107]

The on-demand cleaning industry has also seen litigation. More specifically, Homejoy was an on-demand start-up that connected independent cleaners with customers.[108] The business classified its 1,000-plus cleaners as independent contractors.[109] Early on, the company enjoyed considerable growth and raised a significant amount of venture capital financing.[110] Despite its early successes, workers filed a series of lawsuits, including three class actions, against Homejoy, alleging that the company's cleaners were misclassified as independent contractors.[111] Each complaint asserted that Homejoy exerted a substantial amount of control over its cleaners, and, therefore, improperly classified its workers as independent contractors.[112] A class-action complaint filed on March 19, 2015, in the Northern District of California alleged that Homejoy failed to compensate cleaners for overtime and work-related expenses that the company should have reimbursed.[113] A separate class-action complaint filed in California state court alleged that the company's cleaners could not "negotiate their pay," and had no discretion over which homes to clean or the amount of time spent cleaning at each home.[114] Additionally, Homejoy could fire a cleaner at any time or place a cleaner on a "performance improvement plan[]."[115] The complaint further alleged that Homejoy could change a cleaner's schedule with very little notice,[116] determined the cleaning fees,[117] mandated a "minimum number of jobs" per week,[118] and required cleaners to wear a shirt with the company's logo.[119] Furthermore, the cleaners were required to stick to a cleaning checklist provided by Homejoy and could not determine "cleaning tasks" within the home.[120] In July 2015, Homejoy announced that it would cease operations primarily due to pending lawsuits over the worker classification issue.[121]

And even on-demand laundry services have seen class-action efforts. Washio was an on-demand dry cleaning and laundry service that hired drivers to pick up and deliver laundry to customers.[122] Washio drivers filed a class action lawsuit on June 29, 2015, in California state court arguing that drivers were misclassified as independent contractors.[123] The complaint alleged that Washio required its drivers to stick to rules dictating client interactions and how drivers should "store clothes in their vehicles."[124] Moreover, Washio drivers were evaluated on how quickly they completed pick-ups and drop-offs, and the company could fire workers at will.[125] The complaint further alleged that Washio required drivers to consent to an exclusivity agreement, which prohibited drivers from working for Washio's competitors.[126] Washio ceased operations in August 2016,[127] though the company cited reasons other than the employment-related litigation for shutting down.[128]

As these cases illustrate, there is a large amount of litigation against technology-sector companies related to the worker classification issue. This litigation has had differing results: some cases have been allowed to proceed, others have been dismissed, others have settled, and still others have found their way into arbitration.

Most importantly for purposes of this text, these cases emphasize the varied fact patterns that can give rise to technology-sector working relationships. While the ultimate question is one of control, there is no single set of facts in these cases that will help provide guidance on how that control should be evaluated. These cases thus emphasize how this question is highly individualized in nature. With regard to control in this economy, we see that GrubHub controls where its workers are to report, how to dress, where to pick up deliveries, and how to address timeliness issues.[129] Amazon Prime Now controlled the application that the drivers used, the appearance of drivers, and their rate of pay.[130] Yelp apparently maintains almost *no control* over its reviewers.[131] And, there is an additional swath of businesses that have yet to see litigation in this area but that are ripe for a potential dispute on this question of worker classification.

Regardless of the potential business involved, the worker classification question will continue to arise in numerous contexts within the technology sector until more guidance is provided in this area. This chapter seeks to provide a framework with which to address these classification issues on a classwide basis in technology-sector cases.

4.5 THE CLASS-ACTION INQUIRY REVISITED: WEIGHING INDICIA OF EMPLOYMENT

The difficulty associated with litigating class action cases in the technology sector is also one of the greatest benefits associated with this type of employment: worker flexibility.[132] Workers in the technology sector enjoy an unprecedented level of flexibility in their work, and often choose when, where, and how to carry out their job duties.[133] While this workplace flexibility often benefits individuals, it can make aggregation of claims far more difficult. Unlike a traditional brick-and-mortar type place of business, or a factory assembly line setting, workers in the tech industry are unequal and often do not perform identical services or work similar hours.[134]

4.5.1 *Indicia of Employment*

A significant problem with *O'Connor* (and the cases following its analysis) is the lack of commonality that often exists among workers in technology-sector cases. The key inquiry of whether a worker is an employee or an independent contractor is very difficult to answer on an aggregate level; the workers are often too varied to answer this question in a single way. This is not to say that in certain circumstances (or in particular employment settings) such claims cannot be aggregated. However, each case must be examined on an individualized basis. Indeed, there may be groups of workers that have similar employment characteristics that would allow them to be aggregated for purposes of systemic litigation. Or, there may be subclasses that would work in the particular litigation. The overarching point, however, is that there is typically no "one-size-fits-all"[35] answer to this question for technology-sector cases. Rather, the best that we can hope to do is to provide some general guidelines on how – and when – to aggregate these claims.

This chapter suggests a framework that helps identify those technology-sector cases that would be appropriate for aggregation on the employee classification question. Through an extensive review of the case law, several factors emerged that help clarify which cases should be permitted to proceed on a systemic level. The key component of this framework is an emphasis on the level of commonality of the workers as required by the Supreme Court's decision in *Wal-Mart* discussed above. Those workers who have more in common with one another share a number of similar characteristics, which are identified in the model identified below.

This framework sets forth five different characteristics that the courts and litigants should consider when evaluating class action litigation on the employee classification question. These characteristics should only serve as a guideline and are not dispositive. Each case – particularly in this emerging economy – is unique and should be evaluated on its own merits. The model below, however, is sufficiently comprehensive to help the courts navigate this complex area of the law. It also provides some basic guidelines to consider when evaluating the appropriate scope of a class on this with respect to the commonality question. Each of the five factors below should be carefully evaluated by the court when addressing this type of systemic litigation.

These factors can help shape a class action case when considering the employee classification issue and should be evaluated when any aggregate litigation is proposed on this question. It is important to note that these factors should not be confused with the test discussed earlier for determining the *existence* of an employment relationship. Rather, these factors are intended primarily to help evaluate the more precise question of whether worker claims should be aggregated on the employment classification issue. Each factor should be evaluated separately when examining this issue, and the weight given to any specific factor will depend on the particular case. These factors are not exhaustive, and it is entirely possible that factors not even contemplated here may still play a major role in shaping a proposed class. Nonetheless, the following framework attempts to provide some basic guidelines for aggregating a class in the technology sector.

These five factors – which are unweighted – are set forth below:

1. *The time that the work occurs*: When an individual performs work is a critical component of that individual's status as an employee.[136] When aggregating claims, the courts should closely examine the timing of the work itself. If an individual works exclusively on evenings, that individual's experience may be far different than someone who works only during the day.[137] Thus, individuals who perform work at similar times will be more likely to satisfy the commonality component of the Federal Rules. Timing is only one factor – but an important indicium of employment – and should be considered when grouping plaintiffs in systemic litigation on the employment classification question.

2. *The place where work is performed*: The place where the work is performed is a critical factor which helps differentiate individuals. Workers will likely vary in where their job duties are executed, such as at home, in an office, or even in their car.[138] Those that carry out their tasks in a similar physical location will be far more likely to satisfy the commonality necessary to be part of a class action. Individuals who work at different locations may be too different from one another to warrant class certification.

3. *The frequency of work*: Frequency may well be the most important factor in the five-part framework, as it helps clarify which workers are truly similar to each other. Frequency is a term that can change given the specific workplace, but in most contexts – as in the technology sector – it can be more simply defined as how often the work is performed. In the context of Uber, for example, the frequency of work would mean the number of hours that a driver performs her duties – how often the driver is actually on the road transporting customers, as well as any time spent waiting.[139]

The frequency factor – at least in the technology sector – is where employees will likely differ substantially from one another. Some drivers might work forty to sixty hours a week, whereas other drivers may treat their employment as a part-time job, working only a few hours a week to make extra money on the side. Frequency of work is driven by a number of different criteria; individuals who are suddenly unemployed may see being a full-time Uber driver as an excellent employment opportunity. Individuals who are currently employed in other parts of the economy may quit their jobs to make more money at Uber full-time. Or, workers might have other full-time employment, be full-time students, or simply only want to work for the company for a more limited number of hours per week. Irrespective of the particular worker's situation or motivation, however, how often the work is performed will be a critical criterion for aggregation on the employee classification question.

4. *Manner of work*: The manner of work performed can more simply be defined as *how* a worker performs her job.[140] This factor is important, but often not likely to differ among workers in technology-driven work. In the Uber case, for example, courts could look at whether the individual drives her own car, or whether she utilizes a vehicle owned by the company. Or, the court could look at whether some workers perform their jobs under particularly high-stress conditions, such as during peak times, whereas others do not face the same obstacles or difficulties. How a particular individual's work is evaluated or supervised can be yet another critical factor that forms part of this inquiry. Like the other factors, those who perform work in a similar manner will be more likely to satisfy the commonality component of the Federal Rules as defined by the Supreme Court. This factor should thus be carefully considered when evaluating the scope of a particular class action in the workplace.

5. *Pricing models*: Price is a particularly important part of the framework set forth in this book.[141] The other factors – time, place, frequency, and manner – all go to the core of how work is performed. Pricing questions can reveal the level of control a worker exerts in her relationship with the business. Those individuals who are able to set their own pricing models for their services will be far more likely to be independent contractors than those who do not have this amount of control. Similarly, class actions on the question of the employee classification issue may be grouped among workers who have similar levels of control over setting their own pricing structures for their particular services. Those workers who have different levels of power in setting prices should not be considered as part of the same class on this question, as they are far different in their status as employees.

The five-part model set forth above is intended to serve only as a guide and to provide some common markers for courts (and litigants) to look to when evaluating the scope of a class claim. The framework addresses the appropriate scope of employment classification. The model should not be used to evaluate the different question of whether workers are actually employees or independent contractors. Nonetheless, the same factors used to shape a class action in this area will typically be relevant to the ultimate issue of whether a worker is an employee or an independent contractor.

Trying to define an appropriate class on this issue can be a difficult task, and the model offered here is simply one approach to this type of aggregate litigation. This model should serve as a guide to systemic litigation in this area of the law – one of many tools practitioners and the judiciary can use to help establish the parameters of this now fairly common type of class action litigation. There are certainly other approaches to analyzing class action cases, and there are surely other indicia the courts can look to when considering the employee classification issue. The model offered here is thus not intended to be exhaustive and serves only as a single formulation to help better define this complex area of the law.

The technology cases in this area are highly individualized. The model offered here attempts to be broad enough in scope to help account for specific variances in the cases. However, the model is flexible and will need to be adjusted in specific situations that do not fit neatly within its parameters. As the modern economy is constantly evolving, the framework offered here must only be considered a guide, and some employers may fall outside of the factors contemplated. Each case will present a unique set of facts and should be considered accordingly. In sum, no model can account for all of the potential variances in a constantly changing technology industry. This chapter offers a basic framework to address the bulk of the cases but should be considered malleable and it may need to be adapted to more unique or novel situations. Nonetheless, this model provides an important framework for evaluating the scope of much of the class action litigation in the platform-based economy.

4.5.2 Applying the Proposed Model to O'Connor

The proposed framework set forth here is meant to apply to all cases arising in the technology sector. The proposed model is broad enough to be adapted to each of these cases. However, it is helpful to understand the contours of the test by applying it to the facts of one particular claim: the O'Connor case.

When evaluating the framework in this context, we see that the time in which the work is performed will vary substantially across the Uber workforce. Some drivers work during the day, others at night, and some drivers work exclusively on weekends. Similarly, the place where drivers perform the work will vary as well; some will drive in specific areas of the city or primarily near particular venues or attractions. Frequency differs among workers here too: some drivers will work full-time schedules while others will only spend a few hours a week driving for the business.[142] The manner in which the work is performed can also vary; those driving during rush hour, high-peak times, or during nighttime hours will have a far different experience than those working during the day or on weekends. Finally, the pricing model appears to be largely consistent across the proposed Uber class, as the fares and reimbursements are established by the company itself.[143]

As we see from the Uber example, then, perhaps the greatest advantage of the model proposed here is its simplicity. Through this model, we are able to quickly identify and assess some of the unifying and differing characteristics of the proposed class. We can readily identify what factors would make drivers similar – and different – from one another. We can find the "glue" holding the purported class together as demanded by the Supreme Court in Wal-Mart. Four of the five factors of the framework – time, place, frequency, and manner – highly suggest that allowing a single, aggregated class of all 160,000 Uber drivers would likely be too excessive, at least under the Wal-Mart test. There is too much variance present in the example to satisfy the commonality necessary for a class-action claim under the Supreme Court's heightened standard.

This is not to say that a class action would never be appropriate against Uber (or in other technology-sector cases). Rather, the class-action mechanism could still be used to litigate several smaller systemic cases where workers are grouped together in similar classes.[144] The courts and litigants must approach each case from the standpoint of commonality – how workers can be aggregated in classes where they share sufficiently similar characteristics. The touchstone for this inquiry should be the five-part framework set forth above. If drivers work a similar number of hours at the same times of the day, in similar geographic locations, they are far more likely to represent an adequate – and fair – class of litigants.

In the O'Connor example specifically, it is impossible to say how many class cases should be properly used to aggregate the workers (or whether subclasses could be properly utilized in the matter). It may be that five or ten classes of workers would be appropriate and would help to more similarly situate the workers together. This would still represent average classes of well over 10,000 workers each, which are still massive claims for the company to defend. If situated in the framework presented above, however, such classes would be far easier to conceptualize and would make the determination of whether such workers were independent contractors or employees much easier to resolve. Until we have a better idea of how many workers share similar characteristics with one another, however, it will be impossible to know precisely how many class cases should be pursued. The precise number of cases is irrelevant for purposes of this text; the more important consideration is a focus on the elements of the Federal Rules and assuring that all of the claimants share sufficient commonality. If this commonality requirement is satisfied, then the cases will be far easier to define.

This will also mean that aggregation is inappropriate for some workers. Many of the 160,000 drivers will work completely unique schedules, drive in particular geographic areas, or otherwise perform their services in a way that sets them apart from other workers.[145] These drivers should not be considered as part of a group with other workers, and their claims should be litigated and resolved independently.[146] Whether these drivers are employees or independent contractors must thus be considered on an individual rather than a class basis. Where these drivers fail to share common characteristics with the other workers, their claims must be resolved separately.

Given the *Wal-Mart* standard, then, a more narrow grouping of workers is likely necessary under the heightened commonality standard adopted by the Supreme Court. Others – such as the district court in *O'Connor* – will likely argue that the commonality standard is already satisfied and that a 160,000 class of workers is acceptable. The Supreme Court would likely reject this analysis given the *Wal-Mart* precedent.

4.5.3 Implications of the Proposed Framework

Adopting the framework suggested here would have several important implications for the courts and the litigants. There are a number of specific advantages of the model that are worth noting. Perhaps most importantly, the proposed framework offers a level of certainty to an otherwise confused area of the law. It navigates a complex field and breaks down the cases in this area into a workable five-part test that can easily be followed. The straightforward model thus synthesizes the law and Federal Rules and allows the courts to aggregate cases pursuant to a much more simple formula. The proposed framework thus makes the process much more straightforward and less susceptible to error.

While simplicity is an important advantage of the proposed analysis, the framework further assures the existence of commonality in diverse cases frequently brought in the technology sector. Technology cases are notoriously difficult to navigate and identifying common threads with which to aggregate these matters can be hard. The Supreme Court's definition of commonality in the *Wal-Mart* case has made aggregating employment cases difficult under the Federal Rules of Civil Procedure.[147] The Court's heightened commonality standard is particularly difficult to apply to claims brought in the platform-based economy. The framework offered here helps assure that commonality is achieved in these complex cases, and that the Supreme Court's standard is adequately satisfied. The framework proposed here thus makes certain that workers share enough similar characteristics to proceed in a class action case.

The proposed framework also helps balance the interests of all parties in the litigation.[148] By providing a fair and equitable test, it allows the scope of the litigation to be framed in an appropriate way. Similarly, the model provides fairness to defendants, who can more precisely defend against this more focused systemic litigation. The proposed model is far more useful than the approach currently used in the courts, which essentially involves varied attempts by the judiciary to make sense of a hodgepodge of case law in this evolving area.

There are admittedly some drawbacks to the offered approach. Though the framework offered here would bring much-needed simplicity to this area, it would also lead to additional litigation in some instances. As noted by the *O'Connor* example, the class of 160,000 Uber drivers would need to be broken down into smaller classes, leading to additional (albeit smaller) cases on the dockets of the courts.

And, this would also mean that individual, nonsystemic litigation would also be preferred in many technology-sector cases. More cases – both individual or otherwise – likely means more litigation time for the courts and the parties, and less efficiency.[149] Nonetheless, the importance here is on the courts "getting it right." By assuring that only similar claimants with common characteristics are aggregated as part of the same class, the framework offered here helps achieve the proper result under existing Supreme Court precedent. And, by proposing a more straightforward, streamlined approach, the model offers many efficiencies that are not currently realized by the current system.

Some might also argue that by adding an additional framework to certain class action cases, the model proposed here adds an additional layer of complexity to an already complex process. While it is a fair concern that the proposed framework could make the class-action process more difficult, that is not the goal of the model. Indeed, the factors suggested here are simply meant to serve as nonexhaustive, unweighted guidelines to assist the courts in constructing a proper class in technology-sector cases. The framework is not intended to introduce an additional rigid, inflexible test into an already complex process. It is meant only to serve as a tool to assist the courts in working through cases in an emerging, ill-defined area of the law.[150]

At the end of the day, and as noted earlier in this text, no approach is perfect. The model offered here simplifies a cumbersome area of the law, proposes a straightforward framework for the courts to follow, and assures that Supreme Court case law and the Federal Rules are being followed. The approach should strongly be considered for this type of technology-driven litigation.

As a final consideration, it is worth noting that the approach described in this book could apply to cases brought outside of the platform-based economy.

The worker classification question pervades many areas of the law beyond the technology sector. While this test could certainly be adapted to other areas of the economy, it was formulated specifically for cases brought in the technology sector. As this is the area that is currently the most divisive and complex, and as the cases are rapidly evolving in this sector, this chapter attempts to bring clarity to this specific field. The considerations addressed here, however, could certainly be tailored to other areas of the law.

4.6 THE ISSUE CLASS

This chapter offers a framework for litigating class-action claims on the employee classification question in technology-sector cases. The framework helps define classes of workers who can litigate systemically and thus assists in resolving these claims. While the model here proposes a way for workers to bring their claims together, there is another approach to this type of litigation that is often overlooked: issue class certification.

Federal Rule of Civil Procedure 23(c)(4) allows for issue class certification where specific issue(s) can be resolved on a classwide basis.[151] The rule allows a particular issue to be resolved in an entire class of cases, while still permitting these cases to proceed individually on the other issues involved.[152] Under Rule 23(c)(4), "[w]hen appropriate, an action may be brought or maintained as a class action with respect to particular issues."[153] Issue class certification has the advantage of resolving specific issues across a broad spectrum of cases a single time, while not requiring the complete resolution of the other facts or issues involved in individual cases.[154] Unlike other class action cases, claims brought under Rule 23(c)(4) do not "involve 'an all-or-nothing decision to aggregate individual cases.'"[155] Rather, specific issues can be addressed that are common to a number of cases, while allowing the rest of each claim to proceed individually.

Issue class certification tends to be appropriate when "there are common issues present in the case that would apply to the entire class, even where other questions will need to be resolved individually in specific cases."[156] Technology-driven cases often fit neatly within these parameters, as many of the workers share a basic common set of facts/characteristics but have been harmed in varying ways.

By way of example, in the *O'Connor* case, drivers have many overlapping commonalities that include using the same technology platform, having similar pay/compensation schemes, and sharing other terms, conditions, and privileges of the working relationship. The drivers also have suffered varying degrees of harm. As discussed earlier, these individuals have a number of identifiable differences with regard to how and when they perform their work, leading to differing amounts of damages. As further noted, these drivers perform their duties in a number of different locations, at differing times, and under varying working conditions. Issue class certification would therefore often be appropriate in technology-sector cases. These types of cases frequently offer overlapping legal issues and varying factual nuances. Rule 23(c)(4) fits perfectly with these types of cases to allow the courts to streamline this litigation by resolving the specific overlapping issues a single time, while still permitting the differing facts and issues in the case to be resolved independently.

Without more precise information, it is impossible to frame precisely how the issue class could be used in a particular platform-based case, but it offers enormous potential. A court could, for example, resolve the issue – across a case such as *O'Connor* – of whether workers who fit a specified set of parameters would be employees or independent contractors. This would help streamline much of the controversy currently present in the case, while still preserving litigation on the identified differences that also exist.

Issue class certification offers the courts enormous flexibility and efficiency. It permits the judge overseeing the matter another case management tool when adjudicating these issues. The court can determine which issue(s) can be resolved on a broader basis, while leaving the remaining claims to be addressed individually.[157] Additionally, issue class certification can provide efficiency to the proceedings, as common questions are resolved a single time without the need to revisit these particular issues. This procedural tool thus provides "a happy medium between individual cases and a global class action."[158]

As the cases continue to emerge in this complex area, issue class certification should be strongly considered, as it seems particularly appropriate for many technology-sector claims. As the litigation presents common company-wide policies, personnel, and workplace practices, issue class certification should be considered as a possible procedural tool in these cases. Issue class certification has already been used effectively in employment class action litigation after *Wal-Mart*. Indeed, Judge Posner approved the use of this tool in a class case brought against a major brokerage house.[159] As the court stated in that case, "[A] single proceeding ... could not resolve class members' claims. Each class member would have to prove that his compensation had been adversely affected by the corporate policies But at least it wouldn't be necessary in each of those trials to determine whether the challenged practices were unlawful."[160]

Similarly, many cases that arise in the technology sector will present over-arching corporate policies that can be litigated in an aggregate proceeding. The individual issues, damages, and other factual differences can similarly be litigated independently.[161]

Thus, while this chapter proposes a model for assisting the courts in determining the breadth of a class-action claim in the technology sector, it also encourages the use of issue class certification to help peel off issues where appropriate. Issue class certification can be used independently with the model offered here, or in conjunction with it. While the complete extent of the appropriate use of issue class certification in technology cases is well beyond the scope of this text, it is helpful for the courts and litigants to consider using this procedural tool. This chapter thus simply identifies this tool as an additional way to help sort through this complex litigation.

4.7 CONCLUSION

This chapter attempts to provide some clarity to the complex area of class-action worker misclassification issues in the technology sector. These cases – even before the onset of the pandemic – were a source of substantial litigation in the virtual economy, as discussed in great detail throughout this chapter. In the modern economy, we have experienced an increase in these cases given the varied and uncertain status of the workers involved. Class-action efforts have spanned the entire spectrum of the platform economy, including grocery and restaurant delivery services, home-cleaning providers, and laundry services. The Supreme Court's jurisprudence in *Wal-Mart* v. *Dukes* has only further confused the area and raised the bar on certification issues arising in the workplace context. This chapter provides a streamlined five-part framework to help analyze systemic litigation on the worker misclassification issue arising in technology-sector cases.

Application of this framework helps make clear that the class-action mechanism should be used only cautiously in technology-sector cases. As these cases typically involve highly specific fact patterns, it will often be more appropriate to litigate these claims on an individualized or more narrow class-action basis.[162] The factors identified here are not exhaustive, and the framework is only one way of evaluating these cases. This chapter thus seeks to open a discussion in this important and emerging field.

Like other technology and platform-based workers, individuals forced to work at home (or outside of the office) as a result of COVID-19 will have many common (as well as differing) characteristics. Both during and after this pandemic, we can expect to see class action litigation from these workers on a wide range of employment issues. The principles articulated in this chapter for technology-based workplace claims will therefore be applicable to this new and growing set of cases as well.[163]

NOTES

This chapter draws heavily from Joseph A. Seiner, "Tailoring Class Actions to the On-Demand Economy," *Ohio State Law Journal* 78 (2017): 21–71; Joseph A. Seiner, "Weathering *Wal-Mart*," *Notre Dame Law Review* 89 (2014): 1343–81; Joseph A. Seiner, "The Issue Class," *Boston College Law Review* 56 (2015): 121–58; Benjamin Means and Joseph A. Seiner, "Navigating the Uber Economy," *University of California at Davis Law Review* 49 (2016): 1511–46; and Joseph A. Seiner, *The Supreme Court's New Workplace* (New York: Cambridge University Press, 2017).

1 Margaret Atwood, *The Handmaid's Tale* (New York: Houghton Mifflin Harcourt Publishing Co., 1986).

2 See, e.g., "Apply Now," *Lyft*, www.lyft.com/drive-with-lyft; "Driving Jobs vs Driving with Uber," *Uber*, www.uber.com/driver-jobs.

3 Marisa Kendall, "Uber Battling More Than 70 Lawsuits in Federal Courts," *Mercury News*, July 4, 2016, www.mercurynews.com/business/ci_30091649/uber-faces-attacks-multiple-fronts.

4 See *O'Connor v. Uber Techs., Inc.*, No. C-13-3826 EMC, 2015 WL 5138097, *1, *37 (N.D. Cal. September 1, 2015) (amended order granting in part and denying in part plaintiffs' motion for class certification); *O'Connor v. Uber Techs., Inc.*, 58 F. Supp. 3d 989, 994 (N.D. Cal. 2014).

5 See *O'Connor*, 2015 WL 5138097, *1; *O'Connor*, 58 F. Supp. 3d 994.

6 See, e.g., *Cobarruviaz v. Maplebear, Inc.*, 143 F. Supp. 3d 930, 934 (N.D. Cal. 2015); *Iglesias v. Homejoy, Inc.*, No. 15-cv-01286-EMC, 2015 WL 5698741, *1 (N.D. Cal. September 29, 2015) (order granting plaintiff's motion for entry of default); *Loewen v. Lyft, Inc.*, 129 F. Supp. 3d 945, 956 (N.D. Cal. 2015); *Zenelaj v. Handybook Inc.*, 82 F. Supp. 3d 968, 970 (N.D. Cal. 2015); First Amended Collective & Class Action Complaint & Jury Demand ¶¶1–2, *Singer v. Postmates Inc.*, No. 4:15-cv-01284 (N.D. Cal. March 19, 2015) (hereinafter Singer Class Action Complaint); Class Action Complaint & Jury Demand ¶¶1–2, *Taranto v. Washio, Inc.*, No. CGC-15-546584 (Cal. Super. Ct. June 29, 2015) (hereinafter Taranto Class Action Complaint); Amended Class Action Arbitration Demand ¶¶1–2, *Tang v. Shyp, Inc.*, No. 01-15-0004-0358 (Am. Arbitration Ass'n July 17, 2015); Patrick Chu, "Labor Cases Filed against Shyp, Washio, Postmates," *San Francisco Business Times*, July 1, 2015, www.bizjournals.com/sanfrancisco/news/2015/07/01/shyp-washio-postmates-sued-uber-lyft-caviar.html.

7 Class Action Complaint ¶2, *Kissner v. DoorDash, Inc.*, No. CGC-15-548102 (Cal. Super. Ct. September 23, 2015) (hereinafter Kissner Class Action Complaint); Class Action Complaint ¶2, *Tan v. GrubHub, Inc.*, No. CGC-15-548103 (Cal. Super. Ct. September 23, 2015) (hereinafter Tan Class Action Complaint).

8 See Amy L. Groff et al., "Platforms Like Uber and the Blurred Line between Independent Contractors and Employees: Facing the Challenges to Employment Law Presented by Seemingly Intermediary Platforms of the Modern On-Demand Economy," *Computer Law Review International* 16 (2015): 166, 171, www.klgates

.com/files/Publication/04dcde30-9c10-4003-b663-f7f5f2cdec32/Presentation/
PublicationAttachment/805ddc72-69b2-426b-ad51-fe92be45434e/CLRI_2016.pdf.

9 See, e.g., Tricia Gorman and Rebecca Ditsch, "Q&A: The Uber Settlement and Its
Impact on Worker Classification in the Gig Economy," *Westlaw Journal Computer
& Internet* (May 20, 2016), *1, *2, *10.

10 *NLRB* v. *Hearst Publ'ns, Inc.*, 322 U.S. 111, 121 (1944), overruled in part by
Nationwide Mut. Ins. Co. v. *Darden*, 503 U.S. 318 (1992).

11 *Wal-Mart Stores, Inc.* v. *Dukes*, 564 U.S. 338 (2011).

12 Cf. Means and Seiner, "Navigating the Uber Economy," 1511, 1515 (presenting a
new approach to the problem of worker misclassification). There has been excellent
recent scholarship on class actions more generally. See, e.g., Robert H. Klonoff,
"The Decline of Class Actions," *Washington University Law Review* 90 (2013): 729,
755–58; Arthur R. Miller, Keynote Address, "The Preservation and Rejuvenation of
Aggregate Litigation: A Systemic Imperative," *Emory Law Journal* 64 (2014): 293; cf.
Megan Carboni, Note, "A New Class of Worker for the Sharing Economy,"
Richmond Journal of Law and Technology 22 (2016): 11, 47, http://scholarship
.richmond.edu/jolt/vol22/iss4/2.

13 *O'Connor* v. *Uber Techs., Inc.*, No. C-13-3826 EMC, 2015 WL 5138097 (N.D. Cal.
September 1, 2015) (amended order granting in part and denying in part plaintiffs'
motion for class certification).

14 See Bloomberg News, "California Judge Sides with Ex-Uber Driver over Arbitration
Clause," *Washington Post*, September 21, 2015, www.washingtonpost.com/business/
economy/california-judge-sides-with-ex-uber-driver-over-arbitration-clause/2015/09/
21/7e5403la-6087-l1e5-8e9e-dce8a2a2a679_story.html; Chelsey Dulaney, "Uber
Ruling Adds More Drivers to Class Action Suit," *Wall Street Journal*, December
9, 2015, www.wsj.com/articles/uber-ruling-adds-more-drivers-to-class-action-suit-
1449699041; Mike Isaac et al., "Seattle Considers Measure to Let Uber and Lyft
Drivers Unionize," *New York Times*, December 13, 2015, www.nytimes.com/2015/12/
14/technology/seattle-considers-measure-to-let-uber-and-lyft-drivers-unionize.html?
_r=O; Dan Levine, "In US Driver Lawsuit, Uber Must Live with Class Action
Order for Now," *Reuters*, November 17, 2015, www.reuters.com/article/us-uber-tech-
classaction-idUSKCNOT62IA2015lll7; Tracey Lien, "Uber Sued by Drivers
Excluded from Class-Action Lawsuit," *Los Angeles Times*, January 4, 2016, www
.latimes.com/business/technology/la-fi-tn-uber-lawsuit-driver-misclassification-
20160104-story.html; Laura Lorenzetti, "Everything to Know About the Uber Class
Action Lawsuit," *Fortune*, September 2, 2015, http://fortune.com/2015/09/02/uber-
lawsuit; Reuters, "Judge Expands Driver Class Action Lawsuit against Uber," *New
York Post*, December 9, 2015, http://nypost.com/2015/12/09/judge-expands-driver-
class-action-lawsuit-against-uber; Joel Rosenblatt and Pamela MacLean, "Uber
Judge Taps Brakes on California Drivers' Suit Outcome," *Bloomberg*, December
22, 2015, www.bloomberg.com/news/articles/2015–12-23/uber-wins-conditional-halt-
to-part-of-california-drivers-lawsuit; Katy Steinmetz, "Judge Lets Drivers' Class
Action Lawsuit against Uber Go Forward," *Time*, September 1, 2015, http://time
.com/4019439/uber-judge-class-action; Matt Thompson, "The Class Action Lawsuit

against Uber Is a Case to Watch," *Atlantic*, September 7, 2015, www.theatlantic
.com/notes/2015/09/the-class-action-lawsuit-against-uber-is-a-case-to-watch/404116.

15 See Martin H. Redish and Andrianna D. Kastanek, "Settlement Class Actions, the
Case-or-Controversy Requirement and the Nature of the Adjudicatory Process,"
University of Chicago Law Review 73 (2006): 545–46.

16 See *Hansberry v. Lee*, 311 U.S. 32, 41–43 (1940).

17 See Joshua D. Blank and Eric A. Zacks, "Dismissing the Class: A Practical
Approach to the Class Action Restriction on Legal Services Corporation,"
Pennsylvania State Law Review 110 (2005): 10–12.

18 Fed. R. Civ. P. 23(a); see also J. Douglas Richards and Benjamin D. Brown,
"Predominance of Common Questions – Common Mistakes in Applying the
Class Action Standard," *Rutgers Law Journal* 41 (2009): 163.

19 *Wal-Mart Stores, Inc. v. Dukes*, 564 U.S. 338 (2011).

20 See, e.g., ibid., 349–52.

21 See Joseph A. Seiner, "Weathering *Wal-Mart*," *Notre Dame Law Review* 89 (2014):
1343, 1344.

22 See ibid.

23 Ibid.

24 See *Wal-Mart*, 564 U.S. 345.

25 See Fed. R. Civ. P. 23(a)(2).

26 *Wal-Mart*, 564 U.S. 350.

27 Ibid., 356.

28 Ibid.

29 Ibid., 357.

30 Ibid., 352.

31 *Tyson Foods, Inc. v. Bouaphakeo*, 136 S. Ct. 1036 (2016).

32 See, e.g., Klonoff, "The Decline of Class Actions," 775–76; Catherine M. Sharkey,
"The Future of Classwide Punitive Damages," *University of Michigan Journal of
Law Reform* 46 (2013): 1127, 1143; Sherry E. Clegg, Comment, "Employment
Discrimination Class Actions: Why Plaintiffs Must Cover All Their Bases after
the Supreme Court's Interpretation of Federal Rule of Civil Procedure 23(a)(2) in
Wal-Mart v. Dukes," *Texas Tech Law Review* 44 (2012): 1087, 1108; see also
Stephanie S. Silk, Note, "More Decentralization, Less Liability: The Future of
Systemic Disparate Treatment Claims in the Wake of *Wal-Mart v. Dukes*,"
University of Miami Law Review 67 (2013): 637, 658.

33 Valerio De Stefano, "The Rise of the 'Just-in-Time Workforce': On-Demand Work,
Crowdwork, and Labor Protection in the 'Gig-Economy,'" *Comparative Labor Law
and Policy Journal* 37 (2016): 471, 481.

34 See 29 U.S.C. § 216(a)–(c) (2012).

35 See 29 U.S.C. §§ 203, 206, 207, 212 (providing three primary areas of protection for
minimum wage, maximum hours, and child labor provisions).

36 See 29 U.S.C. § 203(r)–(s); see also Wage & Hour Division, *Fact Sheet #14:
Coverage under the Fair Labor Standards Act (FLSA)* (Washington, DC: U.S.
Department of Labor, 2009).

37 See David Weil, *Administrator's Interpretation No. 2015-1, The Application of the Fair Labor Standards Act's "Suffer or Permit" Standard in the Identification of Employees Who Are Misclassified as Independent Contractors* (Washington, DC: U.S. Department of Labor, 2015), 15; Bruce Goldstein et al., "Enforcing Fair Labor Standards in the Modern American Sweatshop: Rediscovering the Statutory Definition of Employment," *University of California at Los Angeles Law Review* 46 (1999): 983, 1004–05.

38 See 29 U.S.C. § 203(e)(1) (defining "employee" generally as "any individual employed by an employer").

39 29 U.S.C. § 203(g).

40 Cf. Weil, *Application of FLSA's "Suffer or Permit" Standard*, 1.

41 Ibid. (citing *Sec'y of Labor v. Lauritzen*, 835 F.2d 1529, 1534–35 [7th Cir. 1987]); see also *Nationwide Mut. Ins. Co. v. Darden*, 503 U.S. 318, 323–24 (1992).

42 See Greg Ip, "As the Gig Economy Changes Work, So Should Rules," *Wall Street Journal*, December 9, 2015, www.wsj.com/articles/as-the-gig-economy-changes-work-so-should-rules-1449683384; Arun Sundararajan, "The 'Gig Economy' Is Coming. What Will It Mean for Work?," *Guardian*, July 25, 2015, www .theguardian.com/commentisfree/2015/jul/26/will-we-get-by-gig-economy; see also Jennifer Ludden, "The End of 9-to-5: When Work Time Is Anytime," *NPR*, March 16, 2010, www.npr.org/templates/story/story.php?storyId=1 24705801.

43 *Cotter v. Lyft, Inc.*, 60 F. Supp. 3d 1067, 1081 (N.D. Cal. 2015) (order denying cross-motions for summary judgment).

44 See Means and Seiner, "Navigating the Uber Economy," 1536–45. See generally *O'Connor v. Uber Techs., Inc.*, 82 F. Supp. 3d 1133, 1153 (N.D. Cal. 2015) (order denying defendant's motion for summary judgment).

45 See *AT&T Mobility LLC v. Concepcion*, 563 U.S. 333, 352 (2011).

46 See *Bell Atlantic Corp. v. Twombly*, 550 U.S. 544, 556 (2007).

47 Ibid., *8 (quoting *Wal-Mart Stores, Inc. v. Dukes*, 564 U.S. 338, 351 [2011]).

48 Ibid., *8.

49 Ibid.

50 Ibid.

51 See generally Joel Rosenblatt, "Uber's $100 Million Driver Pay Settlement Rejected by Judge," *Bloomberg*, August 18, 2016, www.bloomberg.com/news/articles/2016-08-18/uber-s-100-million-driver-pay-settlement-is-rejected-by-judge.

52 See "Uber Drivers," *Uber Law Suit*, http://uberlawsuit.com (last visited June 9, 2020).

53 See Fed. R. Civ. P. 23(a)(2); *Wal-Mart Stores, Inc. v. Dukes*, 564 U.S. 338, 349 (2011).

54 *Wal-Mart*, 564 U.S. 350. The question presented must therefore "resolve an issue that is central to the validity of each one of the claims in one stroke." Ibid.

55 Ibid.

56 *Wal-Mart Stores, Inc. v. Dukes*, 564 U.S. 338, 352 (2011).

57 See Sarah Kessler, "The Gig Economy Won't Last Because It's Being Sued to Death," *Fast Company*, February 17, 2015, www.fastcompany.com/3042248/the-gig-

economy-wont-last-because-its-being-sued-to-death; A. J. Kritikos, "A Lawsuit to Break the Gig Economy," *Wall Street Journal*, September 20, 2015, www.wsj .com/Essays/a-lawsuit-to-break-the-gig-economy-1442788712; Tracey Lien, "Meet the Attorney Suing Uber, Lyft, GrubHub and a Dozen California Tech Firms," *Los Angeles Times*, January 24, 2016, www.latimes.com/business/technology/la-fi-class-action-lawyer-20160124-story.html; see also, e.g., Jeff Bercovici, "Why the Next Uber Wannabe Is Already Dead," *Inc.com*, November 2015, www.inc.com/maga zine/201511/jeff-bercovici/the-1099-bind.html; Therese Poletti, "Uber Drivers' Class Action Lawsuit Endangers Much More Than Uber," *Marketwatch*, September 1, 2015, www.marketwatch.com/story/uber-drivers-class-action-lawsuit-endangers-much-more-than-uber-2015-09-01; Cole Stangler, "Why the Uber, Lyft Driver Union Push Could Disrupt the Gig Economy," *International Business Times*, December 18, 2015, www .ibtimes.com/why-uber-lyft-driver-union-push-could-disrupt-gig-economy-2232778. See generally Means and Seiner, "Navigating the Uber Economy."

58 "About Us," *DoorDash*, www.doordash.com/about; "About Us," *GrubHub*, http:// about.grubhub.com/about-us/what-is-grubhub/default.aspx.

59 Tan Class Action Complaint, ¶¶6–7.

60 Ibid., ¶2.

61 Ibid., ¶10; see also Scott Holland, "Drivers Deliver Class Action Saying GrubHub Needs to Treat Them as Employees, Not Contractors," *Cook County Record*, July 11, 2016, http://cookcountyrecord.com/stories/510955592-drivers-deliver-class-action-saying-grubhub-needs-to-treat-them-as-employees-not-contractors.

62 Tan Class Action Complaint, ¶10.

63 Ibid., ¶12.

64 Kissner Class Action Complaint, ¶2.

65 "What Is Instacart?," *Instacart*, www.instacart.com/help/section/200758544#204426950 (last visited June 9, 2020); see also Farhad Manjoo, "Grocery Deliveries in Sharing Economy," *New York Times*, May 21, 2014, www.nytimes.com/2014/05/22/technology/ personaltech/online-grocery-start-up-takes-page-from-sharing-services.html?_r=0.

66 "What Is Instacart?"; see also Manjoo, "Grocery Deliveries."

67 See Brian Solomon, "America's Most Promising Company: Instacart, the $2 Billion Grocery Delivery App," *Forbes*, January 21, 2015, www.forbes.com/sites/briansolo mon/2015/01/21/americas-most-promising-company-instacart-the-2-billion-grocery-delivery-app/#5e4092544858.

68 See Complaint, ¶29, *Bynum v. Maplebear Inc.*, 160 F. Supp. 3d 572 (E.D.N.Y. 2016) (No. 15-CV-6263); Complaint, ¶29, *Moton v. Maplebear Inc.*, No. 1:15-cv-08879-CM, 2016 WL 616343 (S.D.N.Y. February 9, 2016); Class Action Complaint for Damages and Demand for Jury Trial, ¶20, *Cobarruviaz v. Maplebear, Inc.*, 143 F. Supp. 3d 930 (N.D. Cal. 2015) (No. 3:15-cv-00697-EMC); Class Action Complaint, ¶11, *Sumerlin v. Maplebear, Inc.*, No. BC 603030 (Cal. Super. Ct. December 2, 2015).

69 See Class Action Complaint for Damages and Demand for Jury Trial, ¶63.

70 See ibid., ¶¶31, 39, 44, 51.

71 See ibid., ¶24.

72 See ibid., ¶22.

73 See ibid., ¶23.
74 See ibid., ¶27.
75 See ibid., ¶32.
76 See ibid., ¶23.
77 See, e.g., *Bynum v. Maplebear Inc.*, 160 F. Supp. 3d 527, 529 (E.D.N.Y. 2016) (order granting motion to compel arbitration); *Cobarruviaz v. Maplebear, Inc.*, 143 F. Supp. 3d 930, 935 (N.D. Cal. 2015) (order granting defendant's motion to compel arbitration).
78 Class Action Complaint, ¶¶2, 4, *Truong v. Amazon.com, Inc.*, No. BC598993.
79 Ibid., ¶1.
80 Ibid., ¶¶18, 25.
81 See ibid., ¶19.
82 Ibid. ¶20.
83 Ibid., ¶21.
84 Ibid., ¶23.
85 "About Us," *Yelp*, www.yelp.com/about (last visited June 14, 2019).
86 Ibid.
87 Ibid.; see also Lydia O'Connor, "Yelp Reviewers File Class-Action Lawsuit Claiming They Are Unpaid Writers," *Huffington Post*, October 31, 2013, www .huffingtonpost.com/2013/10/30/yelp-lawsuit-_n_4179663.html.
88 See *Jeung v. Yelp, Inc.*, No. 15-CV-02228-RS, 2015 WL 4776424, *1 (N.D. Cal. August 13, 2015) (order granting motion to dismiss, granting motion to strike, and denying motion for sanctions).
89 Ibid., *3.
90 Ibid., *2.
91 "About Us," *Handy*, www.handy.com/about (last visited May 26, 2020).
92 *Zenelaj v. Handybook Inc.*, 82 F. Supp. 3d 968, 975 (N.D. Cal. 2015) (order granting defendant's motion to compel arbitration).
93 Ibid.
94 Ibid., 970; see also Maya Kosoff, "Two Workers Are Suing a Cleaning Startup Called Handy over Alleged Labor Violations," *Business Insider*, November 12, 2014, www.businessinsider.com/handy-cleaning-lawsuit-2014-11.
95 *Zenelaj*, 82 F. Supp. 3d 970.
96 Ibid.
97 "About Postmates," *Postmates*, https://postmates.com/about (last visited May 26, 2020).
98 See Singer Class Action Complaint, ¶2; Class Action Complaint ¶1, *Peppler v. Postmates, Inc.*, No. 1:15-cv-05145-RCL (D.C. Super. Ct. August 25, 2015); Complaint ¶1, *Marable v. Postmates, Inc.*, No. BC589052 (Cal. Super. Ct. July 23, 2015); see also Katy Steinmetz, "Homejoy, Postmates, and Try Caviar Sued over Labor Practices," *Time*, March 19, 2015, http://time.com/3751745/postmates-homejoy-try-caviar-lawsuits.
99 Singer Class Action Complaint, ¶¶2–3.
100 Ibid., ¶21.
101 Ibid., ¶23.

102 "AI for Your Business," *Crowdflower*, www.crowdflower.com.

103 "Platform Overview," *figure eight*, www.figure-eight.com/platform (When users upload their data, figure eight "provide[s] the annotations, judgments, and labels [they] need to create accurate ground truth for [their] models.") (last visited May 26, 2020).

104 Ibid.

105 *Otey v. CrowdFlower, Inc.*, No. 12-cv-05524-JST, 2014 WL 1477630, *1 (N.D. Cal. April 14, 2014) (order denying motion for approval of settlement without prejudice).

106 Ibid., *2.

107 Craig Johnson, "Crowdsourcing Supplier Settles Class Action Lawsuit," *Staffing Industry Analysts*, July 8, 2015, www.staffmgindustry.com/Research-Publications/ Publications/CWS-3.0/July-2015/July-8-2015/Crowdsourcing-supplier-settles-class-action-lawsuit. See court docket for full history of case and settlement.

108 See Lora Kolodny, "Homejoy Raises $38M for House Cleaning on Demand," *Wall Street Journal*, December 5, 2013, http://blogs.wsj.com/venturecapital/2013/12/ 05/homejoy-raises-38m-for-house-cleaning-on-demand.

109 See ibid.; see also Kia Kokalitcheva, "Home Cleaning Startup Homejoy Bites the Dust – Literally," *Fortune*, July 17, 2015, http://fortune.com/2015/07/17/homejoy-closing-cleaning-google.

110 See Kolodny, "Homejoy Raises $38M."

111 Collective & Class Action Complaint & Jury Demand, ¶¶15–17, *Iglesias v. Homejoy, Inc.*, No. 3:15-cv-01286-LB (N.D. Cal. March 19, 2015); Class Action Complaint for Damages, ¶¶1–2, *Ventura v. Homejoy, Inc.*, No. CGC-15-544750 (Cal. Super. Ct. March 16, 2015); Class Action Complaint, ¶3, *Malveaux-Smith v. Homejoy, Inc.*, No. 37-201500005070-CU-OE-CTL (Cal. Super. Ct. February 13, 2015).

112 See Class Action Complaint for Damages, ¶¶32–33, 44.

113 Ibid., ¶3.

114 Ibid., ¶43.

115 Ibid.

116 See ibid., ¶37.

117 See ibid., ¶44.

118 Ibid., ¶35.

119 Ibid., ¶39.

120 Ibid., ¶40.

121 See Kokalitcheva, "Home Cleaning Startup"; see also Ellen Huet, "Homejoy Shuts Down, Citing Worker Misclassification Lawsuits," *Forbes*, July 17, 2015, www .forbes.com/sites/ellenhuet/2015/07/17/cleaning-startup-homejoy-shuts-down-citing-worker-misclassification-lawsuits/#I006dcb87780.

122 See Brian Solomon, "Washio, the On-Demand Laundry Startup, Washes Out," *Forbes*, August 30, 2016, www.forbes.com/sites/briansolomon/2016/08/30/washio-the-on-demand-laundry-startup-washes-out/#97aa85a68361 [https://perma.cc/LW6F-FY9T].

123 Taranto Class Action Complaint, ¶2; see Biz Carson, "The Lawyer Fighting for Uber and Lyft Employees Is Taking the Fight to Four More Companies," *Business Insider*, July 1, 2015, www.businessinsider.com/postmates-shyp-and-washio-hit-with-legal-action-from-contractors-2015-7; see also Class Action Complaint for Damages

& Injunctive Relief, *Bennett v. Washio, Inc.*, No. BC603067 (Cal. Super. Ct. December 8, 2015) (a separate case brought against Washio).

124 Taranto Class Action Complaint, ¶11.

125 Ibid., ¶¶11–12.

126 Ibid., ¶14.

127 See Solomon, "Washio."

128 See ibid.; see also Shan Li, "On-Demand Laundry Start-Up Washio Shuts Down," *Los Angeles Times*, August 30, 2016, www.latimes.com/business/la-fi-washio-startup-20160830-snap-story.html.

129 Taranto Class Action Complaint, ¶10.

130 Class Action Complaint, ¶¶18, 23, *Truong v. Amazon.com, Inc.*, No. BC598993.

131 See *Jeung v. Yelp, Inc.*, No. 15-cv-02228-RS, 2015 WL 4776424, *2 (N.D. Cal. 2015) (order granting motion to dismiss, granting motion to strike, denying motion for sanctions, and denying motion for preliminary certification of collective action).

132 Noam Scheiber, "Growth in the 'Gig Economy' Fuels Work Force Anxieties," *New York Times*, July 12, 2015, www.nytimes.com/2015/07/13/business/rising-eco nomic-insecurity-tied-to-decades-long-trend-in-employment-practices.html.

133 Ibid.; "There's an App for That," *Economist*, December 30, 2014, www.economist .com/news/briefing/21637355-freelance-workers-available-moments-notice-will-reshape-nature-companies-and; see also James Surowiecki, "Gigs with Benefits," *New Yorker*, July 6, 2015, www.newyorker.com/magazine/2015/07/06/gigs-with-bene fits. Though this chapter focuses on a handful of illustrative examples of class action cases in the technology sector, there are many more cases that have been filed.

134 See, e.g., Elka Torpey and Andrew Hogan, "Working in a Gig Economy," *Bureau of Labor Statistics*, May 2016, www.bls.gov/careeroutlook/2016/article/what-is-the-gig-economy.htm.

135 Groff et al., "Platforms Like Uber," 171.

136 *Nationwide Mut. Ins. Co. v. Darden*, 503 U.S. 318, 323 (1992); see, e.g., *Kramer v. Cash Link Sys.*, 715 F.3d 1082, 1088–89 (8th Cir. 2013); *O'Connor v. Uber Techs., Inc.*, 82 F. Supp. 3d 1133, 1152 (N.D. Cal. 2015) (order denying defendant's motion for summary judgment). But see *Estate of Suskovich v. Anthem Health Plans of Va., Inc.*, 553 F.3d 559, 566 (7th Cir. 2009).

137 See, e.g., Laura A. Stokowski, "Nurses Are Talking About: Working the Night Shift," *Medscape*, January 11, 2013, www.medscape.com/viewarticle/777286.

138 See Katy Steinmetz, "Exclusive: See How Big the Gig Economy Really Is," *Time*, January 6, 2016, http://time.com/4169532/sharing-economy-poll (exploring the size of various gig economy workplaces, including cars, bedrooms, and kitchens).

139 See Jonathan V. Hall and Alan B. Krueger, "An Analysis of the Labor Market for Uber's Driver-Partners in the United States" (National Bureau of Economic Research, Working Paper No. 22843, 2016), 10.

140 *In re FedEx Ground Package Sys., Inc. (FedEx II)*, 869 F. Supp. 2d 942, 973 (N.D. Ind. 2012).

141 See *FedEx. I*, 662 F. Supp. 2d 1088, 1100, 1106 (N.D. Ind. 2009); see also, e.g., *Simpkins v. Unigard Mut. Ins. Co.*, 203 S.E.2d 742, 745 (Ga. Ct. App. 1974).

142 See *O'Connor* v. *Uber Techs., Inc.*, No. C-13-3826 EMC, 2015 WL 5138097, *17 (N.D. Cal. September 1, 2015) (amended order granting in part and denying in part the motion for class certification); Frizell, "Uber Just Answered."

143 Dan Kedmey, "This Is How Uber's 'Surge Pricing' Works," *Time*, December 15, 2014, http://time.com/3633469/uber-surge-pricing; "Uber Moves: Columbia, SC," *Uber*, www.uber.com/cities/columbia.

144 Suzette M. Malveaux, "How Goliath Won: The Future Implications of *Dukes* v. *Wal-Mart*," *Northwestern University Law Review Colloquy* 106 (2011): 44.

145 Hall and Krueger, "An Analysis," 10, 21.

146 Jon Romberg, "Half a Loaf Is Predominant and Superior to None: Class Certification of Particular Issues under Rule 23(c)(4)(A)," *Utah Law Review* (2002): 249, 299.

147 A. Benjamin Spencer, "Class Actions, Heightened Commonality, and Declining Access to Justice," *Boston University Law Review* 93 (2013): 441, 475–87.

148 See Romberg, "Half a Loaf," 258–59.

149 See ibid., 258 (quoting James Wm. Moore et al., *Moore's Federal Practice* § 23.02, Vol. 5, 3rd ed. [New York: Matthew Bender, 1998]).

150 See Groff et al., "Platforms Like Uber," 171.

151 Fed. R. Civ. P. 23(c)(4); see also Jenna G. Farleigh, Note, "Splitting the Baby: Standardizing Issue Class Certification," *Vanderbilt Law Review* 64 (2011): 1585, 1588 (discussing issue class certifications under federal rules).

152 See Farleigh, "Splitting the Baby," 1624, 1624 n.250.

153 Fed. R. Civ. P. 23(c)(4).

154 Seiner, "The Issue Class," 133.

155 Ibid., 132–33 (quoting Romberg, "Half a Loaf," 251); Jenna C. Smith, Comment, "'Carving at the Joints': Using Issue Classes to Reframe Consumer Class Actions," *Washington Law Review* 88 (2013): 1187, 1212–25.

156 Seiner, "The Issue Class," 133, 135–36.

157 See Charles Alan Wright et al., *Federal Practice and Procedure* § 1790, Vol. 7AA, 3rd ed. (St. Paul, MN: Thomson West, 2005).

158 Romberg, "Half a Loaf," 299.

159 See *McReynolds* v. *Merrill Lynch, Pierce, Fenner & Smith, Inc.*, 672 F.3d 482, 491–92 (7th Cir. 2012), *abrogated by Phillips* v. *Sheriff of Cook Cty.*, 828 F.3d 541 (7th Cir. 2016).

160 Ibid., 490–91; see also Seiner, "The Issue Class," 148–49.

161 See Wright et al., *Federal Practice and Procedure*, § 1790.

162 See Romberg, "Half a Loaf," 299.

163 This chapter also benefited greatly from the scholarship and work of numerous other authors. See Bibliography.

5

Collective Bargaining Agreements and Unions in the Modern Economy

A nation that successfully moved from farm to factory to mainframe can certainly find a way to harness new digital technologies and data-driven decision making in a way that ensures workers are fairly treated and prosperity is broadly shared. We can't fall into the trap of believing that the latest innovation is so transformational that we simply can't accommodate and acclimate.

—Former US Secretary of Labor[1]

In the face of a COVID-19 pandemic, we saw many employment opportunities evaporate, and many other jobs move out of the office and into the home. Where there is no physical, brick-and-mortar facility to report to, it can – as a practical matter – be difficult for workers to act collectively. It is simply far more difficult for employees to organize when they do not interact regularly on a daily or weekly basis. The same is true for many workers in the technology sector and this was the case even before the rise of the virus. The pandemic, as well as the increasing levels of employment in the virtual economy, will therefore make it much more difficult for workers to organize collectively and to unionize. This chapter thus explores the difficulty of these organizational efforts in this evolving economy and discusses alternative approaches to traditional unionizing.

As seen in the prior chapters, workers in the on-demand technology sector represent a new breed of employees, and courts are still struggling to define this hybrid working relationship. While the law grapples with the rights that should be afforded to these workers, many employee protections are simply falling through the cracks. One clear example of this phenomenon can be seen with respect to union rights in this emerging sector. Involvement in traditional union activity has seen a steep decline across all industries. In the on-demand economy, it is almost nonexistent.[2] This has forced workers to consider alternative ways to have their voices heard when pursuing workplace change. The decline of traditional unionism has been well documented and widespread.[3] Union density rates have faced steep declines in the United States – and, to a lesser extent, in many other countries – over the last couple of decades.[4] Yet, worker demand for representation and voice in the employment setting appears as strong as ever. Nowhere is this demand more pronounced than in the emerging on-demand economy.[5] This growing industry presents unique problems for workers as the employment status of these individuals is remarkably ill-defined. This chapter explores possible ways to bridge the gap between workers' desires for representation in the technology sector and the severe limitations of the traditional collective-bargaining arrangement envisioned by the National Labor Relations Act (NLRA).[6]

Perhaps the best-case example of nontraditional unionization efforts again involves Uber, a major technology-sector company. As discussed in prior chapters, Uber is a massive transportation business that provides an on-demand platform for drivers to use across the country. While the courts still struggle with the issue of whether these workers should be treated as employees or independent contractors, workplace protections remain in flux. It is unclear which, if any, federal laws protect these workers, including the NLRA. In the face of these challenges, Uber, and many of its drivers, has agreed to engage in a nontraditional collective relationship – the Uber Guild. This book explores the import of this relationship, critiquing the model and explaining its implications for the broader technology-sector economy.

Other alternative models also exist, and this chapter examines these additional "alt-labor" relationships. In particular, this chapter explores the model adopted by the Freelancers Union – a collective group of workers who pursue benefits despite not having employment status under the law. Similarly, this chapter examines "Working America," a group that does not actively represent workers but instead promotes political action. Finally, this chapter explores attempts at quasi-union arrangements in the more traditional brick-and-mortar employment relationships and looks at efforts by General Electric and Volkswagen to create alt-labor agreements.

It is important to note at the outset that although such alternative union options exist, they do not hold much hope for substantial increases in unionization nationwide. The barriers to union representation are quite high and, especially given the important role of global trade, are largely outside the bounds of any realistic reform measures.[7] The options explored here are not panaceas for the labor movement. Instead, they are alternatives to the traditional collective-bargaining process that seem likely to do a better job at fulfilling some of workers' unmet desires.

Given this gloomy status quo, why seek any improvements? Although no magic bullet exists, expanding worker voice and opportunities to participate in employment decision-making promises gains for workers, as well as society as a whole. The NLRA and other labor laws were enacted, at least in part, to improve the US economy and the living standards of workers.[8] Those policy goals still resonate – particularly given recent economic trouble – yet, the traditional NLRA model leaves many of them unmet. Addressing these short-comings, even only in part, could have a real, positive impact for many people. Efforts to circumvent the outdated model set forth in the statute have resulted in various alternative bargaining relationships between companies and workers. At times, these new models even include workers who would not be considered "employees" under traditional employment laws.

The starting point for possible reform is the traditional labor union. Although traditional, private-sector unionization has been particularly weak in the last couple of decades, the fact remains that unions are the largest, best-organized, and most well-funded employee-side groups in the United States. Thus, the initial question is what unions can do to change the current dynamic. This book discusses nontraditional groups and their potential con-tribution to expanding worker participation and voice, but those groups are nowhere close to having the strength of unions.

Ultimately, no model will be perfect, but nontraditional unionization efforts are imperative if workers in the technology sector want any semblance of a collective voice. The Uber Guild simply represents one joint attempt by workers and management to create a model that comports with the technol-ogy sector. Given the high-profile nature of this business, however, this example provides an excellent platform for discussing how traditional union benefits can be molded to fit nontraditional companies. The modern union suggested by this chapter contemplates this example and offers a broader approach for the technology sector, which could be applied in many other sectors as well. Navigating the existing attempts at quasi-union arrange-ments, this chapter suggests the development of a modern union for the technology sector.

Section 5.1 identifies the need for more cooperation between workers and management in light of the steep national decline in unionization. Section 5.2 then examines how the lack of formal collective bargaining has directly impacted workers in the technology sector. It further explores the nontradi-tional efforts at worker organization, including the Freelancers Union, Working America, and the Uber Guild. Section 5.3 looks at workplace participation groups and discusses their role in the employment setting. It also explains the potential advantages and disadvantages of quasi-unions in the technology sector, exploring how the alt-labor strategy can fit within the contours of the modern economy. Section 5.4 concludes by examining what quasi-unions should look like in the modern economy and describes the three primary forms such groups could assume. It is time to revisit the current union model as applied to the virtual economy, particularly in light of the recent pandemic. The NLRA was developed at a far different time in a much different environment. Put quite simply, times have changed, and the law should keep pace in this area.

5.1 MORE COOPERATION NEEDED

The history of labor regulation in the United States – particularly the NLRA, which governs most private-sector workplaces – embodies cooperation as an overarching policy goal.[9] Throughout the late nineteenth and early twentieth centuries, the largely unregulated labor relations were marked by a rash of strikes, widespread boycotts, and violence by unions and employers alike.[10] Congress responded to the economic turmoil that resulted from this labor unrest by enacting statutes limiting courts' ability to enjoin labor activity;[11] regulating labor relations in the railroad industry;[12] and most importantly, in 1935, enacting the Wagner Act (or NLRA).[13] Although Congress recognized that labor strife cannot be completely removed, the NLRA's aim was to regulate the conduct of unions and employers so that harm to the national economy would be mitigated.[14]

As Congress made explicit in section I of the NLRA – the introductory portion, which sets forth its policies – the primary aim of the law was to create a new way of settling employment disputes that would help the national economy. Among the threats to the economy at that time were employer denials of employees' right to engage in collective action; unequal bargaining power; and unions' use of strikes and other labor unrest that, among other things, impeded commerce, contributed to business depressions, and depressed wages.[15] The solution is a system that encourages the "friendly adjustment" of labor disputes by protecting employees' right to organize and to seek collective representation and by limiting strikes and other labor unrest. Although the NLRA expressly protected the right to strike, this option was to be more of a last resort, replaced by the less harmful process of collective bargaining. Although it is difficult to prove causation, by many measures this solution was successful for quite a while.[16]

Image Credit: Harold M. Lambert/Contributor/Getty Images

Unions gained significant strength and power through their strong opposition to employers and their treatment of workers.[17] Armed with the Wagner Act's protections, union membership and influence increased exponentially.[18] The large number of union members gave organized labor tremendous resources in terms of both finances and individuals committed to fighting for their and other employees' working conditions. Ironically, this early increase in strength for unions initially resulted in more work stoppages, not fewer.[19] That said, these work stoppages were far less violent and disruptive than before. Moreover, with enhanced union power came significant wage increases and declines in wage inequality.[20] Ultimately, however, unions' strength fell precipitously, accompanied by fewer strikes, declining employee wages, and falling wage equality.[21]

The steep decline in those numbers is accompanied by a similar decrease in unions' power.[22] But there is another, less obvious cost to this decline. As union membership dwindled, the public became less aware of the unions' role. Many, if not most, individuals are not immediately related to anyone in a union so they lack an appreciation for the benefits that unions can provide. Combine this lack of awareness with the strong public relations campaigns that employers use to attack unions, and it is no surprise that their popularity has weakened over the years.[23] This weakness, in turn, has reduced employees' ability to participate in the workplace and to seek improvements in their working conditions.

Although many of the causes of this declining power are structurally economic and largely outside of unions' control, it also seems apparent that a contributing factor is a serious public relations problem for unions. Unions have been under political assault in recent years. For instance, they have been the subject of substantial legislative and political attacks in Michigan, Ohio, and Wisconsin – three states long known for union strength – which illustrates the degree to which unions have lost political and popular support.[24] The story is more complex, of course. Unions still wield significant political power; they remain among the most important campaign contributors (and sources of campaign labor) for Democratic politicians. In addition, voters in Ohio overturned the legislature's antiunion measures and Wisconsin witnessed an outpouring of opposition against that state's antiunion legislation. But the overall sharp decline in union density over the last few decades has largely been met with a collective yawn from the public. Indeed, the fact that these antiunion legislative measures occurred in the first place speaks volumes about unions' overall lack of support from the public.

Given the low density rate and poor public perception, unions should consider ways to bolster their popular support. As the state-level attacks on unions and the debate over the Employee Free Choice Act[25] show, support among the public – even individuals who are not union members or likely targets of future union campaigns – can have a significant impact on organized labor. Traditional NLRA organizing strategies are simply not enough in this economy to maintain broad support for unions. The difficulty is how unions might turn that trend around.

The modern economy's technology sector presents several additional hurdles. Most notably, employers in this industry have fought fiercely in court to define these workers as independent contractors rather than employees. In the absence of true employment status, which is required for NLRA coverage,[26] there are few opportunities for such workers to gain the protection of labor unions.

Although there is no magic bullet for turning around unions' fortunes and increasing employee voice, there does appear to be more that unions can do to achieve greater support than their current conflict-oriented model. One option is a broad public relations campaign. Through advertising and other types of outreach, unions could attempt to bolster their image among the general public in the hopes that it will stave off some of the attacks that seem to be cropping up more frequently. But the focus of this chapter is on other measures, particularly those that implicate ways in which unions, and other advocates for workers, can help to expand employees' participation at work. The common theme to these alternatives is the need for these groups to adopt a more cooperative strategy. That is not to say that conflict with employers is unwise; indeed, unions should still fight hard for employees when warranted. But a permanently adversarial posture does not seem to be serving unions well. A willingness to engage in cooperative relationships with employers and, at times, to forgo some goals normally associated with unionization may result in greater gains. If employers view unionization as being less costly than they do now, in many instances they may be more accepting, or at least less resistant, to unions. Corporate resistance will always remain a serious issue. For many employers there is nothing a union can do to mitigate that hostility. Yet, other employers may view the costs of fighting unionization – costs that include financial expenditures and decreased employee morale – as being less worthwhile if the prospect of a union presence is less restrictive than it appears to be now. Few employers are likely to welcome unionization, but even a reduction in the level of hostility could have a significant impact on unions' ability to represent or assist workers. Cooperation also allows independent contractors – in addition to employees – to have a voice in the organization. This distinction is critical for attempts at collective action in the modern economy, where the use of contingent workers is pervasive.

There are many ways in which unions and employee-side groups could engage in more cooperation with employers, both large and small. This chapter discusses a few more prominent options, such as unions being more open to nontraditional employee-voice mechanisms and unions and employee groups focusing more on the provision of services rather than classic collective representation. This chapter further identifies how these options would prove advantageous for workers in the technology sector, who currently face the most difficult hurdles with respect to traditional union representation.

5.2 TECHNOLOGY COMPANIES, THE UBER GUILD, AND OTHER NONTRADITIONAL UNION AGREEMENTS

Although traditional unions remain the most robust form of worker representation, it is not a realistic possibility for many, if not most, American workers – particularly those in the technology sector. Taking into account the political barriers to substantial reform of US labor law, this chapter argues that, in many cases, seeking more cooperative strategies will be the best way to increase worker voice and representation. These strategies can, but generally need not, involve assistance from traditional unions. However, such assistance would likely benefit both unions and workers. Unions possess considerable expertise in representing workers, which would be of great value to workers involved with these alt-labor organizations. In turn, interest in unions would likely increase, particularly from workers who have positive experiences, employers that see the potential for a more cooperative relationship with unions, and the public that has more exposure and experience with the gains to be had by increased worker voice.

This chapter first explores the unique problem facing workers in the technology sector in obtaining the employment status required to achieve protections under the NLRA and other workplace statutes. Given these challenges, workers in this sector have much to gain from more nontraditional unionization efforts. This chapter then examines one such quasi-union effort by one of the largest technology-sector companies – the Uber Guild. It further navigates attempts by workers to organize outside of the NLRA. In particular, through the Freelancers Union, contingent workers have achieved some control over the working relationship. And, Working America has provided workers a platform from which to pursue political actions. Finally, this chapter examines how more traditional brick-and-mortar-type companies have also pursued quasi-union arrangements and looks at how General Electric and Volkswagen have provided workers with a collective voice outside of the protections of the NLRA. While much has been written on quasi-unions,[27] there is little literature extensively examining alt-unions in the context of the technology sector.

5.2.1 Contingent Workers

One increasingly large group of employees in particular need of workplace protections consists of independent contractors and other contingent workers. Employers' ability and willingness to classify workers as independent contractors has had an enormous impact on those workers. Aside from the often lower pay and lesser benefits that many employers unilaterally choose to provide, the independent contractor classification also means that most employment laws do not apply to these workers. Thus, independent contractors neither have a right to collective action or bargaining nor any protection against, among other things, discrimination and pay that would violate the minimum wage or overtime rules. Efforts to assist independent contractors, such as the Uber Guild, show potential options for all workers to improve their working conditions, even in the current economic climate.

As discussed in prior chapters, workers in the technology sector face an increasingly steep battle in their attempts to be recognized as employees under state and federal employment statutes. These workers are difficult to define as the nature of their employment is nontraditional and not easily categorized. The employment laws, such as the Fair Labor Standards Act of 1938 (FLSA),[28] were conceptualized at a time when the technologies that have enabled the success of Uber and others were nonexistent. The laws were thus not developed for these workers in the technology sector, and the courts have struggled in their efforts to define these individuals as either independent contractors or employees. The litigation in *O'Connor v. Uber Technologies, Inc.*,[29] discussed in prior chapters, makes this clear.

5.2.2 *The Traditional Standard*

As the Uber and Lyft cases make clear, courts and litigants have faced immense struggles when applying the employee/independent contractor analysis to workers in the technology sector. The Uber and Lyft cases in no way stand out as anomalies, and class action litigation on the employee classification issue has been widespread in the technology sector. As noted in the prior chapter, cases have been brought against numerous on-demand companies,[30] including GrubHub,[31] Amazon,[32] Handy (previously Handybook),[33] CrowdFlower,[34] Homejoy,[35] Postmates,[36] Instacart,[37] and Washio.[38] As discussed, an unsuccessful class action claim was even brought against Yelp, arguing that online reviewers of local businesses should be considered employees.[39] Much of the difficulty for courts in these cases is in the application of a traditional legal standard to a developing, ill-defined segment of workers in the technology sector of the economy.

The worker classification issue extends well beyond the FLSA to other employment statutes. Indeed, for coverage, individuals must generally be considered employees for purposes of discrimination claims brought under Title VII of the Civil Rights Act of 1964,[40] the Americans with Disabilities Act,[41] and the Age Discrimination in Employment Act.[42]

The debate over whether technology workers are employees or independent contractors will likely be waged for years with varying outcomes depending upon the particular employer or jurisdiction where the claim is brought. Ultimately, the Supreme Court may have to weigh in on this issue. In the meantime, however, these technology-sector workers are left in an untenable position. With their employment status in flux, it will be difficult for them to obtain proper employment protections and to have their collective interests adequately represented. These workers can substantially benefit from less traditional methods of organizing.

Looking beyond the typical statutory protections, there are a number of avenues still available to such workers. A number of these are addressed below, including the Freelancers Union and Working America. Nontraditional attempts of workers to have their collective voice heard with their employers through informal mechanisms is also outlined in this chapter. In the technology sector, the best example of this is the Uber Guild, though other examples are highlighted here as well. There can be no perfect approach to organizing outside of the statutory protections that Congress has provided to so many workers. Nonetheless, more workers should attempt to bargain for informal protections where these traditional protections are unavailable.

5.2.3 *The Freelancers Union*

One of the higher profile approaches to servicing contingent workers has been the Freelancers Union.[43] Founded in 1995, this organization has been described as the fastest-growing labor organization in the country, with over 200,000 independent contractors, part-time workers, and temps as members primarily in New York State but expanding to other areas of the country.[44] The union does not engage in collective bargaining on behalf of its members: instead, it provides services to individuals who wish to purchase them, although membership is free. Central among those services is health insurance, which the union identified as its members' primary concern.[45]

The Freelancers Union's lack of traditional collective bargaining and representation certainly limits its ability to change its members' work conditions. In spite of declining union density, unions have remained surprisingly capable of increasing their members' wages,[46] and their role in pursuing grievances on behalf of employees can be immensely important. But the insurance and other benefits obtainable through the Freelancers Union can make a real difference for independent contractors and other workers who would otherwise not be able to afford them. Also, the union allows members to rate "clients" they have worked for, which provides potentially valuable information that these workers would otherwise lack.[47] Moreover, the union has made moves in the political arena that could benefit independent contractors nationwide.[48]

This political action,[49] combined with its ability to attract workers with the option to purchase affordable benefits, gives the Freelancers Union and other organizations like it an opportunity to improve unions' reputations among the public. The union might also provide an important benefit for firms. A significant cost of being an independent contractor or other nonstatutory employee is the lack of benefits often associated with that arrangement. By permitting these workers to purchase benefits at a much lower price than what they could achieve on their own, the Freelancers Union – perhaps ironically – lowers the cost of working under these arrangements. This, in turn, will make the independent contractors and other similar workers even more attractive to firms who are unable or unwilling to provide benefits for those workers.

5.2.4 *Working America*

Traditional unions have also explored the use of nontraditional employee groups. For instance, the AFL–CIO's organization Working America celebrated its fifteenth anniversary in 2018.[50] It described itself as the fastest-growing workers' organization in the country[51] and has claimed to have over three million members. Working America does not formally represent workers; instead, its primary goal is to promote relevant political action.[52] For instance, it mobilized residents in the Albuquerque area to vote for a raise in the minimum wage.[53] It has also distributed information on matters such as companies' legal violations, mass layoffs, and offshoring practices, which may help improve employees' ability to offset some employers' opportunistic use of their information advantages.[54] Like the Freelancers Union, Working America also has potential public relations benefits; as more workers and their families become acquainted with the potential benefits of labor organizations, all such groups may rise in the public's estimation. Indeed, the AFL–CIO has been open about Working America's potential to foster support for more formal unionization efforts as employees gain more positive experiences with representational groups. This could occur by organizing groups of employees who are already members of Working America or other employees learning about Working America and thinking more favorably about unionization as a result of that knowledge. One example of the transition from nontraditional to traditional organizing is the Communication Workers of America's WashTech organization. WashTech started as a non-collective-bargaining group that assisted and lobbied for independent contractors and temporary workers at Microsoft but ultimately developed several groups that sought formal status as a collective-bargaining representative.[55]

These nontraditional worker groups are merely a sample of the various organizations that may help workers outside of the classic Wagner model of collective bargaining. By removing the emotionally charged, formalistic labor law framework, they have an opportunity to assist workers while maintaining a less antagonistic relationship with employers and gaining a more favorable reputation with the general public. However, these groups have limits as well. Although the lack of formal collective bargaining will generally improve relationships with employers, the reason is largely because full-fledged bargaining is more effective at extracting wages and other benefits.[56] In addition, these groups could have funding difficulties without a steady source of dues or other income.[57] Yet, despite these barriers, it seems that unions and other organizations concerned about workers would benefit from more experimentation with nontraditional assistance. The degree to which these experiments will bear fruit is unclear, but it is not likely that they will make things any worse. One such high-profile experiment was undertaken in the technology sector.

5.2.5 The Uber Guild

In May 2016, Uber announced the creation of a drivers' union that it coined the "Independent Drivers Guild,"[58] which operates in New York City. This drivers' association falls far short of providing full union status but will offer workers "a forum for regular dialogue and afford them some limited benefits and protections."[59] This unique organization was created to represent drivers who (purportedly) wanted to remain independent while still being allowed to enjoy the protections and benefits of a collective association of Uber drivers. The guild provides tens of thousands of Uber drivers in the city with a voice in company operations, as well as other new benefits and protections. The Independent Drivers Guild is affiliated with a regional branch of the International Association of Machinists and Aerospace Workers union (IAM).[60]

The IAM represents nearly 600,000 members in aerospace, manufacturing, transportation, shipbuilding, woodworking, and electronics.[61] The organization describes itself as the workers "moving North America."[62] The IAM is split into numerous districts; District 15, where the Uber Guild operates, is one of IAM's largest, representing close to 19,000 active and retired members in various industries throughout the northeast.[63] Its mission is "to negotiate agreements on behalf of its members containing the best possible wages, benefits and protections while continuing to discover ways to better the lives of [its] members outside of their collective bargaining agreements." Additionally, District 15 is "continuously endeavoring to increase union density by organizing the unorganized through traditional and alternative methods of unionization."[64]

The creation of the guild followed a series of lawsuits alleging that the drivers should be considered employees of Uber instead of being classified as independent contractors. The independent contractor classification used by Uber allows the company to keep labor costs low, and it also excludes the drivers from coverage under many labor and employment laws and regulations, including minimum wage and overtime provisions. Independent contractors cannot form traditional unions.[65] The guild agreement reached with the IAM attempted to soften concerns from both drivers' groups and regulators regarding the company's labor model and classification of workers without formally allowing the creation of a union.[66] Moreover, the possibility of unionization has led Uber to enter into agreements with drivers that help ameliorate some of the mounting tension over workplace issues.[67] Uber had hoped to smooth relationships with the drivers after recent fare cuts and policy changes. According to Uber's chief advisor, the agreement was designed to "[i]mprove communication between Uber and our driver-partners; [p]rovide benefits without jeopardizing the independence and flexibility drivers love; and [g]ive drivers who have been barred from the app an additional voice in the deactivation appeals process."[68] This statement reveals the hope that the guild could provide a cooperative relationship that benefits both Uber and its drivers.

The guild was established for a five-year period. During those five years, "a group of drivers who are guild members will hold monthly meetings with Uber management in the city, where they can raise issues of concern."[69] In addition, "[t]he drivers will be able to appeal decisions by Uber to bar them from its platform, and can have guild officials represent them in their appeals."[70] The association also provides drivers with the option of purchasing discounted legal services, discounted life and disability insurance, and discounted roadside help for problems encountered while driving.[71] During the five-year duration of the guild, the IAM has stated that it will halt its efforts to unionize the drivers and will not encourage them to strike.[72]

However, the guild does not provide all of the benefits of a traditional union. Although the drivers will have more of a unified voice, as noted, they will not achieve formal union or employee status.[73] Guild members cannot bargain with Uber over contractual provisions concerning wage, benefits, or other protections.[74] Instead, the company will exclusively determine these provisions. Nevertheless, Uber will receive more input from drivers when considering how to make these important determinations.[75]

But, in joining the guild, drivers have not waived any labor rights. If, during the term of the agreement, it is determined by a court that the drivers are employees, the IAM may still attempt to unionize the drivers. The guild will also work with Uber to lobby for policies on which they agree. Uber has declined to specify how much the company will pay to support the new group,[76] and the IAM plans to pay for some of the administrative costs of the organization. Drivers who join the guild will not be required to pay any membership dues.

In addition, Uber launched new features on its platform to further its attempts to ameliorate the frustrations voiced by many drivers. For instance, under these changes in Uber's mobile application, drivers are afforded the ability to pause rider requests, for a coffee or bathroom break.[77] Drivers will also be paid for wait times that exceed two minutes and, in some markets, can receive other discounts. Moreover, drivers who are commuting may receive trip requests that occur only along their way home or to work. Other changes include "in-app phone support, the ability to view earnings and be paid instantly from the app through an Uber debit card, and a fuel-finder function that allows drivers to find the cheapest gas nearby."[78]

Uber is hoping to build a relationship with its drivers through the guild.[79] According to Uber, the agreement is part of an ongoing effort by the company to work more closely with drivers who use the Uber platform. The guild is purportedly a "win–win" for Uber and its workers-drivers receive a stronger voice while Uber prevents formal organization efforts and simultaneously adds a partner in its lobbying efforts.[80] The Uber Guild forms part of a larger strategy for building the new workforce in the gig economy.[81]

Uber has also teamed up with the Freelancers Union to ensure better relations with drivers. Uber has stated that the "Freelancers Union, a longtime leader in advocating for independent workers, will advise Uber on how to best bring flexible benefits to independent workers in the on-demand economy."[82] These worker-friendly changes, along with the implementation of the guild, further Uber's objective of ameliorating the existing tensions with drivers while maintaining the company's platform, ideals, and cost structure.

5.2.6 *Additional Attempts at Quasi-Union Arrangements*

The Uber Guild is a unique organization that has been tailored to fit the particular concerns raised by the structure of the working relationship of the company with its drivers. While limited, there have been other attempts to provide workers in nonplatform-based sectors with benefits and representation outside of the traditional union setting. This book sets forth two such examples below.

5.2.6.1 The GE Ombudsperson Process

Although many of General Electric's (GE) workers are represented by traditional unions,[83] the company created an ombudsperson process for individuals to ask questions and report integrity concerns.[84] GE employed approximately 600 ombudspersons for all of its businesses. GE workers became familiar with their local and regional ombudsperson through "frequent communications, articles and various Company intranet sites."[85] The GE ombudsperson process allowed workers to voice their integrity questions and concerns, anonymously if they chose, and to avoid concerns over retaliation.[86]

Due to General Electric's global presence, ombudspersons could "speak the local language and understand the culture and business environment of their locations."[87] Ombudspersons underwent training to learn "procedures for receiving concerns, initiating investigations and monitoring case progress and closure."[88] Furthermore, "[o]mbudspersons [were] introduced at all employee meetings within the businesses and regions, including integrity events and trainings."[89]

GE's website provided an online form to submit "an Ombuds concern" by filling out an integrity questionnaire.[90] In 2015, workers reported 3,844 integrity concerns through the ombudsperson process.[91] All concerns raised went through the ombudsperson process, which included an investigation.[92] The investigation process included "assigning an investigation team," "conducting an investigation," "corrective action," and "feedback."[93] The process did not provide any formal union protections, but the ombudsperson program did provide clear benefits to employees. The company maintained that "[t]he GE Ombudsperson process allows [workers] to voice [their] integrity questions and concerns . . . and [they] will receive a response."[94] The goal of the "open reporting environment" was to encourage employees to report without fear of retaliation and for employees to "remain the Company's first and best line of defense for the early detection of potential compliance issues."[95] Typically, "fair employment practices" comprised the majority of concerns reported through the ombudsperson process.

5.2.6.2 Volkswagen "Minority Union" Agreement

In 2014, the United Auto Workers (UAW) lost a union representation election at the Volkswagen (VW) Chattanooga plant in Tennessee.[96] In late 2014, VW implemented a "Community Engagement Program."[97] As part of the program, VW agreed to hold three meetings each month with the UAW despite the UAW's failed attempt to unionize VW's employees. The meetings provided a "forum for the UAW to raise workplace issues, ranging from who works the graveyard shift to how much work the company gives lower-paid temps."[98] The policy attracted widespread media attention, with headlines that included "Minority Unionism (Sort of) Comes to VW Chattanooga,"[99] and "Volkswagen's Sort-of Union in Tennessee."[100] The program thus immediately became controversial based on its structure and the benefits provided to workers as part of the policy.

The arrangement between the UAW and VW is a form of "unionization-lite" in which "VW certified that the UAW represents at least 45 percent of its hourly employees."[101] Under the program, groups that VW had certified as representing 15 percent or 30 percent of employees also met with VW, but less often. Labor activists hoped that the arrangement would grow into a "minority union" arrangement, "where a union represents and negotiates contracts for those employees who sign up, whether or not it has majority support."[102]

Image Credit: Bloomberg/Contributor/Getty Images

The policy did not establish a "true minority unionism at Volkswagen."[103] The policy also did not include any actual bargaining obligations, and VW was only required to "meet" with the organizations to listen to their concerns.[104] In addition, the policy allowed employees to "[d]iscuss and/or promote their interests."[105] Although the policy did not establish a traditional union for workers, it did attempt to build a strong relationship between VW Chattanooga and its employees.[106] Although the door was not opened all the way, labor leaders were hopeful that this policy would eventually grow into a "'minority union' arrangement."[107]

With the exception of the United States, China, and Russia, VW implemented local "works councils" in its operations worldwide.[108] The works councils provided elected blue-collar employees a voice in management and company policies. Although both the UAW and VW have embraced the idea of bringing the works-council model to the United States, federal law prohibiting "company-dominated" unions likely hinders such an arrangement.

5.3 HELPING EMPLOYERS HELP WORKERS: PARTICIPATION GROUPS

As noted, quasi-union arrangements often benefit from the participation of traditional unions but can succeed independently of them. However, one quasi-union strategy that requires some degree of union participation or acquiescence is the expansion of "employee participation groups." These are groups that are housed at a specific workplace and that provide employees with a means to give input to their employers. Many employee participation groups already exist but often operate illegally. Unions could enhance their existence in many ways, although they have been resistant to such efforts thus far. One of the Wagner Act's original provisions was a ban on "company unions." At the time, many employers created and dominated so-called unions that purported to represent employees but were often intended to weaken employees' desire and ability to seek truly independent representation.[109] To combat this problem, Congress added section 8(a)(2), which makes it unlawful for an employer to dominate or interfere with any labor organization.[110]

One of the key conditions for a section 8(a)(2) violation is that the work group at issue qualify as a "labor organization" as defined by section 2(5).[111] Under section 2(5), a group will be considered a labor organization if it has employee participation and its purpose is to deal with an employer over terms and conditions of work.[112] The NLRB has expansively interpreted section 2(5), particularly the requirement that a labor organization have the purpose of "dealing with" an employer. According to the NLRB, "dealing with" is defined as a bilateral process or a "pattern or practice in which a group of employees, over time, makes proposals to management, management responds to these proposals by acceptance or rejection by word or deed, and compromise is not required."[113] Moreover, under NLRB jurisprudence, a group can be a labor organization even if it lacks a formal structure; has no elected officers, bylaws, regular meetings, or dues; and its discussions with an employer fall far short of traditional collective bargaining.[114] As discussed below, section 2(5) has far-reaching effects on nontraditional worker groups, including the result that an employer cannot provide any support to or exercise control over a group considered a labor organization without violating section 8(a)(2).[115] However, employers could lawfully form or support a group made up of workers who are not classified as employees under the NLRA; thus, independent contractors and other similarly situated technology workers have an opportunity for cooperation with their employers that workers classified as employees lack.

The general debate over section 8(a)(2), and calls for its reform, are well known.[116] This book does not revisit this discussion; instead, it argues that section 8(a)(2) represents another area in which a more cooperative approach could be beneficial to unions, not to mention employees and employers. Unions have strongly objected to attempts to narrow section 8(a)(2)'s reach,[117] but reconsideration of that stance may now be appropriate.

Surveys have demonstrated that there is an unmet demand for employee voice (or participation) at work.[118] Workers overwhelmingly want more opportunities to provide input on business operations and to discuss working conditions with their employers.[119] Employers also frequently recognize the value in certain types of worker participation, particularly as the economy relies more on jobs that require independent thinking.[120] For instance, employee input can improve productivity and morale, as well as provide a better way to address workplace grievances. As a result, many – although certainly not all – managers have expressed their support for allowing some form of employee voice in the workplace.[121]

Although the desires of employers and employees are not always congruent – an employer may want employee input on production operations but not on working conditions – there is often enough overlap that some increase in employee participation and voice could be accomplished. That is, of course, if section 8(a)(2) did not prohibit most employee participation groups. The breadth of section 8(a)(2), or more specifically the breadth of section 2(5)'s definition of a "labor organization" that an employer is not allowed to dominate or support, allows for little experimentation – it is largely a choice between traditional union representation or nothing at all.[122] Because employers will often take the lead in organizing these groups, section 8(a)(2)'s expansive reach means that these groups cannot be created lawfully. The result is an unmet demand for employee participation and voice though this unmet demand is not as dire as it initially seems.

Despite the potential of an unfair labor practice finding, it appears that employers frequently use employee participation groups that may violate section 8(a)(2) – likely reflecting the potential advantages for employers and the weak remedies found in the NLRA.[123] There is significant variety in the form that these groups can take, as well as in the amount of employee participation and topics they consider, such as self-managed employee teams and quality circles that focus on production rather than work conditions; quality of work or employee-action committees that often focus on safety, grievances, and other human resource issues; employee caucuses that promote better work conditions; and profit-sharing groups, such as employee stock ownership plans, that usually lack decision-making authority.[124] Many of these groups appear to involve input about working conditions and – perhaps not surprisingly, given that one would expect less hostile employers to be more open to meaningful employee input – employees generally have favorable views of the groups.[125]

Expanding the opportunity for employee participation groups, in addition to removing the specter of illegality on those that currently exist, is challenging but certainly not hopeless. Because many employers want some form of employee voice – enough so that many willingly violate the law to get it – the normal alliances are turned upside down. It is largely unions that oppose reform, while employers are more aligned with the general sentiment of employees. That is not to say that unions and others who oppose weakening section 8(a)(2) have no justification for their position; the potential harm of company unions and the risk that even more benevolent employee participation groups may create a misleading facade of participation is quite real.[126] But the unique alignment between employees and employers on this issue produces a potential for compromise.

Unions must ask themselves how much they really object to section 8(a)(2) reform. In particular, they should consider whether acceding to some changes in section 8(a)(2) could provide benefits that outweigh the feared costs of reform. Those benefits could come in the form of other legislative changes as well as the ability to promote a more cooperative image and relationship with other labor law actors. If a compromise on section 8(a)(2) reform occurred – a political long shot, to be sure – what might it look like?[127] There is general agreement that the prohibition against the most pernicious of company unions, such as sham organizations that employers use to prevent independent unions or to trick employees into believing that they have real representation, should be maintained. But section 8(a)(2) bans organizations that fall short of that concern, leaving ample room for far more narrow coverage that would still respect the provision's central policy concerns.[128] This would be particularly true if an employer's ability to create an employee participation group was tied to the lack of significant labor law violations.[129]

Unions have opposed narrowing section 8(a)(2) in part because of their fear that employer-initiated employee participation groups will compete with traditional unions and mislead employees regarding the actual independence of their representation.[130] Those fears are not unfounded, but they may be exaggerated and stand in the way of an opportunity worth pursuing. The risk of employees being misled about the true nature of their representation is a serious concern, but one that could be addressed by adding information requirements to a limited reform measure – such as requiring employers that use employee participation groups to inform workers of employer involvement and their right to join an independent union.

Additionally, it is difficult to believe that allowing more employer-initiated employee groups would make union density drop substantially below its current historical low. To the contrary, there are valid arguments that the expansion of these groups would actually lead to greater unionization. For instance, employee participation groups might encourage more interest in traditional unionization as employees have positive experiences with collective participation in the workplace.[131] As a result, these groups could represent potential organization targets for unions.[132] Employee participation groups could also encourage unions to improve, which may make them more attractive to employees.[133] Indeed, most other countries with developed labor laws lack section 8(a)(2)'s prohibition against nonunion employee participation groups yet have union density rates that are far greater than what is found in the United States.[134] Many countries also require employee representation in some form.[135] Finally, the reality is that many of these groups already exist (often illegally), so it is unclear how much advantage flows to unions by keeping the broad but weak section 8(a)(2) unchanged.

Unions, of course, are well aware of these considerations and still believe that the uncertainties of section 8(a)(2) reform outweigh the need to change a status quo that does not appear to have hurt them. But the potential benefits of cooperation may be a less obvious, or at least more discounted, factor. In addition to the potential gains resulting from a hypothetical legislative compromise, unions could see benefits flow from a less hostile stance toward employee participation groups. For instance, employers' resistance to unionization might decline if they have a positive experience with an employee participation group.

In the unlikely event that legislative reform is possible, unions need not – indeed, should not – open the door to section 8(a)(2) reform unconditionally. For instance, narrowing section 8(a)(2) in exchange for allowing the NLRB to issue fines, which is particularly important in cases that do not involve direct financial harm, may be a worthwhile trade-off for unions. Similarly, strengthening enforcement against unlawful terminations, expanding unions' organizing capabilities (such as increasing access to employees and decreasing election delays), and developing more types of injunctive relief could also be bargaining chips.[136] Some employer groups may be open to these types of trade-offs, especially representatives of the largest employers, which are better able to create and enjoy the benefits of employee groups. This sweet spot may be illusory, but it is certainly an effort worth pursuing.

If, as is likely in the short term, legislative reform is unattainable, unions could help implement de facto reform. For employers that are interested in employee input and participation and that are not overly hostile to union involvement, a potential compromise exists: An employer can avoid section 8 (a)(2) liability if its employee group is created or partially run by an outside union or other employee group. The most straightforward means of achieving this status is the voluntary recognition of a union that has agreed to limit its bargaining rights with a prerecognition framework agreement. That option has its limits, primarily because many employers will not be willing to recognize a union simply to avoid a potential section 8(a)(2) violation that has little cost.

But there are alternatives to such an arrangement. For instance, unions or quasi-union entities could help establish employee work groups in places where there are no formal collective-bargaining representatives. If the employer does not create an employee group or otherwise unlawfully support it, section 8(a)(2) is not implicated. Moreover, unions – or a quasi-union such as Working America – could simply provide information and assistance to employees interested in gaining more input at work. If these employees work for a firm that is sympathetic to increased worker voice, the employer can agree to discuss issues once the group is formed. As long as the employer does not recognize the group as a collective-bargaining representative and does not provide other unlawful domination or interference, there will generally be no section 8(a)(2) violation.

Whether unions will rethink their opposition to section 8(a)(2) reform remains an open question. But they need not go as far as supporting legislation to test the waters. Exploring opportunities to support employee participation groups could provide unions with more control over groups that already exist, remove some uncertainty about the effects of these groups, and provide opportunities for more cooperation with employers. These possible effects, in addition to others discussed, hold promise for unions and near-certain benefits for the largest employers who want more participation and voice in their workplaces.

If unions do not explore these options, they may find that the ship will sail without them. The desire of both employees and many employers to permit more voice at work can certainly enjoy the aid of unions but may not need unions to expand such opportunities. For instance, Professor Cynthia Estlund has discussed the possibility that corporate employers will internalize support for workplace democracy, much as they have done for diversity efforts.[137] As she rightly notes, however, employer antipathy for organized labor means that corporate citizenship will never embrace workers' right to voice if it is tied exclusively to the process of formal unionization.[138] Instead, nonunion groups, such as progressive companies and coalitions of quasi-unions, are more likely to play the primary role in changing corporate culture to favor workplace democracy.[139] Unions can and should be involved with such efforts, but it will require them to put their traditional collective-bargaining interests to the side at times. If they fail to do so and other groups successfully push corporations to internalize workplace democracy, then unions risk further marginalizing themselves.

The strength of employees' desire for workplace voice, and the desire of many employers to listen to their employees, makes the possibility of increased workplace democracy real. A significant number of employers are using worker participation groups, even though many of them are illegal under section 8(a)(2).[140] Moreover, attempts to repeal section 8(a)(2) have already come close to succeeding.[141] Thus, it would be no surprise to see legal change in this area. The question is how such change will occur. Will unions continue to fight any modification of the employee participation rules, or will they try to influence the direction of future reform? Will quasi-unions see workplace democracy as a goal worth the fight? Employers seem to have already concluded that workplace voice should be expanded and, given the current political environment, the chances are that they will ultimately be able to effect change. Unions and other pro-employee groups should ensure that they have influence over that process. If not, the resulting law may be as bad as some of them fear and could fail to accomplish the hopeful goals that workplace democracy promises.

5.4 NAVIGATING THE LEGAL BOUNDARIES OF TRADITIONAL AND NONTRADITIONAL WORKER REPRESENTATION

Given the currently poor prospects for traditional union collective bargaining, organizations that serve employees through other means may hold particular promise. Although generally not an equal substitute for unions' advocacy and influence over working conditions, these quasi-union worker representation organizations can still provide benefits to employees through other means, such as the provision of services, sharing useful employment-related information, and assisting employee attempts to engage in collective activity.[142] They might also give some new life to organized labor. If the Wagner model of collective bargaining has been failing workers and unions, then seeking alternatives could help both groups. The problem with traditional organizing and collective bargaining has not gone unnoticed by unions, which have increasingly explored new ways to organize and represent workers. For example, the Service Employees International Union (SEIU) implemented a successful Justice for Janitors campaign in southern California by focusing heavily on the workers' Mexican culture and seeking assistance from local religious and political leaders.[143] As part of that effort, the SEIU also used a public relations campaign that took advantage of the fact that many of the janitorial companies' clients were well-known retailers. By leading highly publicized demonstrations and boycotts against clients such as Apple, the union was able to exert more pressure on the primary employer than would normally be possible.[144] But a more radical change in strategy may be warranted.

As the Uber Guild and other examples show, quasi-union worker representation groups can achieve gains for workers by being more service-oriented toward members and working with employers to find ways to achieve gains for both employers and their workers. Cooperative strategies will not always be successful or appropriate, but these nontraditional groups are particularly suited to take advantage of instances where they would be beneficial. By providing previously unorganized workers with some level of voice and representation, nontraditional groups could provide significant opportunities for this large segment of the workforce. The degree of voice and representation may be less than what would occur under a formal, traditional collective-bargaining relationship. But in most cases, nontraditional representation will produce far more benefits for workers than currently exist. This is particularly true for the many contingent workers in technology and other fields, such as Uber drivers, who may not be classified as employees under workplace statutes. For these workers, as well as the vast majority of employees who are not unionized, their only opportunity for input on their work conditions exists at the whim of their employers. Finding ways to fill the gap between workers' overwhelming desire for voice and the current dearth of such opportunities should be a central priority for the labor movement.

Beyond the direct advantages to providing workers with voice and representation, nontraditional strategies might provide long-term gains for collective representation generally. As discussed earlier, the labor movement is suffering a serious public relations problem, which has contributed to a sharp decline in unionization rates and increased legislative and judicial barriers to organizing. Although it is unlikely that any strategy can substantially reverse these trends, increasing the number of workers who have experience with some form of collective bargaining will likely help. These workers, as well as their friends and families, may acquire a "taste" for collective representation that could lead to higher unionization rates and more nontraditional representation. Additionally, if these nontraditional representation strategies prove beneficial for employers, or even less negative than they feared, then employer opposition to unions and other types of worker representation may shrink to some extent. More generally, as employers and workers gain a better view of workplace representation, the general public may be less solicitous of political attacks against unions and other pro-worker efforts.

Beyond these strategic issues, however, is the impact of the law on worker representation groups. Because nontraditional quasi-unions straddle the line between traditional unions and nonlabor membership organizations, the legal restrictions that apply are often unclear. This lack of clarity typically results from the difficulty in determining whether a quasi-union should be classified as a labor organization, with the answer imposing significant legal consequences that will sharply affect the type of activities that the group can lawfully pursue. For instance, groups that are not considered labor organizations can avoid many burdensome regulations governing traditional unions and can take advantage of certain types of pressure on employers that unions are prohibited from pursuing. At the same time, avoiding the labor organization classification restricts groups' ability to represent workers and potentially exposes them to antitrust liability. In other words, nontraditional groups act on a knife's edge, on which a move in one direction can expose them to significant monetary or even criminal liability, while a move in the other direction makes them more like traditional unions and prone to the shortcomings that such a designation entails.

The modern economy holds great promise for nontraditional worker groups, but as discussed below, the law has not kept up with changes in the technology sector and other similar industries. Given the current political climate, it is not realistic to hope for legislative reforms; thus, nontraditional groups must be cognizant of the legal consequences of their actions and shape their organizational and representational strategies accordingly.

5.4.1 *The Potential Advantages of Nontraditional Strategies*

There are various legal advantages to nontraditional representation strategies over more formal union representation, particularly for workers in the technology sector. These advantages generally stem from the possibility that most of these groups would avoid classification as a "labor organization" under the NLRA.[145] For example, groups that are not classified as labor organizations under the statute can receive support from an employer without violating section 8(a)(2). In other words, groups that do not engage in bilateral bargaining over wages, hours, and terms and conditions of employment can currently provide workers with some degree of representation with an employers' acquiescence. Although not all employers will be willing to engage in this type of bargaining, for those that are, this quasi-union strategy provides workers with some degree of representation as well as the opportunity to engage in a more cooperative relationship with the employer.

Despite its nontraditional nature, many of these quasi-unions may still enjoy traditional legal protections. For example, although the NLRA's section 8(a)(1)[146] antiretaliation protection for employee collective action is typically associated with union activity, it also applies to nonunion employee attempts to act together to improve their working conditions.[147] Thus, even nonunionized employees who work with nontraditional groups or engage in activities to further their interests as employees will remain protected. However, workers who are not classified as employees lack this NLRA protection. For these workers, collective action remains a serious threat to their job status. This lack of protection can be a significant impediment to collective action, but it also illustrates the importance of efforts such as the Uber Guild, which provide a more cooperative and less risky strategy for collective representation.

Acting outside of the traditional legal framework can have potential liabilities, but there are numerous benefits as well. In particular, nontraditional groups may be able to avoid some of the more restrictive limits placed on traditional unions. Three of the most significant of these restrictions are possible limits on agreements with employers, recordkeeping and structural organizational requirements, and prohibitions against various types of employer pressure.

5.4.1.1 Avoiding Section 302 Attacks on Cooperative Agreements

Nontraditional groups whose actions put them outside of section 2(5)'s definition of a labor organization will have greater freedom to cooperate with employers. In particular, these quasi-unions will likely be able to avoid certain legal challenges to any agreements they secure with employers. Chief among these challenges is the claim that an agreement violates section 302 of the Labor Management Relations Act (LMRA or Taft–Hartley Act).[148] Anti-labor organizations and workers have been increasingly using this provision to attack agreements between unions and employers.

Under section 302(a), it is unlawful for an employer to provide "any … thing of value" to a labor organization or representative of its employees.[149]

This provision is primarily intended to prohibit employer bribes of union officials,[150] but dissenting employees, often acting with anti-union groups, have used private rights of action under section 302 to argue for an expansion of its scope.[151] This expansive interpretation of section 302 could be a significant barrier to traditional union organizing and, in turn, represent an advantage of nontraditional representation efforts.

The recent section 302 strategy centers on the argument that this provision extends beyond traditional bribery and extortion to include actions such as an employer promise to a union that it will remain neutral in an organizing campaign; that it will voluntarily recognize the union if it achieves majority support; or that it will abide by other ground rules, such as providing access to the employer's premises.[152] In the past, courts have rejected claims that such promises are a "thing of value" under section 302.[153] However, in *Mulhall v. Unite Here Local 355*,[154] the Eleventh Circuit appeared to open the door to such claims. In *Mulhall*, the court held that an employer's promise to remain neutral during organizing drives,[155] among other assistance, could be considered a "thing of value."[156]

Union opponents heralded the *Mulhall* decision as a legal tool to attack the use of neutrality and similar agreements between employers and unions, especially after the Supreme Court agreed to hear the case.[157] Unions, in turn, were alarmed by *Mulhall* – so much so that they also sought certiorari.[158] However, both sides may have placed too much weight on the Eleventh Circuit's decision; while it certainly opened the door wider to section 302 claims, the court also seemed to limit potential liability to employer promises that amounted to corruption or extortion.[159] That said, the fact that the Supreme Court agreed to hear the case raised a genuine possibility that it would help usher in a new type of attack on union organizing.

Despite its promise as a potential labor law blockbuster, *Mulhall* ultimately ended with a whimper when the Court dismissed the case as improvidently granted.[160] Nevertheless, as the Supreme Court maintains – and potentially expands – its conservative bent, we can expect to see this issue before the Court again. If it follows *Mulhall*'s lead, or pushes the interpretation of section 302 further, the Court could severely limit a union's ability to cooperate with employers, which they have increasingly done in organizing drives.[161] In the meantime, parties will likely continue to argue that section 302 should be broadly interpreted to cover neutrality and other similar promises. We might see arguments that other types of agreements violate section 302, such as employer promises to provide appeal rights from certain workplace actions – like being dismissed from the Uber platform – or to have periodic meetings with the company.

The Uber Guild agreement implicates many of these potential section 302 promises, but the group and others like it should have little to fear. Indeed, the ability to mitigate the risk of such claims represents one of the advantages of nontraditional representation groups because the distinguishing features that make them nontraditional also serve to inoculate them from section 302 liability. First, if a group represents workers who are not classified as employees, then section 302 – by its own terms – does not apply.[162] Second, even if a group represents workers who are classified as employees, the group would likely still avoid liability as long as it is not categorized as a traditional labor organization under section 2(5) of the NLRA.[163] In other words, as long as nontraditional groups are not "dealing with employers,"[164] they should not be at risk for a section 302 violation. Groups in this situation would have to decide whether reducing section 302 liability is worth the limitations required to avoid dealing with employers.

5.4.1.2 Lowering Organizational and Administrative Legal Burdens

In addition to the mitigation of liability under section 302, nontraditional representation groups, particularly those found in the technology sector, can avoid many of the burdensome requirements of the Labor Management Reporting and Disclosure Act (LMRDA).[165] Although these requirements were intended, at least in part, to promote democracy and fairness for union members, they also impose extra costs for covered organizations – costs that can be significant for smaller organizations.[166]

Among other things, the LMRDA imposes upon covered labor organizations (1) a duty of fair representation to members;[167] (2) a requirement that organizations implement democratic processes, such as conducting regular secret-ballot elections and providing members the right to participate at meetings, to regularly elect leaders, and to vote on dues; and (3) a requirement that members be given due process rights against discipline. The LMRDA also requires detailed reporting on finances and time spent by organization leaders.[168]

If nontraditional groups are not considered labor organizations under the LMRDA, they can incorporate whatever requirements they and their members believe are appropriate while maintaining flexibility to alter or eliminate requirements that are unduly burdensome or need improvement.[169] Whether groups can avoid the labor organization classification is not always clear, however. One complication for nontraditional groups' ability to navigate their legal exposure under the LMRDA is that the law arguably has a broader definition of "labor organization" than does the NLRA. The LMRDA incorporates the definition of labor organization used in section 2(5) but also adds coverage for "any conference, general committee, joint or system board, or joint council so engaged which is subordinate to a national or international labor organization, other than a State or local central body."[170] Particularly for groups working with traditional unions, this addition creates the possibility of being classified as a labor organization for LMRDA purposes, even if they are not considered a labor organization under the NLRA.[171] Indeed, pro-employer groups have already used this argument in an effort to impose LMRDA requirements on nontraditional groups.[172]

The potential for LMRDA coverage creates a double-edged sword for nontraditional groups that represent statutory employees – the more effective they are at representing their members, the more likely they are to be subject to the restrictions that accompany status as a labor organization.[173] But if nontraditional groups are able to avoid this classification, they will be free to pursue a wider variety of financial and organizational models than is currently mandated by the LMRDA – models that would hopefully provide these groups a better opportunity to serve their members.[174]

5.4.1.3 Freedom to Pursue Secondary Pressure and Other Strategies Prohibited by the NLRA

Another set of legal limitations that nontraditional groups may avoid are the limits on the types of pressure that traditional unions can bring to bear against employers. A larger set of pressure tactics is advantageous when groups decide to take a less cooperative stance against employers. However, even cooperative strategies may involve some degree of pressure on employers, particularly when initially attempting to get an employer to participate in discussions. Whether a quasi-union is merely trying to get an employer's attention and interest in cooperation or is attempting to exert more forceful pressure, being nontraditional comes with certain legal advantages.

In the 1947 Taft–Hartley amendments, Congress amended the NLRA by adding section 8(b), which prohibited labor organizations from engaging in various practices, including certain methods that unions had often used to pressure employers.[175] Most important for nontraditional groups are section 8 (b)(4)'s limits on secondary pressure, such as boycotts and strikes that target businesses that deal with the employer at the center of the dispute. Prior to 1947, unions had long targeted businesses in the hopes that they might exert pressure on the "primary employer," the employer with whom the union has the dispute.[176] Under section 8(b)(4), labor organizations can still peacefully publicize a labor dispute, but they are prohibited from boycotting, striking, or picketing other employers who do business with the primary employer.[177]

Although there are questions about section 8(b)(4)'s constitutionality, these restrictions have been repeatedly upheld against unions.[178] Moreover, unlike unfair labor practices in which employees are the victims, employers can bring private lawsuits seeking compensatory damages against unions for violations of section 8(b)(4).[179] However, section 8(b)(4) applies only to labor organizations as defined by the NLRA; thus, nontraditional groups that can avoid that designation are largely free to use secondary pressure to influence the behavior of employers.[180]

Similarly, so-called hot cargo agreements between labor organizations and employers are illegal under section 8(e) of the NLRA.[181] This means that, unlike traditional unions, nontraditional groups that avoid classification as a labor organization can seek and enter into agreements with a company to avoid doing business with another company that has committed unfair labor practices or other acts that the group opposes.

More recent events illustrate how nontraditional groups can engage in activities that might be viewed as violations of section 8(b)(4) had traditional unions been the primary actors. The most high-profile example is the effort taken by the Organization United for Respect at Walmart (OUR Walmart) to improve the pay, benefits, and working conditions of Walmart employees. OUR Walmart's tactics included picketing, which led Walmart to allege that the group violated section 8(b). Walmart argued that this provision was applicable because OUR Walmart was affiliated with a traditional union and should therefore be considered a labor organization.[182] Walmart's willingness to pursue this action illustrates the potential advantages of nontraditional groups. The existence of the suit itself indicates that OUR Walmart's pressure was having an impact. As long as nontraditional groups can avoid classification as labor organizations, or being considered part of such an organization, they will have much more free rein than traditional unions to impose pressure on employers. This is especially true in the technology sector, which has many workers who are not classified as employees[183] and is particularly susceptible to secondary pressure because of the industry's breadth and substantial interaction with many different companies.

5.4.2 *The Potential Disadvantages of Alt-Labor Strategies*

Although nontraditional worker representation comes with certain legal advantages, working outside of the mainstream labor organization structure presents potential legal risks as well. The likely advantages of nontraditional representation greatly outweigh these potential disadvantages – especially given the current anemic state of affairs for workers – but these risks are nonetheless important for groups to keep in mind as they make strategic decisions.

5.4.2.1 Lack of Protection against Retaliation

One of the major risks for workers is that support for collective representation may expose them to employer retaliation or even loss of their jobs. This is less of a concern for statutory employees who, even if advocating or working for nontraditional representation, are typically protected by the NLRA. Seeking redress through the NLRB is often a laborious process with limited monetary remedies, but it does offer a degree of legal protection for employee collective action. In contrast, the NLRA offers no protection against retaliation for workers who are not statutory employees – or, like Uber drivers, workers whose status may be in serious doubt. As a result, it can be difficult to recruit these workers to support and join nontraditional representation efforts, particularly when their employers are openly hostile to such efforts.

This lack of legal protection against retaliation can be a significant barrier to the already difficult task of organizing workers – a task that is particularly hard for contingent and gig workers whose relative lack of physical proximity to coworkers make them less able to bond with each other. However, this issue also illustrates the advantage of more cooperative representation efforts. Because a hostile employer emboldened by a complete lack of NLRA protection is likely to intimidate workers to prevent them from acting together, nontraditional groups that can find ways to work with employers will be able to provide significant value to their members.

5.4.2.2 Antitrust Liability

Among the potential disadvantages of nontraditional groups – and the most significant from a financial and criminal perspective – is antitrust law. Perhaps no issue better represents the knife's edge facing nontraditional groups, which must carefully monitor whether their actions may constitute anticompetitive behavior under antitrust law and, if so, whether they will enjoy protection under the antitrust labor exception. This task is made all the more difficult by the opacity of antitrust law as it applies to nontraditional labor efforts.

Since the initial enactment of federal antitrust legislation, worker collective action has been a concern. Indeed, immediately after passage of the Sherman Act in 1890, employers attacked unions by arguing that their attempts to restrict the supply of labor was an antitrust violation. Ultimately, in 1914, Congress enacted the Clayton Act to provide an exemption for labor, although the Supreme Court has significantly limited its scope.[184] Nevertheless, traditional unions and employers enjoy an antitrust exemption when engaging in most collective bargaining.[185] Whether nontraditional representation enjoys or even needs an exemption is currently an open question.

Under the Sherman Act, "[e]very contract, combination in the form of trust or otherwise, or conspiracy, in restraint of trade or commerce among the several States . . . is declared to be illegal."[186] This law provided employers with an effective tool against unions and their officials, who would frequently face criminal sanctions and treble damages for boycotts that sought to pressure employers to hire union employees and other similar actions.[187] As a result, Congress added an exemption to the Clayton Act, which was intended to remove antitrust liability for typical labor-union activity.[188] Despite its explicit statement that the "labor of a human being is not a commodity or an article of commerce," the Supreme Court has interpreted this exemption narrowly.[189]

There are two categories of antitrust exemptions for labor: a statutory exemption and a nonstatutory exemption.[190] The statutory exemption protects peaceful conduct related to a labor dispute in which "a union acts in its self-interest and does not combine with non-labor groups."[191] This means that the exemption would apply to a union boycott of a company as part of a labor dispute but would not apply when a union acted with an employer to resolve a labor dispute.[192] The statutory exemption is clearly inapplicable to most nontraditional efforts, such as the Uber Guild, which are premised on agreements with employers. Although at first blush the nonstatutory exemption seems to hold more promise for nontraditional groups, the exemption's current interpretation is not particularly helpful. The Court established the nonstatutory exemption in two cases involving union agreements with employers, holding that there was an antitrust exemption for a union that seeks and obtains an agreement about hours, wages, or other terms and conditions of work (that is, "mandatory" subjects of bargaining) with an employer or set of employers, as long as the union is not trying to extend the agreement to other employers.[193] Nontraditional groups, such as the Uber Guild, can argue that the nonstatutory exemption also protects their agreements with employers. The problem, however, is that current judicial interpretations of the labor antitrust exemption have limited their application to groups considered "labor organizations" under federal labor law.[194] In other words, this interpretation refuses to extend antitrust protection unless there is an employer–employee relationship or such a relationship was at the center of the dispute at issue (for instance, if Uber drivers engaged in conduct with the goal of establishing an employer–employee relationship).[195]

This limited scope of the nonstatutory exemption appears to leave most nontraditional collective action outside of its protection. The question, then, is whether a quasi-union's conduct raises antitrust concerns. Strikes and boycotts, as well as threats to engage in this activity, are areas that these groups need to avoid, as they raise significant antitrust risk. What is less clear is whether an agreement between an employer and a nontraditional group, such as the Uber Guild agreement, would also raise antitrust concerns.[196] At present, antitrust law is simply unclear about whether such agreements constitute illegal price-fixing. This lack of clarity poses a threat that nontraditional groups must take into account, but it also presents opportunities to pursue a litigation strategy that might result in favorable decisions that allow these groups leeway to reach some sort of agreement with employers without facing antitrust liability.

This possible antitrust liability for nontraditional worker groups illustrates the paradox in modern labor law. The changing economy begs for more modern and less formal worker collective action, but labor law remains locked in a model that is no longer relevant to an increasing number of workers. As a result, groups are forced to make a decision: (1) to act like a traditional labor union and accept the burdens and hurdles of current labor law that accompanies that choice, or (2) to seek new ways of representing workers but limit their actions out of fear of antitrust liability.[197] Although this paradox begs for legislative or judicial solutions, such help does not appear to be on the horizon. In the meantime, antitrust liability will be a significant factor in shaping nontraditional groups' strategies and actions.

5.5 NONTRADITIONAL REPRESENTATION STRATEGIES

One of the benefits of nontraditional worker representation is that it promises more flexibility to adjust to different circumstances. As described, workers in the modern economy are laboring under a wide variety of conditions. This variance means that there is no one ideal strategy for nontraditional groups to pursue as they navigate the different legal restrictions that might apply to them. However, the conditions under which a group operates – as well as the group's goals and tolerance for risk – may point toward certain general strategies.

There are at least two broad categories of nontraditional groups. One category involves groups that represent workers who are not considered employees under the NLRA or possibly, such as members of the Uber

Guild, are simply not pressing the issue.[198] This scenario provides a relatively straightforward legal analysis. Because the workers are not statutory employees, groups representing them will not be a labor organization.[199] Accordingly, such groups need not worry about the restrictions of sections 8(a)(2), 8(b)(4), and 8(e) of the NLRA, or of section 302 of the LMRA; thus, these groups can receive assistance from employers, pursue secondary pressure, and reach agreements with employers without fear of liability. Moreover, groups with only nonemployee members are not required to comply with the LMRDA and therefore have more flexibility to structure their operations.

Even so, the nonemployee members of such groups lack protection against retaliation, which creates a hurdle to organizing workers. But it also means that groups can provide value by reaching agreements with employers that provide some level of job security, such as the Uber Guild's negotiation of the right to challenge dismissal from the Uber platform. The biggest risk for groups in this category, as noted, is antitrust liability. Although the lack of a labor organization status frees such groups to engage in bilateral negotiations with businesses without the specter of a section 8(a)(2) violation, any resulting agreements could face antitrust challenges. And although the applicability of antitrust law to agreements covering nonemployees is unclear, nontraditional groups must consider their tolerance for risk. Groups that are more risk-averse should avoid agreements that control wages and work stoppages – which could arguably be considered unlawful price-fixing – and focus instead on other work issues, such as the Uber agreement's guarantee of meetings with company officials and the right to challenge exclusion from the platform. Groups with a higher risk tolerance, including those with the means to withstand potential treble damages (or are judgment proof because of a lack of funds), may be more willing to reach agreements on financial and work stoppage issues on the grounds that the benefits to workers outweigh a potential antitrust challenge. In sum, groups that represent nonemployees can more aggressively pressure employers and organize themselves freely, but their members lack protection from retaliation and potential antitrust liability hovers over their negotiations with employers.

The second category involves groups that represent statutory employees. Employee-representation groups should generally consider two separate tracks: either attempt to avoid classification as a labor organization or willingly accept labor organization status. For groups that want to avoid being a labor organization, section 2(5) will be their lodestar. These groups must avoid bilateral negotiations over terms and conditions of work, which may be considered "dealing with" employers. This puts a significant limitation on the degree to which groups can represent employees – making the groups more of a suggestion box for issues involving work conditions than an effective representative body. These groups could engage in more substantive negotiations of other issues – such as contracting out work – but would not be able to engage in significant cooperative bargaining.[200]

However, these groups could still provide services to members without being hampered by the restrictions on secondary pressure from section 8(b)(4) and the requirements of the LMRDA. They could also receive assistance from employers without violating section 8(a)(2). Antitrust liability would remain a theoretical concern, but by avoiding bargaining that would result in labor organization status, the groups would likely avoid any meaningful antitrust challenges. Overall, such groups would enjoy the freedom to organize as they wish, have members who enjoy protection against retaliation, be able to exert pressure on secondary employers, and likely avoid antitrust issues; yet, the groups' ability to bargain with employers would be significantly limited. For employee-representation groups that are willing to accept status as a labor organization, the second track is much different from the first. As these groups represent employees, their members enjoy protection from retaliation. However, unless these groups want to become a traditional union that acts as the exclusive representative of employees, their bargaining options are limited. Under section 8(a)(2), an employer cannot recognize a group as the exclusive bargaining representative of its employees unless that group has majority support.[201] A willing employer would be able to engage in meaningful bargaining and reach an agreement with a labor organization that represents a minority of employees but it must avoid undue assistance or support under section 8(a)(2). Moreover, such agreements could potentially face section 302 challenges if they include access and other promises. These groups would also be prohibited from engaging in secondary pressure and, although nontraditional, they would have to comply with LMRDA requirements. However, such groups would enjoy the same antitrust immunity as traditional unions, which removes a potentially large threat. In sum, these groups would operate under most of the same legal restrictions as traditional unions even though their goals fall short of the exclusive-representation model.

There is thus no ideal quasi-union for technology-sector workers. Rather, the group should be tailored to fit the particular employer as well as the needs and demands of the workers. Many quasi-unions in the technology sector will fit the first category discussed above, as they will be comprised largely of contingent, nonemployee workers. Other groups, however, represent statutory employees and must be mindful of the legal consequences of their representational activity. Ultimately, just like no two labor unions are alike, nontraditional unions must be carefully crafted, each in a unique way, to fit the particular demands of a specific workplace.

5.6 CONCLUSION

Traditional union membership may never return to the levels of its zenith in the 1950s. Yet workers' need for advocacy and assistance is now as strong as, if not stronger than, it was then. This is particularly true in the wake of the COVID-19 outbreak, which saw many workers left with few – or no – employment protections. The virus thus revealed the need for a more collective voice for many workers, particularly as so many jobs were moved away from the traditional workplace and into the home, and often disappeared altogether. The pandemic has thus shone a bright light on the need for workers to bargain together, a need that is particularly difficult to satisfy in the virtual context, as addressed in detail in this chapter.

Given the immense impediments to legislative reform also discussed above, it is unlikely that we will see any wholesale labor law changes that could reverse declining union density in the near future.[202] Thus, unions and other groups concerned with working conditions must seek alternative strategies. Nowhere is this need more pronounced than in the technology sector, where workers' employment status remains in flux. One strategy addressed here is to seek more opportunities for cooperation with employers. This cooperation has the potential to lower employer resistance to formal and informal unionization, increase employee support for unions and nontraditional worker groups, and improve the public's perception of labor organizations. None of these benefits are certain and, even if they come to fruition, are not likely to completely turn the tide in favor of worker collective action. But expanding cooperation as a complement to more combative strategies is an idea that warrants more serious exploration by unions and quasi-unions alike.

The traditional NLRA model of collective bargaining is working for a declining number of unions and workers. As a result, the attachment to that model must weaken. The more adversarial model can still play an important role, but by itself, it appears to be failing a growing percentage of the workforce. Workers need and deserve other options, whether through traditional unions that are willing to change or through other less formal groups. The global economic headwinds will remain a significant barrier to organizing and other attempts to improve working conditions, but this does not mean that workers are helpless. Workers may never see the labor movement return to its former strength, but through more cooperation and quasi-union strategies, workers should be able to overcome the precarious situation they currently face.

The NLRA has unfortunately not been very hospitable to these nontraditional working groups, effectively reducing the choice set for most workers to a binary decision: either engage with traditional unions or submit to complete management control. But there is a third option that can be attractive to both workers and companies – a more flexible, nontraditional labor model. As discussed, this approach makes particular sense in the technology sector, and companies such as Uber should continue to develop and fine-tune these new models. "We can't fall into the trap of believing that the latest innovation is so transformational that we simply can't accommodate and acclimate."[203] A more modern union is needed, particularly in the technology sector, and particularly as so many of us have seen the meaning of work change so quickly in recent times.[204] And the recent pandemic, which clearly exposed the substantial need for a collective voice for workers in the employment setting, only further demonstrates the importance of considering alternative approaches to formal unionization.

NOTES

This chapter draws heavily from Jeffrey M. Hirsch and Joseph A. Seiner, "A Modern Union for the Modern Economy," *Fordham Law Review* 86 (2018): 1727–83. A special thanks to Professor Hirsch for all of his superb work on that article.

1 Memorandum from Thomas E. Perez, former Secretary, Dep't of Labor, to the American People (January 5, 2017), https://obamawhitehouse.archives.gov/sites/whitehouse.gov/files/documents/DOL%20Exit%20Memo.pdf (hereinafter Exit Memorandum).

2 See Barry T. Hirsch and David A. Macpherson, "Union Membership and Coverage Database, Union Membership, Coverage, Density, and Employment by Industry," *Unionstats*, http://unionstats.gsu.edu/Ind_U_2017.htm (last visited June 9, 2020) (hereinafter "Coverage Database"). See generally Barry T. Hirsch and David A. Macpherson, "Union Membership and Coverage Database from the Current Population Survey: Note," *Industry and Labor Relations Review* 56 (2003): 349; Steven Greenhouse, "On Demand, and Demanding Their Rights," *American Prospect*, June 28, 2016, http://prospect.org/article/demand-and-demanding-their-rights; David McCabe, "Labor, Tech Unite Behind Push for 'On Demand' Worker Rights," *Hill*, November 15, 2015, http://thehill.com/policy/technology/260140-labor-tech-unite-behind-push-for-on-demand-worker-rights.

3 See Michael L. Wachter, "Labor Unions: A Corporatist Institution in a Competitive World," *University of Pennsylvania Law Review* 155 (2007): 581, 584–85, 588–90, 598, 606–07, 613 (arguing that decline in unionization is largely the result of the NLRA's failure to adopt a corporatist model).

4 See generally Leo Troy and Neil Sheflin, *U.S. Union Sourcebook: Membership, Finances, Structure, Directory* (West Orange, NJ: Industrial Relations Data and Information Services, 1985), A-1; Hirsch and Macpherson, "Coverage Database."

5 See Patrick Dorrian, "Gig Workers and Job-Related Bias: Are Protections on the Way?," *Daily Labor Report* BNA No. 243 (December 19, 2016): 1 (discussing a survey showing that over one-third of current US workers are contingent and predicting that 43 percent of the US workforce will be contingent by 2020, as well as a report showing that 69 percent of firms in the ride-sharing industry, which typically classifies drivers as independent contractors, have no employees).

6 29 U.S.C. §§ 151–169 (2012).

7 See Douglas MacMillan, "Uber Agrees to Work with a Guild for Its Drivers in New York City," *Wall Street Journal*, May 10, 2016, 4:54 PM, www.wsj.com/articles/uber-agrees-to-work-with-a-guild-for-its-drivers-in-new-york-city-1462913669; Noam Scheiber and Mike Isaac, "Uber Recognizes New-York Drivers' Group, Short of a Union," *New York Times*, May 10, 2016, www.nytimes.com/2016/05/11/technology/uber-agrees-to-union-deal-in-new-york.html; see also "About the IDG," *Independent Drivers Guild*, https://drivingguild.org/about (last visited June 9, 2020).

8 29 U.S.C. § 151 (2012) (stating that "inequality of bargaining power between employees ... and employers ... substantially burdens and affects the flow of commerce. and tends to aggravate recurrent business depressions"); National Labor Relations Act, *NLRB*, www.nlrb.gov/about-nlrb/what-we-do/introduction-to-the-nlrb (last visited May 26, 2020) ("Congress enacted the National Labor Relations Act (NLRA) in 1935 to protect the rights of employees and employers, to encourage collective bargaining, and to curtail certain private-sector labor and management practices, which can harm the general welfare of workers, businesses and the U.S. economy.").

9 See 29 U.S.C. § 151 (2012) (declaring that the policy is to eliminate strife between employers and employees through cooperation); Mark Barenberg, "The Political Economy of the Wagner Act: Power, Symbol, and Workplace Cooperation," *Harvard Law Review* 106 (1993): 1379, 1461.

10 For more detail, see Paul M. Secunda et al., *Mastering Labor Law* (Durham, NC: Carolina Academic Press, 2014), 8–12; Michael L. Wachter, "The Striking Success of the National Labor Relations Act," in *Research Handbook on the Economics of Labor and Employment Law*, ed. Cynthia L. Estlund and Michael L. Wachter (Cheltenham: Edward Elgar, 2012), 427, 429–37.

11 Norris–LaGuardia Act, 29 U.S.C. §§ 101–115 (2012).

12 Railway Labor Act, 45 U.S.C. §§ 151–188 (2012).

13 National Labor Relations Act, 29 U.S.C. §§ 151–169 (2012).

14 Ibid., § 151 ("It is hereby declared to be the policy of the United States to eliminate the causes of certain substantial obstructions to the free flow of commerce and to mitigate and eliminate these obstructions when they have occurred by encouraging the practice and procedure of collective bargaining.").

15 See Wachter, "The Striking Success," 429–30 (indicating that strikes often required intervention by the National Guard and federal troops); see also Irving Bernstein,

"Americans in Depression and War," in *A History of the American Worker*, ed. Richard B. Morris (Princeton, NJ: Princeton University Press, 1983), 151, 159–60 (noting that 1934 saw 1,856 strikes, many of which were coupled with violence, including a coast-wide maritime shutdown in San Francisco and a textile strike in New England and the South that saw 376,000 workers walk off the job); "Employer/Union Rights and Obligations," *National Labor Relations Board*, www.nlrb.gov/rights-we-protect/employerunion-rights-and-obligations (last visited February 14, 2018).

16 Wachter, "The Striking Success," 457–58 (arguing that the NLRA largely fulfilled its goals, particularly in stabilizing the nonunion sector).

17 Ibid., 441, 457–58 (exploring the power of workers to boycott employers until they are allowed to unionize and the use of "closed shop" rules).

18 Private-sector union density (the percentage of employees who are union members) rose quickly from 15 percent in 1936, the year before the Supreme Court approved the constitutionality of the NLRA, to 35.7 percent in 1953. Troy and Sheflin, *U.S. Union Sourcebook*, A-1 (estimating pre-1953 data).

19 Wachter, "The Striking Success," 451 ("In the period between the passage of the Wagner Act and the adoption of the Tali-Hartley amendments, the annual number of strikes was 3.539. Rather than industrial peace, the number of strikes and lockouts nearly doubled under the Wagner Act.").

20 Lawrence Mishel et al., "Wage Stagnation in Nine Charts," *Economic Policy Institution*, January 2015, www.epi.org/publication/charting-wage-stagnation (showing the relationship between increased union membership and decreased wage inequality, and vice versa, since 1917).

21 Ibid.; Wachter, "The Striking Success," 454 (arguing that a major reason for the decline in strikes and union strength was the Taft Hartley amendments, which made the NLRA more neutral and helped the nonunion private sector grow in relation to the union sector).

22 Lawrence Mishel, "Unions, Inequality, and Faltering Middle-Class Wages," *Economic Policy Institution*, August 29, 2012, www.epi.org/files/20 l 2/ib342-unions-inequality-middle-class-wages.pdf; Josh Levs, "Analysis: Why America's Unions Are Losing Power," *CNN*, December 12, 2012, 4:06 PM, www.cnn.com/2012/12/11/us/union-power-analysis/.

23 Gallup has surveyed whether respondents "approve" or "disapprove" of labor unions since 1936. Labor Unions, GALLUP, http://news.gallup.com/poll/12751/labor-unions.aspx [https://perma.cc/8V83-BJPJ]. Approval of unions had been in the 60 to 70 percent range since the early 1970s in all but one year, after which it has moved between as high as 65 percent and as low as 48 percent, with the poll in August 2017 showing that 61 percent of respondents approved of labor unions and 33 percent disapproved. Ibid.; see also Drew DeSilver, "American Unions Membership Declines as Public Support Fluctuates," *Pew Research Center*, February 20, 2014, www.pewresearch.org/fact-tank/2014/02/20/for-american-unions-membership-trails-far-behind-public-support/ (citing a 2013 poll finding that 51 percent of respondents had a favorable opinion of labor unions and that 42 percent had an unfavorable opinion).

24 See generally *Janus v. Am. Fed'n of State, Cty, and Mun. Emps., Council 31*, 138 S. Ct. 2448 (2018).

25 Employee Free Choice Act of 2009, H.R. 1409, 111th Cong. (2009).

26 29 U.S.C. § 152(3) (2012).

27 See, e.g., Michael C. Duff, "Alt-Labor, Secondary Boycotts, and Toward a Labor Organization Bargain," *Catholic University Law Review* 63 (2014): 837, 843–49; Dayne Lee, "Bundling 'Alt-Labor': How Policy Reform Can Facilitate Political Organization in Emerging Worker Movements," *Harvard Civil Rights-Civil Liberties Law Review* 51 (2016): 509, 529–35; Michael M. Oswalt, "Improvisational Unionism," *California Law Review* 104 (2016): 597, 609–10; Brishen Rogers, "Libertarian Corporatism Is Not an Oxymoron," *Texas Law Review* 94 (2016): 1623, 1631–35 (detailing the rise of the alt-labor movement and its current shortcomings).

28 29 U.S.C. § 201 (2012).

29 82 F. Supp. 3d 1133 (N.D. Cal. 2015).

30 See Joseph A. Seiner, "Tailoring Class Actions to the On-Demand Economy," *Ohio State Law Journal* 78 (2017): 21, 46–53 (summarizing cases).

31 See Class Action Complaint at 1, *Tan v. GrubHub, Inc.*, No. CGC-15-548102 (Cal. Super. Ct. September 23, 2015).

32 See Class Action Complaint at 1, *Truong v. Amazon.com, Inc.*, No. BC598993 (Cal. Super. Ct. October 27, 2015).

33 See *Zenelaj v. Handybook, Inc.*, 82 F. Supp. 3d 968, 970 (N.D. Cal. 2015).

34 See *Otey v. CrowdFlower, Inc.*, No. 12-cv-05524-JST.2014 WL 1477630, *I (N.D. Cal. April 14, 2014).

35 See Collective & Class Action Complaint & Jury Demand at 1, *Iglesias v. Homejoy, Inc.*, No. 3: 15-cv-01286-LB (N.D. Cal. March 19, 2015); Class Action Complaint for Damages at 1, *Ventura v. Homejoy, Inc.*, No. CGC-15-544750 (Cal. Super. Ct. March 16, 2015); *Zenelaj v. Homejoy, Inc.*, No. CGC-15-544599 (Cal. Super. Ct. March 9, 2015); Class Action Complaint at 1, *Malveaux-Smith v. Homejoy, Inc.*, No. 37-2015-00005070-CU-OE-CTL (Cal. Super. Ct. February 13, 2015).

36 See First Amended Collective & Class Action Complaint & Jury Demand at 1, *Singer v. Postmates, Inc.*, No. 4:15-cv-01284 (N.D. Cal. March 19, 2015); Complaint at 1, *Marable v. Postmates, Inc.*, No. BC589052 (Cal. Super. Ct. July 23, 2015); Class Action Complaint at 1, *Peppler v. Postmates, Inc.*, No. 1:15-cv-05145-RCL (D.C. Super. Ct. August 25, 2015).

37 See Complaint at 1, *Bynum v. Maplebear, Inc.*, 160 F. Supp. 3d 527 (E.D.N.Y. 2016) (No. l5-cv-6263): Complaint at 1, *Moton v. Maplebear, Inc.*, No. 1:15-cv-08879-CM, 2016 WL 616343 (S.D.N.Y. February 9, 2016); Class Action Complaint for Damages & Demand for Jury Trial at 1, *Cobarruviaz v. Maplebear, Inc.*, 143 F. Supp. 3d 930 (N.D. Cal. 2015) (No. 3:15-cv-00697-EMC); Class Action Complaint at 1, *Sumerlin v. Maplebear, Inc.*, No. BC 603030 (Cal. Super. Ct. December 2, 2015).

38 See Class Action Complaint & Jury Demand at 1, *Taranto v. Washio, Inc.*, No. CGC-15-546584 (Cal. Super. Ct. June 29, 2015).

39 *Jeung v. Yelp, Inc.*, No. 15-CV-02228-RS. 2015 WL 4776424, *3 (N.D. Cal. August 13, 2015).

40 42 U.S.C. § 2000e-2(a)(2) (2012) ("It shall be an unlawful employment practice for an employer . . . to limit, segregate, or classify his employees or applicants . . . which would deprive or tend to deprive any individual of employment opportunities or otherwise adversely affect his status as an employee, because of such individual's race, color, religion, sex, or national origin.").

41 42 U.S.C. § 12112(b)(l) (2012) ("As used in subsection (a) of this section, the term 'discriminate against a qualified individual on the basis of disability' includes limiting, segregating, or classifying a job applicant or employee.").

42 29 U.S.C. § 623(a)(1) (2012) ("It shall be unlawful for an employer to fail or refuse to hire or to discharge any individual or otherwise discriminate against any individual with respect to his compensation, terms, conditions, or privileges of employment, because of such individual's age.").

43 *Freelancers Union*, www.freelancersunion.org (last visited May 26, 2020).

44 Steven Greenhouse, "Tackling Concerns of Independent Workers," *New York Times*, March 23, 2013, www.nytimes.com/2013/03124/business/freelancers-union-tackles-concerns-of-independent-workers.html.

45 The union also provides other types of insurance, operates a health clinic, and has a 401(k) plan. "Save Some Green," *Freelancers Union*, www.freelancersunion.org/resources/financial-tools/retirement/ (last visited June 9, 2020).

46 See David G. Blanchflower and Alex Bryson, "Changes over Time in Union Relative Wage Effects in the UK and the US Revisited," in *International Handbook of Trade Unions*, ed. John T. Addison and Claus Schnabel (Cheltenham: Edward Elgar Publishing, 2003), 197, 207–21 (concluding that the US union wage premium has declined only slightly over time).

47 See Gabrielle Wuolo, "New Tool Lets Freelancers Rate Clients and Companies," *Freelancers Union*, May 31, 2011, https://blog.freelancersunion.org/2011/05/31/new-tool-lets-freelancers-rate-clients-and-companies/; see, e.g., *IRateMyBoss*, www.iratemyboss.com (last visited June 9, 2020).

48 Noam Scheiber, "As Freelancers' Ranks Grow, New York Moves to See They Get What They're Due," *New York Times*, October 27, 2016, www.nytimes.com/2016/10/28/nyregion/freelancers-city-council-wage-theft.html.

49 See Greenhouse, "Tackling Concerns of Independent Workers."

50 "About," *Working America*, www.workingamerica.org/about (last visited June 9, 2020).

51 See generally Greenhouse, "Tackling Concerns of Independent Workers."

52 See Alan Hyde, "New Institutions for Worker Representation in the United States: Theoretical Issues," *New York Law School Law Review* 50 (2006): 385, 389; Harold Meyerson, Opinion, "Labor Wrestles with Its Future," *Washington Post*, May 8, 2013, www.washingtonpost.com/opinions/harold-meyerson-labor-wrestles-with-its-future/2013/05/08/852192d6-b74f-11e2-b94c-b684ddao7add_story.html; Richard B. Freeman, "From the Webbs to the Web: The Contribution of the Internet to Reviving Union Fortunes"

(National Bureau of Economic Research, Working Paper No. 11298, 2005), 8, 19–20, www.nber.org/papers/w11298.

53 See Doug Foote, "40,000 Workers in Albuquerque Get a Raise This Week (You Built That)," *Working America Main Street Blog*, January 3, 2013, 10:40 AM, http://blog.workingamerica.org/2013/01/03/40000-workers-in-albuquerque-get-a-raise-this-week-you-built-that/.

54 For instance, Working America used to run a "JobTracker" website that allowed searches of over 400,000 companies and their labor practices. See "Working America Exposes Outsourcing Culprits," North Carolina State American Federation of Labor and Congress of Industrial Organizations, October 13, 2010, http://aflcionc.org/working-america-exposes-outsourcing-culprits/.

55 See Katherine V. W. Stone, *From Widgets to Digits: Employment Regulation for the Changing Workplace* (New York: Cambridge University Press, 2004), 235; Hyde, "New Institutions," 390–91.

56 See Paul M. Secunda, "The Wagner Model of Labor Law Is Dead – Long Live Labor Law," *Queen's Law Journal* 38 (2013): 580.

57 See Joni Hersch, "A Workers' Lobby to Provide Portable Benefits," in *Emerging Labor Market Institutions for the Twenty-First Century*, ed. Richard B. Freeman et al. (Cambridge, MA: National Bureau of Economic Research, 2005), 207–11.

58 Natalie Foster, "Uber's Major Step Forward for Workers," *CNN*, May 25, 2016, 6:14 PM, www.cnn.com/2016/05/25/opinions/uber-guild-agreement-portable-benefits-natalie-foster/index.html; "About the IDG," *Independent Drivers Guild*, https://drivingguild.org/about/ (last visited May 26, 2020). The Uber Guild and its membership obviously continue to evolve over time. The information and research provided here are current as of the date of the articles and other support cited in this chapter.

59 Scheiber and Isaac, "Uber Recognizes New York Drivers' Group."

60 Ibid.

61 Machinists Union, "About," *Facebook*, www.facebook.com/MachinistsUnion/about (last visited May 26, 2020). The IAM also represents workers in the federal sector. Ibid.

62 Ibid.

63 "About Us," *Machinists Union District 15*, www.iamdistrict15.org/#!about-us/c5r0 (last visited May 26, 2020).

64 Ibid.

65 See 29 U.S.C. § 152(3) (2012) (excluding independent contractors from the definition of "employee").

66 See "About Us," *Machinists Union District 15*.

67 See Ted Hesson, "NLRB Argues against Uber," *Politico*, November 3, 2016, 10:00 AM, www.politico.com/tipsheets/morning-shift/2016/11/nlrb-argues-against-uber-217214.

68 David Plouffe, "David Plouffe Remarks on Creation of Independent Drivers Guild," *Uber*, May 10, 2016, www.uber.com/newsroom/plouffe-idg-remarks/.

69 Scheiber and Isaac, "Uber Recognizes New York Drivers' Group."

70 Ibid.

71 Jing Cao and Eric Newcomer, "Uber and Union Agree to Form Drivers Guild in New York City," *Bloomberg*, May 10, 2016, www.bloomberg.com/news/articles/2016-05-10/uber-and-union-agree-to-form-drivers-guild-in-new-york-city.

72 Kia Kokalitcheva, "Uber Strikes Deal with New York City Union to Create Driver Guild," *Fortune*, May 10, 2016, http://fortune.com/2016/05/10/uber-nyc-driver-guild/.

73 Cao and Newcomer, "Uber and Union Agree."

74 Scheiber and Isaac, "Uber Recognizes New York Drivers' Group."

75 See Cao and Newcomer, "Uber and Union Agree."

76 Ibid.

77 Faiz Siddiqui, "Uber Launches New Features Aimed at Improving Driver Experience," *Washington Post*, June 7, 2016, www.washingtonpost.com/news/dr-gridlock/wp/2016/06/07/uber-launches-new-features-aimed-at-improving-driver-experience/.

78 Ibid.

79 Plouffe, "David Plouffe Remarks on Creation."

80 Cao and Newcomer, "Uber and Union Agree"; Scheiber and Isaac, "Uber Recognizes New York Drivers' Group."

81 Ibid.

82 Plouffe, "David Plouffe Remarks on Creation."

83 Donna Brazile, "Why Union?," *General Electric Workers United*, www.geworkersunited.org/why (last visited June 9, 2020).

84 "GE Investors," GE, www.ge.com/investor-relations/governance/ombudsperson-process (last visited February 14, 2018). The ombudsman program may have changed since the research initially performed for this chapter. Ibid.

85 Ibid.

86 General Electric Co., Annual Report, exhibit 14.2 at 3 (Form 10-K) (June 2005).

87 "GE Investors," GE.

88 Ibid.

89 "Integrity & Compliance: A Strong Culture of Integrity," *GE Sustainability*, http://gesustainability.com/how-ge-works/integrity-compliance/a-strong-culture-of-integrity (last visited February 14, 2018).

90 "Raise an Ombuds Concern," *GE Energy Connections*, www.geenergyconnections.com/raise-ombuds-concern [https://perma.cc/9CAD-R5BV].

91 "GE Investors," GE.

92 General Electric Co., Annual Report.

93 Ibid.

94 Ibid.; see also 29 U.S.C. § 158(a)(2) (2012) (providing an exception to a company union ban: "an employer shall not be prohibited from permitting employees to confer with him during working hours without loss of time or pay").

95 "GE Investors," GE.

96 Josh Eidelson, "Union-ish: VW and UAW Are Odd Bedfellows at a Southern U.S. Plant," *Bloomberg Businessweek*, February 19, 2015, 21. The descriptions of the Volkswagen agreement are accurate as of the date of the articles and research cited herein.

97 Ibid.

98 Ibid.

99 Benjamin Sachs, "Minority Unionism (Sort of) Comes to VW Chattanooga," *Onlabor*, November 12, 2014, https://onlabor.org/2014/11/12/minority-unionism-sort-of-comes-to-vw-chattanooga/.

100 Eidelson, "Union-ish."

101 Ibid.

102 Ibid.

103 Sachs, "Minority Unionism."

104 Ibid.

105 Krishnadev Calamur, "New Volkswagen Policy Oks Interactions with Unions at U.S. Factory," *The Two-Way*, NPR, November 12, 2014, www.npr.org/sections/thetwo-way/2014/11/12/363590584/new-volkswagen-policy-oks-interactions-with-unions-at-u-s-factory.

106 Mike Pare, "Labor Groups Support New VW Policy as Volkswagen Opens Way for Talks, Meetings with UAW and ACE," *Times Free Press* (Tenn.), November 13, 2014, www.timesfreepress.com/news/business/aroundregion/story/2014/nov/13/lahor-groups-support-new-vw-policyvolkswagen/273310/.

107 Eidelson, "Union-ish." A "minority union agreement" would have to be limited to employees who agreed to have the union act as their representative: section 8(a)(2) prevents an employer such as VW from reaching a broader agreement with a union that does not have support from a majority of employees in the relevant bargaining unit. See *Int'l Ladies Garment Workers' Union v. NLRB*, 366 U.S. 731, 737–38 (1961).

108 Eidelson, "Union-ish," 1–2.

109 See Electromation, Inc., 309 N.L.R.B. 990, 992–94 (1992), *enforced*, 35 F.3d 1148 (7th Cir. 1994); Samuel Estreicher, "Employee Involvement and the 'Company Union' Prohibition: The Case for Partial Repeal of Section 8(a)(2) of the NLRA," *New York University Law Review* 69 (1994): 125, 129–33; Alan Hyde, "Employee Caucus: A Key Institution in the Emerging System of Employment Law," *Chicago-Kent Law Review* 69 (1993): 149, 174–76.

110 29 U.S.C. § 158(a)(2) (2012) (making it an unfair labor practice for an employer "to dominate or interfere with the formation or administration of any labor organization").

111 Ibid., § 152(5) (defining "labor organization" as "any organization of any kind, or any agency or employee representation committee or plan, in which employees participate and which exists for the purpose, in whole or in part, of dealing with employers concerning grievances, labor disputes, wages, rates of pay, hours of employment, or conditions of work").

112 *Electromation*, 309 N.L.R.B. 994 (concluding that group will be "a labor organization if (1) employees participate, (2) the organization exists, at least in part, for the purpose of 'dealing with' employers, and (3) these dealings concern 'conditions of

work' or concern other statutory subjects, such as grievances, labor disputes, wages, rates of pay, or hours of employment").

113 E. I. Du Pont De Nemours & Co., 311 N.L.R.B. 893. 894 (1993): see also *Electromation*, 309 N.L.R.B. 995 n.21 (concluding that "dealing with" exists when there is "a bilateral mechanism involving proposals from [an] employee committee concerning the subjects listed in Sec[tion] 2(5), coupled with real or apparent consideration of those proposals by management").

114 See *Electromation*, 309 N.L.R.B. 993–94 (concluding that the legislative history of section 8(a)(2) required a broad interpretation of "labor organization" in order to ban "employee representation committees," which had little formal structure); see also *Sahara Datsun, Inc. v. NLRB*, 811 F.2d 1317, 1320 (9th Cir. 1987).

115 See *E. I. Du Pont*, 311 N.L.R.B. 897–98; *Electromation*, 309 N.L.R.B. 995.

116 See Jeffrey M. Hirsch and Barry T. Hirsch, "The Rise and Fall of Private Sector Unionism: What Next for the NLRA?," *Florida State University Law Review* 34 (2007): 1152–67 (describing this issue).

117 See Johanna Oreskovic, "Capturing Volition Itself: Employee Involvement and the TEAM Act," *Berkeley Journal of Employment and Labor Law* 19 (1998): 229, 276, 278.

118 See, e.g., Richard B. Freeman and Joel Rogers, *What Workers Want* (Ithaca, NY: Cornell University Press, 1999), 32–33, 81–84; Oreskovic, "Capturing Volition Itself," 247–49.

119 See Cynthia L. Estlund, "Why Workers Still Need a Collective Voice in the Era of Norms and Mandates," in *Research Handbook on The Economics of Labor and Employment Law*, ed. Cynthia L. Estlund and Michael L. Wachter (Cheltenham: Edward Elgar, 2012), 463–90 (arguing that workers still have significant need for collective voice, despite an increase in individual protections).

120 See Matthew T. Bodie, "Workers, Information, and Corporate Combinations: The Case for Nonbinding Employee Referenda in Transformative Transactions," *Washington University Law Review* 85 (2007): 871, 900 (stating that employees can provide valuable information to employers); Kenneth G. Dau-Schmidt, "Promoting Employee Voice in the American Economy: A Call for Comprehensive Reform," *Marquette Law Review* 94 (2011): 765, 804.

121 See Freeman and Rogers, *What Workers Want*, 131–35 (describing survey results showing managerial support); Paul C. Weiler, "A Principled Reshaping of Labor Law for the Twenty-First Century," *University of Pennsylvania Journal of Labor and Employment Law* 3 (2001): 177, 198–200. But see David I. Levine, *Reinventing the Workplace: How Business and Employees Can Both Win* (Washington, DC: Brookings Institution, 1995), 63.

122 See Cynthia L. Estlund, "The Ossification of American Labor Law," *Columbia Law Review* 102 (2002): 1546.

123 See Freeman and Rogers, *What Workers Want*, 119, 120; Levine, *Reinventing the Workplace*, 7; Orley Lobel and Anne Marie Lofaso, "Systems of Employee

Representation: The US Report," in *Systems of Employee Representation at the Enterprise: A Comparative Study*, ed. Roger Blanpain et al. (New York: Kluwer Law International, 2012), 205, 208 (citing studies); Estlund, "Why Workers Still Need a Collective Voice," 468; John Godard and Carola Frege, "Labor Unions, Alternative Forms of Representation, and the Exercise of Authority Relations in U.S. Workplaces," *Industrial and Labor Relations (ILR) Review: The Journal of Work and Policy* 66 (2013): 142, 151–52; Bruce E. Kaufman, "Does the NLRA Constrain Employee Involvement and Participation Programs in Nonunion Companies?: A Reassessment," *Yale Law and Policy Review* 17 (1999): 729, 747, 776–77. But see Kaufman, "Does the NLRA Constrain?," 753, 777–78.

124 Lobel and Lofaso, "Systems of Employee Representation," 224.

125 See Godard and Frege, "Labor Unions," 153.

126 See Electromation, Inc., 309 N.L.R.B. 990, 992–94 (1992), *enforced* 35 F.3d 1148 (7th Cir. 1994); Estreicher, "Employee Involvement," 129–33; Hyde, "Employee Caucus," 174–76 (discussing the possible rationales of section 8(a)(2)); Michael H. LeRoy, "Employee Participation in the New Millennium: Redefining a Labor Organization under Section 8(a)(2) of the NLRA," *Southern California Law Review* 72 (1999): 1651, 1661–62.

127 Duff, "Alt-Labor," 875–76 (proposing a union–employer compromise).

128 See Hirsch and Hirsch, "The Rise and Fall," 1158–59.

129 Estlund, "Why Workers Still Need a Collective Voice," 489.

130 See Jonathan P. Hiatt and Laurence E. Gold, "Employer-Employee Committees: A Union Perspective," in *Nonunion Employee Representation: History, Contemporary Practice, and Policy*, ed. Bruce E. Kaufman and Daphne Gottlieb Taras (New York: M.E. Sharpe, 2000), 498, 507–08.

131 See Mark Barenberg, "Democracy and Domination in the Law of Workplace Cooperation: From Bureaucratic to Flexible Production," *Columbia Law Review* 94 (1994): 831–35; Julius Getman, "The National Labor Relations Act: What Went Wrong; Can We Fix It?," *Boston College Law Review* 45 (2003): 125, 145; LeRoy, "Employee Participation," 1702, 1710–11; Clyde W. Summers, "Employee Voice and Employer Choice: A Structured Exception to Section 8(a)(2)," *Chicago-Kent Law Review* 69 (1993): 138; see also Hyde, "Employee Caucus," 160.

132 Cf. Kaufman, "Does the NLRA Constrain?," 805–08.

133 Estlund, "The Ossification," 1544, 1551, 1601; cf. Kye D. Pawlenko, "Reevaluating Inter-Union Competition: A Proposal to Resurrect Rival Unionism," *University of Pennsylvania Journal of Labor and Employment Law* 8 (2006): 651, 681–88.

134 See Charter of Fundamental Rights of the European Union Art. 27, 2012 O.J. C 326/391, 401; Samuel Estreicher, "Nonunion Employee Representation: A Legal/Policy Perspective," in *Nonunion Employee Representation: History, Contemporary Practice, and Policy*, ed. Bruce E. Kaufman and Daphne Gottlieb Taras (New York: M. E. Sharpe, 2000), 196; Dau-Schmidt, "Promoting Employee Voice," 811–19.

135 Estlund, "Why Workers Still Need a Collective Voice," 468.

136 Estreicher, "Employee Involvement," 155: Hirsch and Hirsch, "The Rise and Fall," 1163–64; Weiler, "A Principled Reshaping," 189–90, 205–06.

137 See Cynthia L. Estlund, "Citizens of the Corporation? Workplace Democracy in a Post-Union Era," in *Corporations and Citizenship*, ed. Greg Urban (Philadelphia: University of Pennsylvania Press, 2014), 179–80.

138 Ibid., 180.

139 See ibid., 179.

140 See Tara Mahoney and Allison Drutchas, "Could Your Employee Participation Program Be Illegal? Two Laws You Should Know," *Society of Human Resource Management*, June 9, 2016, www.shm1.org/resourcesandtools/hr-topics/labor-relations/pages/could-your-employee-participation-program-be-illegal.aspx (providing examples of illegal employee participation programs).

141 See Heather M. Whitney, "Rethinking the Ban on Employer-Labor Organization," *Cardozo Law Review* 37 (2016): 1510 ("Both narrowing and repealing sections 8(a)(2) directly were proposed by scholars in the 1990s.").

142 See Secunda, "The Wagner Model," 579–81.

143 See Stone, *From Widgets to Digits*, 224–25; Alan Hyde, "Employee Organization in Silicon Valley: Networks, Ethnic Organization, and New Unions," *University of Pennsylvania Journal of Labor and Employment Law* 4 (2002): 493, 496–97.

144 See Christopher L. Erickson et al., "Justice for Janitors in Los Angeles and Beyond: A New-Form of Unionism in the Twenty-First Century?," in *The Changing Role of Unions: New Forms of Representation*, ed. Phanindra V. Wunnava (New York: M. E. Sharpe, 2004), 22, 29; Whitney, "Rethinking the Ban," 1479–80 (describing consumer-based campaigns for workers); see also Estlund, "The Ossification," 1604–06 (discussing union "corporate campaigns"); Hyde, "Employee Organization," 497.

145 See 29 U.S.C. § 152(5) (2012); Duff, "Alt-Labor," 866.

146 29 U.S.C. § 158(a)(l) (2012).

147 See *NLRB v. Wash. Aluminum Co.*, 370 U.S. 9, 14–17 (1962).

148 29 U.S.C. § 186; 29 U.S.C. § 186.

149 Ibid., § 186(a).

150 *Toth v. USX Corp.*, 883 F.2d 1297, 1300 (7th Cir. 1989); *Turner v. Local Union, No. 302*, 604 F.2d 1219, 1227 (9th Cir. 1979).

151 See Nicholas M. Ohanesian, "Does 'Why' or 'What' Matter: Should Section 302 Apply to Card Check Neutrality Agreements?," *University of Memphis Law Review* 45 (2014): 249, 250–53, 257–61.

152 See, e.g., *Mulhall v. Unite Here Local, 355*, 667 F.3d 1211, 1216 (11th Cir. 2012); *Adcock v. Freightliner LLC*, 550 F.3d 369, 371 (4th Cir. 2008); *Hotel Emps. & Rest. Emps. Union, Local 57 v. Sage Hosp. Res., LLC*, 390 F.3d 206, 207–08 (3d Cir. 2004).

153 See, e.g., *Adcock*, 550 F.3d 377; *Hotel Emps. & Rest. Emps. Union, Local 57*, 390 F.3d 218–19.

154 667 F.3d 1211 (11th Cir. 2012).

155 Ibid., 1213.

156 Ibid., 1215.
157 See Sean P. Redmond, "Supreme Court Considers NLRA Case ('Mulhall Case')," *U.S. Chamber of Commerce*, January 18, 2013, 4:29 PM, www.uschamber.com/article/supreme-court-considers-nlra-case-mulhall-case.
158 See Petition for Writ of Certiorari by Unite Here at 1, *Unite Here Local 355 v. Mulhall*, 134 S. Ct. 594 (2013) (No. 12-99), 2012 WL 3027183.
159 *Mulhall*, 667 F.3d 1215.
160 *Unite Here Local 355 v. Mulhall*, 134 S. Ct. 594, 594 (2013) (per curiam).
161 For instance, in the majority of campaigns, unions seek agreements with employers to voluntarily recognize the union if it gains majority support, rather than use an NLRB election. See James J. Brudney, "Neutrality Agreements and Card Check Recognition:·Prospects for Changing Paradigms," *Iowa Law Review* 90 (2005): 819, 839–40.
162 Section 302 covers only an "employer" giving something of value to (1) "any representative or any of his employees"; (2) "any labor organization . . . which represents . . . any of the employees of such employer"; (3) "any employee or group or committee of employees of such employer"; and (4) "any officer or employee of a labor organization." 29 U.S.C. § 186(a) (2012).
163 See *United States v. Ryan*, 350 U.S. 299, 301 (1956). Groups should also avoid being so closely entwined with a labor organization that they are considered a subsidiary covered by LMRA section 302.
164 See 29 U.S.C. § 152(5) (2012) (defining a "labor organization" for the purposes of the NLRA's § 8(a)(2) prohibitions).
165 See 29 U.S.C. § 431 (2012) (establishing reporting and disclosure obligations); ibid., § 439 (permitting imposition of fines or incarceration for failure to file required reports).
166 J. Ralph Beaird, "Employer and Consultant Reporting under the LMRDA," *Georgia Law Review* 20 (1986): 533, 536–37 (describing the purpose of LMRDA); Thomas I. M. Gottheil, Note, "Not Part of the Bargain: Worker Centers and Labor Law in Sociohistorical Context," *New York University Law Review* 89 (2014): 2228, 2263.
167 See *Air Line Pilots Ass'n, Int'l v. O'Neill*, 499 U.S. 65, 73–78 (1991).
168 29 U.S.C. §§ 411, 431(b), 436, 481.
169 Cf. Hirsch and Hirsch, "The Rise and Fall," 1161–62 (arguing that groups not covered by LMRDA would still incorporate protections for members because groups would need support from workers to maintain credibility and effectiveness).
170 29 U.S.C. § 402(i); see also 29 U.S.C. § 152(5) (2012).
171 See Catherine L. Fisk, "Workplace Democracy and Democratic Worker Organizations: Notes on Worker Centers," *Theoretical Inquiries in Law* 17 (2016): 101, 120–22.
172 Compare Stefan J. Marculewicz and Jennifer Thomas, "Labor Organizations by Another Name: The Worker Center Movement and Its Evolution into Coverage under the NLRA and LMRDA," *Engage*, October 2012, 79, 84–85, with Cynthia

Estlund, "Are Unions a Constitutional Anomaly?," *Michigan Law Review* 114 (2015): 169, 229–30, and Eli Naduris-Weissman, "The Worker Center Movement and Traditional Labor Law: A Contextual Analysis," *Berkeley Journal of Employment and Labor Law* 30 (2009): 232, 287–91.

173 David Rosenfeld, "Worker Centers: Emerging Labor Organizations – Until They Confront the National Labor Relations Act," *Berkeley Journal of Employment and Labor Law* 27 (2006): 469, 482–95, 502–03.

174 See Fisk, "Workplace Democracy," 120–22.

175 29 U.S.C. § 158(b) (2012).

176 See Richard A. Bock, "Secondary Boycotts: Understanding NLRB Interpretation of Section 8(b)(4)(b) of the National Labor Relations Act," *University of Pennsylvania Journal of Labor and Employment Law* 7 (2005): 905, 908–18.

177 *Edward J. DeBartolo Corp. v. Fla. Gulf Coast Bldg. & Constr. Trades Council*, 485 U.S. 568, 583–84 (1988).

178 See Charlotte Garden, "Labor Values Are First Amendment Values: Why Union Comprehensive Campaigns Are Protected Speech," *Fordham Law Review* 79 (2011): 2617, 2638.

179 See 29 U.S.C. § 187(b) (2012); *Local 20, Teamsters, Chauffeurs & Helpers Union v. Morton*, 377 U.S. 252, 258 (1964).

180 See 29 U.S.C. § 152(5).

181 29 U.S.C. § 158(e).

182 See Duff, "Alt-Labor," 838–43.

183 See *Di Giorgio Fruit Corp. v. NLRB*, 191 F.2d 642, 648–49 (D.C. Cir. 1951) (holding that section 8(b)(4) did not apply to an agricultural workers' group because the workers were not employees under the NLRA).

184 Secunda, *Mastering Labor Law*, 8–12.

185 Susan Schwochau, "The Labor Exemptions to Antitrust Law: An Overview," *Journal of Labor Research* 21 (2000): 535, 536–37.

186 15 U.S.C. § 1 (2012).

187 See, e.g., *Loewe v. Lawlor*, 208 U.S. 274, 290–91 (1908).

188 See 15 U.S.C. § 17 (2012).

189 See Sanjukta M. Paul, "The Enduring Ambiguities of Antitrust Liability for Worker Collective Action," *Loyola University of Chicago Law Journal* 47 (2016): 969, 1020–33 (discussing the development of the antitrust exemption).

190 See *Brown v. Pro Football, Inc.*, 518 U.S. 231, 236 (1996).

191 See *United States v. Hutcheson*, 312 U.S. 219, 232 (1941).

192 See *Allen Bradley Co. v. Local Union*, No. 3, Int'l Bhd. Electrical Workers, 325 U.S. 797, 808 (1945) (holding that "mutual help" under the Clayton Act did not include unions' use of "employer-help").

193 *Local Union No. 189, Amalgamated Meat Cutters & Butcher Workmen of N. Am. v. Jewel Tea Co.*, 381 U.S. 676, 688 (1965); *United Mine Workers of Am. v. Pennington*, 381 U.S. 657, 660 (1965).

194 Courts have held that the labor exemptions only cover "labor organizations" as that term is used in the Norris–LaGuardia Act, prohibiting federal court injunctions in cases arising out of most labor disputes. 29 U.S.C. §§ 101, 107 (2012).

195 See *Milk Wagon Drivers' Union, Local No. 753* v. *Lake Valley Farm Prods, Inc.*, 311 U.S. 91, 102–03 (1940); *New Negro All.* v. *Sanitary Grocery Co.*, 303 U.S. 552, 562–63 (1938); *Taylor*, 353 F.2d 604–05.

196 See Chris Opfer, "Gig Worker Organizers Find Hurdle in Antitrust Laws," *Antitrust and Trade Regulation Report* (BNA) 110 (November 25, 2016): 1365.

197 Cf. Paul, "Enduring Ambiguities," 982.

198 Groups with members who are arguably employees risk the possibility that the NLRB or a court will subsequently determine that the workers are statutory employees.

199 29 U.S.C. § 152(5) (2012) (defining a "labor organization" as an entity "in which employees participate").

200 The terms and conditions of work referred to in section 2(5) are equivalent to "mandatory subject[s] of bargaining" under the NLRA, which are distinct from permissive subjects that include agreements regarding most contracting out of work, among other matters. See *First Nat'l Maint. Corp.* v. *NLRB*, 452 U.S. 666, 678 (1981).

201 *Int'l Ladies Garment Workers' Union (Bernhard-Altmann Tex. Corp.)* v. *NLRB*, 366 U.S. 731, 737–38 (1961).

202 See Estlund, "The Ossification," 1527–28.

203 Exit Memorandum, 13.

204 This chapter also benefited from the scholarship and work of numerous other authors. See Bibliography.

6

Harassment and the Virtual Workplace

When you talk about sexual harassment in tech or in any other industry, it's like dropping a nuclear bomb on your career. That fear of retaliation, of it impacting your business in some way, is so, so real. We have a financial responsibility to do what's best for our business, and if speaking out is going to harm our business, is that OK?
— Susan Ho, cofounder, Travel Startup Journy[1]

6.1 INTRODUCTION

Over the last thirty years, Silicon Valley has been comprised of a mostly male workforce.[2] The rising modern economy in the technology sector has generated billions of dollars and thousands of jobs across all fifty states. The technology sector provides tremendous opportunities for workers to individualize their employment experience and tailor it to their lives and family needs. The flexibility inherent in this economy offers benefits never seen before in the traditional brick-and-mortar employment setting. This flexibility – particularly with respect to the number of hours worked – was illustrated by one study which reported that technology-sector workers spend about five hours a month performing platform-based work.[3] The massive reach of this emerging industry is also impressive; the same study revealed that almost one-third of adults had participated in some form of platform-type employment during the prior month. The quick rise and exponential expansion of the sector have placed it on unique legal footing. Indeed, traditional employment laws have struggled to keep up with the dynamic and growing environment of the technology sector. This was clearly seen in the face of the pandemic, which illustrated how many labor and employment laws in the United States leave workers vulnerable and unprotected.

   The culture of employment in the technology sector is still defining itself. One thing that is abundantly clear about this culture, however, is that it is on a collision course with workplace discrimination doctrine. The quick rise of many of these multimillion-dollar companies has occurred without the type of sound structural underpinnings that are often found at businesses of these sizes. Reports of widespread discrimination in these industries, then, is not uncommon, as the types of training and reporting mechanisms are not yet fully developed for many of these corporations.[4] Indeed, one study reported that about 90 percent of females working in the technology industry have observed sexist-type behaviors and 60 percent have been subjected to sexual harassment directly.[5] Another study found that substantially more platform-based workers had experienced workplace harassment than their counterparts in other industries.[6]

Image Credit: BRYAN R. SMITH/Contributor/Getty Images

   While discrimination in the technology sector appears disproportionate in a number of areas – most notably age – this chapter focuses on the widespread issues in this industry that have occurred with respect to gender.[7] In particular, there appears to be a disproportionate level of sex discrimination across the technology sector when compared to other industries. Sexual harassment, gender discrimination, and even sexual assault are often rampant at companies within the technology sector.

This chapter examines why gender discrimination has created so much difficulty for employers in the technology sector. It explores exactly what it is about the technology sector that creates such a prevalence of these types of problems. This chapter further examines what can be done to address these problems, and how employers – and the general public – can work to minimize the types of gender discrimination issue that currently exist in this modern economy. This ongoing issue should be looked at more closely by technology companies given the potential for this type of harm across the sector. Much can be done to reduce these types of occurrences and to limit the potential liability for companies and employers.

This chapter is limited to identifying some of the basic rationales explaining the existing culture in the technology sector, raising some possible avenues of redress, and beginning a discussion about the very real problem of sexual harassment (and even assault) that faces this industry. A more thorough analysis is needed in all of these areas, and this chapter seeks only to start this important discussion. Section 6.2 explores the prevalence of gender discrimination in the technology sector. It examines why there is such widespread sex discrimination in this field, providing several markers that explain its occurrence, and it looks at specific incidents where harassment has occurred. Section 6.3 proposes a number of different avenues that could be explored to help resolve this pervasive problem, discussing several ways to begin recognizing and addressing these abusive workplace environments. While not exhaustive, these suggestions provide several possible solutions to the present problem of hostile work environments in the technology industry. This section also explores the very important issue of sexual assault in the technology sector and briefly looks at how customers can be victimized by the existing culture in this industry. It further explores the potential liability companies and employers are exposed to in the face of this situation.

As a note before beginning the heart of this chapter, it is worth pointing out that there are many well-intentioned employers in the technology sector that have gone out of their way to create a respectful and professional working environment. These employers have addressed gender discrimination issues quickly and effectively. This chapter does not seek to disparage these employers by association. Though this chapter makes broad strokes in its characterizations of the widespread discrimination in this industry, these should be considered only as a generalization of an ongoing problem. Like any industry, there are many good actors in the technology sector as well. This chapter really attempts only to highlight the prevalence of this problem in the technology sector and to offer possible solutions.

6.2 SEX DISCRIMINATION IN THE TECHNOLOGY SECTOR

Gender discrimination is widespread and prevalent in the technology sector, and numerous reports of this type of inappropriate workplace behavior will be described in further detail below. Among the more high-profile instances of such conduct are the experiences of Susan Fowler, an engineer working for Uber.[8] Ms. Fowler detailed her experience at the company, noting that it was obvious that her manager "was trying to get me to have sex with him, and it was so clearly out of line that I immediately took screenshots of the[] chat messages and reported him to HR." With respect to other female workers at Uber, Ms. Fowler stated that "[w]omen were transferring out of the organization, and those who couldn't transfer were quitting or preparing to quit. There were two major reasons for this: there was the organizational chaos, and there was also the sexism within the organization."[9]

Similarly, in another well-known claim of harassment in the technology sector, a former vice president at the dating app Tinder, Whitney Wolfe, alleged that she had been subjected to threats and a sexually hostile working environment.[10] Ms. Wolfe alleged that she had been referred to as a "whore" in the presence of the company CEO by her supervisor,[11] and she further produced text messages with her supervisor and the CEO that were both racist and sexist in nature.[12] Pursuant to her allegations and experience at the company, while "it is tempting to describe the conduct of Tinder's senior executives as 'frat-like,' it was in fact much worse – representing the worst of the misogynist, alpha-male stereotype too often associated with technology startups." The case was eventually settled for over a million dollars, with her former supervisor resigning from the company.[13]

This type of behavior is not only unethical but also a clear violation of federal employment discrimination law under Title VII of the Civil Rights Act of 1964 (Title VII). Title VII covers all workplaces with fifteen or more employees and prohibits employers from taking an adverse action against a worker on the basis of race, color, sex, national origin, or religion. Sex discrimination has been specifically covered by the statute since its inception, and the protections afforded by the statute have been interpreted in subsequent years to include both sexual harassment and hostile work environments. Indeed, the Supreme Court has expressly adopted both theories of discrimination. Gender discrimination and sexual harassment, then, are among the broadest and most comprehensive concepts and theories of discrimination, including not only prohibitions against discriminatory tangible actions but environments that are hostile in nature as well.

The technology sector – just like any other employment setting – is covered by these same Title VII protections. Thus, employers in the technology sector that have a large enough workforce are prohibited by federal law from discriminating against workers on the basis of gender. Similarly, tech-based companies are prohibited by Title VII from establishing or permitting a hostile work environment on the basis of sex. These provisions seem to have particular importance to this emerging economy that, as a general matter, appears to be facing disproportionate levels of gender-based discrimination. And, just like any other area of the law, technology-sector companies are similarly liable when they create sexually hostile or abusive environments, even where female employees are not denied any tangible benefits, or do not suffer any demonstrated psychological harm. An important question to ask in attempting to resolve the gender discrimination that exists in this area is why the technology sector creates such a unique setting for perpetuating this type of inappropriate activity. What is it behind the culture in this workplace that creates so many inherent problems? This section will explore some of the basic characteristics of the technology sector that will act as markers to help explain the problems in this industry.

6.2.1 *Why Does This Problem Exist in the Industry?*

There is no objective empirical basis for explaining the prevalence of sex discrimination issues in the technology sector. Indeed, it may even be possible to explain away these types of claims as receiving disproportionate levels of media attention and/or plaintiffs having a desire to bring claims against employers with particularly deep pockets. While there is some plausibility to these different rationales, on its face the more straightforward explanation for the rise of gender discrimination claims in the industry is that there is something inherent in the culture of the technology sector that is creating an abusive environment. This would not be a completely unique result. In the past, certain industries and businesses have operated in an environment that has – in practice – practically cultivated sexually hostile working environments. The airline industry, for example, is notorious for having subjected its female flight attendants and other airline personnel to different forms of sex discrimination over the years in pursuit of higher profits.

The current culture of the technology sector seems to be a bit different from the airline model, however. Indeed, the hostile work environment and sex discrimination created in this industry does not appear to be one that – on its face – was established to generate higher revenues. Rather, the discrimination seems to stem more from the backgrounds of the individuals who created these companies. There are a number of different factors that likely explain the prevalence of sex discrimination in technology as well as the culture of harassment that exists. No single factor completely explains this environment, and there are a number of different reasons that have led to the creation of what has been called the "tech boys' club."[14]

6.2.2 *The Problem of Education*

Part of the problem likely can be found in the academic setting and the early educational opportunities available to both genders. Notably, there tends to be a disproportionate number of men who enter and continue to study in the fields of computer science, mathematics, information technology, and other science-based topics that are often necessary to form the fundamental building blocks needed by workers to make advancements and excel in this industry. Early on, then, females are at a disadvantage when pursuing these different fields of study and often find themselves channeled to other educational opportunities. Indeed, existing research suggests that males are much more strongly encouraged to pursue studies in the science-related fields critical to success in the technology sector.

6.2.3 *The Problem of a Disproportionate Workforce*

Given that more males pursue and obtain the credentials necessary in this area, it is not surprising that over the past two decades the technology industry has lacked female workers and has consisted of a largely male-based workforce. The discriminatory culture is established at an early age and reinforces itself, as women often pursue nonscience-based educational opportunities and fields of study. Gender biases and stereotypes create a number of problems for women long before they even begin to consider a career in technology. Our educational structure thus disadvantages women at an early age, channeling more men into the types of fields that will ultimately lead to employment in this sector. Retention can also be a big problem in this field. Even when women do navigate the many educational and employment boundaries that exist and successfully enter the technology sector, some choose not to stay. This, too, is not a surprising result, given the unpleasant working environments and discriminatory cultures often seen at technology companies. One study concluded that females are not leaving as a result of family concerns or a distaste for the job itself but because of "workplace conditions, a lack of access to creative roles, and a sense of feeling stalled in one's career."[15]

As a result of these types of cultural bias and educational opportunities, it is also not surprising that there are a disproportionate number of men who have pursued science-based studies at the more prestigious academic institutions. Those who excel at these colleges also tend to be those who either self-select or are identified as having the potential for success in the technology sector. These factors have resulted in a so-called "Brotopia" in the technology industry.[16] Regardless of whether this environment is seen as a "boys' tech club" or "Brotopia," the result is that we can observe an industry that has established the ultimate glass ceiling and is largely dominated by males with science-based backgrounds who have done extremely well in college. This industry is one that, unfortunately, also appears to invite sexual harassment, as it appears to be an almost "frat-like" environment that extends from the college setting to the workplace.[17] The quick success and male-dominated workforce of many of these companies have established overly relaxed working environments that are often conducive to this type of abusive behavior. Indeed, in many ways the technology sector is now the new Wall Street – a male-oriented working environment that has led to quick success for many employees and the negative treatment of women generally. The largely male-based workforce is also helping to create an atmosphere that is more conducive to harassment.

6.2.4 *The Problem of Investors*

This discriminatory atmosphere is only enhanced by the nature of the companies themselves. Many of these startups rely on financing from outside investors. These investors, by and large, are often comprised of males or male-dominated groups. Thus, the discrimination is cyclical, and even those on the sidelines looking to invest in this area tend to be made of a single demographic group. Where successful, these investors and companies are thus created, supervised, and dominated by males – many of whom are only shortly removed from college and who have quickly gained widespread financial success in this emerging industry.

The picture that is drawn here is of an industry that has arisen quickly with little diversity in its makeup. The sector tends to consist largely of males, many of whom are reaping financial successes for the first time. The companies have often only been founded in recent years and lack many institutional norms. And, the individuals at the upper echelons of these companies do not come with the same professional background and experience found in other industries. Indeed, "diversity numbers have barely budged in recent years, and many women say that while sexism has become somewhat less overt, it's just as pernicious as ever."[18] This result is a recipe for disaster when considered in the harassment context and explains the "Brohood"-type label given to this sector. This is not to say that all male workers in the technology sector consider harassment to be some type of "entitlement" that comes with the job. However, the widespread lack of diversity in this area almost necessarily lends itself to many of the difficulties experienced by this industry. And, combined with the many other unique aspects of a sector that is still grappling with its identity, we are left with an image of the "tech boy's club,"[19] which is so often negatively portrayed in the media and popular culture, usually for good reason.

6.2.5 *The Problem of Transparency*

In addition to a culture that has been created from the ground up through a largely male-dominated grip, there is also a distinct problem with transparency in this field, particularly with the platform-based part of this industry. This lack of transparency only fosters the abusive nature of the workplace environment in this sector and plays out in a number of different ways. To begin, platform-based companies often operate with a strong sense of anonymity. Workers may not know who their customer is going to be on any given day and may have very few repeat customers. Thus, at least in the platform-based component of the technology sector, there is a built-in sense of anonymity that leads to a lack of accountability. It may be far more difficult in this type of environment to detect and report customer-based harassment.

Also, within the platform-based part of this industry, as well as other areas of the tech sector, workers may have limited interaction with one another. This lack of interaction can result in a general lack of knowledge of the workforce or the extent to which any workplace problems may exist. Individuals may know that they are personally facing discrimination or harassment but may be unaware that it is a company-wide problem. In the advent of the #MeToo movement, this lack of transparency runs directly counter to current societal and cultural efforts to bring an understanding of harassment out into the open.

Similar transparency-based problems arise with workplace arbitration in this area. The technology sector is well known for requiring workers to utilize arbitration when bringing disputes rather than allowing workers to sue in court. One key aspect of such agreements is their secrecy. Indeed, one of the primary advantages many employers identify in the use of arbitration over state or federal court litigation is the ability to keep any workplace misconduct private. Not only does arbitration prevent harassment and other workplace misconduct from being generally known by the public, it also keeps quiet these types of disputes from fellow coworkers. Workers may believe that they are the only ones being targeted or harassed and feel isolated and too afraid to bring a particular claim. By limiting disputes to the arbitral forum, there is a lack of transparency in this industry, which would encourage others to come forward when subjected to an abusive environment. This is not to say that there are not a number of inherent benefits with respect to arbitration – most notably lower costs and increased speed in resolving claims. Nonetheless, the privacy of the arbitral setting runs counter to the #MeToo movement, which is based largely on creating transparency and knowledge of harassment in the workplace.[20] As the widespread use of arbitration agreements in the industry can lead to limited and restricted information in the public and for the workers themselves as to the general nature of harassment and other problems in this sector, there may also be found to be a general lack of reporting of harassment that occurs in this sector.

6.2.6 *The Problem of Regulation*

The lack of regulation and oversight in the technology sector is also undoubtedly a factor that leads to the failure to address hostile working environments. This sector continues to emerge and evolve quickly and lacks the basic foundational elements of many brick-and-mortar companies. Given the fast rise of these businesses, as well as their quickly changing natures, the industry is one that is difficult to regulate. Without consistent, fundamental regulation and oversight, there is a lack of accountability in the technology sector that can be found in most traditional workplaces. Indeed, there is a substantial question for many technology workers as to whether or not they should be considered employees or independent contractors. Without definitive employment status, these workers cannot be certain to have the ability to avail themselves of many workplace laws. These statutes include such provisions as wage and hour regulations, as well as employment discrimination laws that would address sexual harassment and hostile working environments.

Without proper oversight and accountability, there is less incentive for these corporations to be proactive in preventing and correcting hostile working environments. The very nature of many technology-sector companies is that they are amorphous and quite hard to define. Without these traditional working relationships and statutory oversight, many workers find themselves unable to prevent or change the types of hostile working environments that have become so prevalent in this sector.

In sum, it is difficult to quantify precisely why we see such a definitive presence of hostile working environments in the technology sector when compared to other industries. A number of factors discussed above likely lead to this result. There can be little doubt that discriminatory educational opportunities, gender-biased capital investors, lower levels of female-based employment opportunities, a lack of transparency in the industry, and lower levels of reported violations and administrative/legal oversight, all contribute to this result. This combination of factors makes it far more difficult in trying to address the existing problem. As there is no single factor squarely responsible for the discriminatory result – rather it is a mix of cultural and educational elements at fault – providing a precise solution in this area is difficult, if not impossible. Nonetheless, there are certainly a number of different approaches that can be used to create a much more gender-friendly working environment in this industry. These approaches are discussed in greater detail below.

6.3 CREATING A MORE GENDER-FRIENDLY TECHNOLOGY CULTURE

As discussed above, the existence of abusive working environments in the technology sector has created a pervasive and ongoing problem in this industry. The problem is widespread, sometimes even crossing the line into sexual or physical assault. While there is no quick, single way to resolve this very real problem, there are a number of different approaches that could be implemented that would help to alleviate these types of abusive environments. As one writer noted, "It's time for Silicon Valley to realize that being a good employee means more than just being good at your job – and that being good *to* employees means more than just stock options, free snacks, and a foosball table."[21] Effectuating change in this industry will take time, particularly given how ingrained gender-based disparate treatment has become over the years. This chapter will address some of these approaches, keeping in mind that there are a number of different avenues that can be used to help address this issue. And, it is important to note that the facts and circumstances of each specific company must be closely considered and evaluated before implementing any of the approaches offered here.

6.3.1 *Breaking Down Educational Stereotypes*

As discussed earlier, one problem in the technology field is that more men than women pursue educational opportunities in the types of core fields that lend themselves to subsequent careers in that industry. With this in mind, one long-term approach would be to address some of the myths and stereotypes that still persist with respect to education, and to encourage more diversity in these areas. This may likely be one of the most difficult proposals to actually implement, because it would take much longer and would require a dedication of time and resources. Many states or educational institutions may not have the necessary resources to address this type of program. In many ways, these efforts may involve more of an awareness campaign in this area. To be sure, there have already been many attempts to encourage more gender equality in the science and computer fields.[22] And such efforts are certainly a great start. Companies themselves must further accept responsibility in this area and help to provide the financial resources necessary to encourage these types of educational opportunities for all.[23] Thus, trying to break down educational stereotypes will be a heavy lift, but it is one that is absolutely necessary as part of any comprehensive effort to eradicate inequality in the technology sector. Such efforts should also go beyond gender and include comprehensive diversity in all areas.

6.3.2 *Recruiting and Retention from Diverse Backgrounds*

Along the same lines, greater efforts must be made to recruit from a diversity of backgrounds, including gender, if any real difference is to be made in this area. Until greater changes are made in the educational arena, recruiting will likely take on primary importance. And, until those educational changes have any impact, recruiting will present a number of unique challenges as companies will have to be creative in finding ways to attract talent from an already smaller pool of diverse candidates. Technology-sector businesses, then, must actively find ways to attract more female candidates and hire a more broad-based female workforce. How this recruiting is actually accomplished will be company- and geography-specific. Businesses must find ways to tailor their recruiting to enhance the diversity of the applicant pool. No two companies will be alike in this regard, and they must remain flexible in their approach. Ideas such as encouraging internships and mentoring opportunities for female workers could go a long way toward addressing the gender gap in this area, but companies themselves must take ownership of this process and evaluate ways of enhancing gender diversity within their own operations.

Image Credit: Smith Collection/Gado/Contributor/Getty Images

Similarly, once workers are actually hired, technology businesses must do a better job of retaining these employees. It is not simply enough to garner a more diverse pool of applicants or to simply hire at a higher rate from this pool. Rather, once more female workers are employed at these companies, the businesses must actively assure the more positive workplace experience of these individuals. Steps will have to be taken to make certain that the working environment and workplace experience of these individuals is one in which they will want to continue to work and grow in their careers. Of course, this goes beyond simply preventing an abusive environment and includes equality in all terms, conditions, and privileges of employment such as competitive pay, leave, and other workplace benefits.

6.3.3 *Increased Awareness and Training*

This chapter has in many ways painted a picture of a high-tech workforce that is discriminatory and lends itself to hostile work environments. Often, the root of many of these issues is directly related to ignorance. This may be particularly true in the technology sector where many of the industry leaders have formed their corporations without sufficient professional experience running a company or working with businesses more generally.[24] Fortunately, there are many ways to successfully address this lack of experience, particularly where businesses welcome these types of educational opportunities. Unconscious bias training is one area that is already being pursued and that can render real results.[25] Many workers may be unaware of the discrimination and bias that they have, perhaps unknowingly, fostered, and these training programs can bring to light many of these issues.

Beyond this, however, technology-sector companies can certainly do a much better job of integrating more generalized training in the workplace on gender issues, which is greatly needed in the field. Training should be implemented that seriously considers the particular working environment and discusses some of the challenges that the businesses may face with respect to gender discrimination.[26] Even basic reviews of the laws on sexual harassment and gender bias could be discussed to raise awareness in this area. Particular emphasis should be made with respect to assuring that supervisors understand their role in cultivating a healthy working environment, and upper management and business owners should be open to such training as well. Existing and potential discrimination must therefore be addressed at all levels of the company.

Training can help educate what appears to be an oftentimes inexperienced workforce on these issues. Similarly, workers must understand how gender discrimination is defined, what it looks like, the many different forms it can take, and what should be done to report abusive work environments. All workers should understand the role that they play in the company with respect to detecting and preventing such discrimination and fully understand what to do if they see such behavior or are informed that discrimination exists. Additionally, this training should go beyond gender, although sex-based issues must be a primary focus given the existing culture in the technology sector. Training should also include an overview of discrimination that can occur on the basis of race, color, national origin, religion, age, disability, sexual orientation, and marital status, among others. The goal should be a workplace that deters *all* forms of discrimination and includes a broad-based diversity of workers.

Gender discrimination is a topic that should be fully and openly discussed at technology-sector companies, and a continuing dialogue on this topic should be strongly encouraged. Training that targets these types of abusive environments must regularly occur as well. It is not enough to institute a single training session in this area. Rather, awareness is an ongoing endeavor.[27] Periodic attempts to educate a company's workforce against all forms of discrimination – gender or otherwise – should regularly occur and be required.[28] When needed, such training should also occur on a much more frequent basis. The importance of awareness in this area cannot be overstated. Any real change in this field will only occur when companies, and their workers, understand and are well informed of the problems that exist at their place of business and in the industry generally.

6.3.4 *Enhanced Reporting and Response*

Directly related to the issue of training is the assurance that technology-sector companies create numerous avenues for reporting potential claims, and further establish aggressive means of responding to allegations that are made. This will undoubtedly require a change in culture for many technology companies. Given the current environment present at many of these companies, these businesses will want to establish several avenues of reporting for workers. This is critically important as, to the extent there is an abusive environment at a company, workers will feel hesitant to report harassment for fear of potential reprisal. As one article surmised, in the technology sector, "the prevailing advice is to stay silent and avoid repercussions – both financial and emotional. There's fear of earning a reputation as someone who's difficult to work with, which could make it difficult to secure funding. Investors may avoid financing a company with a founder they don't 'trust' if they're nervous she may speak out about their behavior, too."[29]

Avenues of reporting should be spread throughout the company. At larger companies, for example, reporting avenues could include a worker's direct supervisor, designated human resource professionals, supervisors outside of the employee's direct reporting line, and even members of the board of directors or company president.[30] Companies should further consider the potential benefit of creating anonymous avenues for workers to complain of discrimination and harassment. To the extent there is a hostile work environment that is well ingrained at a company, workers may only feel comfortable reporting in an anonymous fashion.

Regardless of the ultimate avenues of reporting established, the company must make sure to create a culture that invites complaints of inappropriate behavior. Through training and education, technology-based companies can create a climate that encourages workers to come forward with potential issues. This is of critical importance because when workers are afraid to complain, the conduct may go undetected and the employer will not have the ability to appropriately identify and address adverse conduct.

Similarly, when complaints do arise, employers must take them seriously and effectively investigate and address any concerns. Independent, objective investigations are key to making certain that the allegations are fully addressed. Internal human resources employees, well trained in this area, may be able to effectively take on this type of investigatory role. Outside legal counsel or consulting firms may also be better equipped to handle these types of situations and should be further considered by technology businesses when looking into employee complaints. At the conclusion of a thorough and fair investigation, the business must then act. The information gathered during the investigation cannot simply be swept under the rug, and employers must address any existing harassment (or other concerns) at the company. Strong corrective measures must be taken to resolve any existing issues and to further prevent any additional hostile conduct from taking place at the company.

Enhanced reporting, thorough and fair investigations, and a commitment to taking effective corrective measures will be the cornerstones to creating a more equitable working environment. The technology sector is not the first industry to encounter hostile work environments, and the best practices already developed for addressing harassment in other areas can prove useful for technology companies. The technology sector must learn from the mistakes of other industries and craft a well-thought-out approach that will tailor these measures to this particular sector.

6.3.5 *Diverse Funding and Investor Training*

The technology sector also relies heavily on capital investment and resources provided by outside groups.[31] In this sector in particular, the investors also tend to be males, only further leading to the gender-based environment that we see in this industry.[32] This presents a somewhat unique problem for technology startups, and though speculative, it is probably fair to conclude that many of these investors hold the same types of male-based bias that we see present at the companies in this industry.[33]

There is unfortunately no easy fix for this problem. And again, awareness and education may be the only realistic solutions here. Investors are entirely aware of the existing problems in the industry, and as a practical matter, they are also well aware of the legal liabilities that flow from these problems. These investors have an obvious financial stake in the success of these companies and certainly would like to avoid employment discrimination lawsuits, other potential bias claims, and bad publicity. If these investors would consider engaging in training themselves that would address potential gender bias, it would go a long way toward resolving some of these issues. Also, investors should strongly consider soliciting the advice from a diverse group of individuals when determining which companies to invest in. This would help assure that bias is being removed from the process of selecting which startups should be funded.

Again, as capital investors have a direct financial interest in the success of these companies, they should be open to making any necessary changes to their role in the process. Education is likely the hardest part of bringing about this change, however, and given the strong and appropriate backlash we have seen against harassment in the technology sector, investors may now be more likely than ever to help engage in this process.

Certainly, if more female investors would consider entering into this industry, it would further help head off many of these problems. A more diverse source of capital investment in this area would likely lead to a more welcoming and less hostile gender-based environment for technology workers.[34] And of course, diversity on all levels would lead to a better working environment in the technology sector.[35] A more diverse group of venture capitalists could further help pressure the companies themselves to increase gender equality, and these investors could demand that startups establish a more fair and equitable working environment.

6.3.6 *Stronger Industry Regulation*

As discussed earlier, there is very little regulation or oversight in this area. Indeed, there is an ongoing debate in the courts over whether workers in this industry should be considered employees or independent contractors. Without employment status, technology workers will lack many of the protections that are offered by federal employment laws. In particular, Title VII prohibits employers from engaging in sexual harassment or perpetrating a hostile work environment on the basis of sex. This law, however, which is the primary source of recourse for workers facing abusive environments, does not protect independent contractors – or others failing to satisfy the statutory definition of "employee." This result leaves literally millions of workers vulnerable in the platform-based economy to being subjected to a hostile working environment without the necessary legal standing to help correct the situation or effectuate any type of meaningful recovery.

From a policy standpoint alone, the courts should strongly consider categorizing workers in this sector as employees afforded all of the protections of Title VII. From a legal standpoint, this result will often make sense as well, as these companies frequently exercise the necessary control over workers to satisfy the employee definition. Where workers do not satisfy this definition, they will have little recourse when facing environments that are hostile on the basis of sex or other protected grounds.

Where platform-based workers do not have these protections, state and local governments should step in to afford technology workers the opportunity to prevent abusive working relationships. State laws, or city ordinances, could be further defined to protect all workers from hostile working environments, irrespective of their status as employees. States and cities with disproportionately high numbers of technology-sector workers should act quickly to adopt reforms that would protect all workers from being subjected to a hostile working environment. This would allow all technology workers to raise any concerns about abusive environments without fear of any type of reprisal.

This type of regulation goes hand in hand with the encouraged reporting of harassment. If workers feel vulnerable to discipline or are unable to achieve recovery when discriminated against, they will be unlikely to come forward to raise concerns to their employer.[36] Regulation, then, through federal, state, and local anti-discrimination laws, is a critical component to changing the culture of an industry that has permitted far too much discrimination.

6.3.7 *Other Approaches*

There are a number of other possible approaches to addressing hostile work environments that exist in the technology sector. This chapter does not purport to provide an exhaustive list of these approaches, and others have already weighed in with suggestions. Hostile work environments have been a problem for decades. However, the technology sector presents additional barriers and complications for harassment claims. The scholars, courts, and companies themselves must think outside the box, then, in attempting to address this topic.

One suggested approach would include encouraging companies to use and adopt "decency pledges."[37] These pledges would require workers, officers, and other company officials to sign an agreement to create an appropriate workplace environment and to not engage in any abusive type behavior.[38] While such agreements are likely not enforceable on their face, they certainly emphasize the importance of creating and encouraging nonhostile working environments. There are obvious shortcomings to this type of approach, and it is easily critiqued.[39] Nonetheless, there really is only upside to adopting these types of agreements, and few, if any, drawbacks exist other than the potential for creating false senses of security.

As noted, in addition to decency pledges, other approaches to resolving this issue exist. Some of these suggestions go hand in hand with the approaches already offered in this chapter. As a sampling, there have been suggestions to increase the use of technology to counter hostile environments,[40] better utilize online platforms to address the issue,[41] increase diversity levels and understanding of the problem, and develop and adopt best practices in the area.[42]

Some technology businesses have made more transparent their gender employment statistics and pay, and other companies have explored advancing females at the company into management positions.

6.3.8 A Word about Sexual Assault

This chapter has focused on hostile working environments created or permitted by employers that run afoul of the rights of individual workers. The technology sector, however, has also encountered a number of specific incidents with respect to customers.[43] Indeed, some customers have alleged that they have been sexually assaulted by workers of technology-based companies. It is unclear the extent to which these types of assaults are the direct result of the current culture in the technology sector or are more simply the acts of individual workers who are not related to this workplace environment. While this chapter does not attempt to fully address the issue of the sexual assault of technology-sector customers, it is certainly a topic that cannot be ignored and is one of great social and legal/criminal importance.[44] Indeed, any steps that are taken to create an overall culture that is less abusive and more diverse may likely lead to fewer legal problems, potentially even reducing the number of these awful criminal acts that occur.[45] And of course, increased training and education are critical on this topic as well. Furthermore, from a civil liability standpoint, this topic also implicates the question of whether these workers are employees or independent contractors of the company.[46] The specific question of how agency principles would work in these instances is thus not only important for hostile work environment claims but also directly involved in the question of liability for criminal sexual assault by technology workers and platform-based employees. Related to this topic, the issue of the sexual assault of customers also raises questions of negligent hiring by technology-sector companies as well as more general questions of employer negligence.[47] Again, however, this topic is quite nuanced and is well beyond the scope of the issues addressed here.

6.4 CONCLUSION

Gender discrimination is an ongoing and undeniable problem in the technology sector. To help resolve this issue, we must begin a dialogue on why this problem exists. There are numerous factors that lead to a discriminatory culture in this industry. Once we begin to better understand the reasons for the discrimination that exists, we can begin to formulate solutions to this problem. There is no quick fix, but with better education, training, and other approaches, the industry can begin to face this problem head on.[48]

NOTES

This chapter draws heavily from Joseph A. Seiner, "Harassment, Technology, and the Modern Worker," *Employee Rights and Employment Policy Journal* 23 (2019): 85–113.

1 Sara O'Brien and Laurie Segall, "Money, Power & Sexual Harassment," *CNN Tech*, https://money.cnn.com/technology/sexual-harassment-tech/ (last visited June 9, 2020).

2 See Andrea M. Matwyshyn, "Silicon Ceilings: Information Technology Equity, the Digital Divide and the Gender Gap among Information Technology Professionals," *Northwestern Journal of Technology and Intellectual Property* 2 (2003): 35, 37–38.

3 *Report on the Economic Well-Being of U.S. Households in 2017* (Washington, DC: Board of Governors of the Federal Reserve System, 2018), 19, www.federalreserve .gov/publications/files/2017-report-economic-well-being-us-households-201805.pdf.

4 See generally Matwyshyn, "Silicon Ceilings"; *Elephant in the Valley*, www .elephantinthevalley.com/ (last visited June 9, 2020).

5 Liza Mundy, "Why Is Silicon Valley So Awful to Women?," *Atlantic*, April 2017, www.theatlantic.com/magazine/archive/2017/04/why-is-silicon-valley-so-awful-to-women/517788/; *Elephant in the Valley*.

6 Alexsandra Bargiacchi et al., *Sexual Harassment in the Workplace: #Metoo, Women, Men, and the Gig Economy* (Edison Research and Marketplace, 2018), 3, www .edisonresearch.com/wp-content/uploads/2018/06/Sexual-Harassment-in-the-Workplace-metoo-Women-Men-and-the-Gig-Economy-6.20.18-1.pdf; "The Criminal Justice System: Statistics," *RAINN*, www.rainn.org/statistics/criminal-justice-system (last visited June 9, 2020).

7 See Peter Gosselin and Ariana Tobin, "Cutting 'Old Heads' at IBM," *ProPublica*, March 22, 2018, https://features.propublica.org/ibm/ibm-age-discrimination-ameri can-workers/.

8 See Susan Fowler, "Reflecting on One Very, Very Strange Year at Uber," *SusanJFowler*, February 19, 2017, www.susanjfowler.com/blog/2017/2/19/reflecting-on-one-very-strange-year-at-uber.

9 Ibid.; see generally Sheelah Kolhatkar, "The Tech Industry's Gender-Discrimination Problem," *New Yorker*, November 13, 2017, www.newyorker.com/magazine/2017/11/20/the-tech-industrys-gender-discrimination-problem.

10 Abby Phillip, "Read the Most Surprising Allegations from the Tinder Sexual Harassment Lawsuit," *Washington Post*, July 1, 2014, www.washingtonpost.com/news/the-switch/wp/2014/07/01/read-the-most-surprising-allegations-from-the-tinder-sexual-harassment-lawsuit/?noredirect=on&utm_term=.d46a7d40b16f.

11 Ibid.; see Complaint at 44, *Wolfe v. Tinder*, No. BC550105 (Super. Ct. Cal. September 5, 2014), www.rezlaw.com/News-Events/06-30-14_Complaint_with_Exhibits-1.pdf.

12 See Complaint exhs. 1–10, *Wolfe v. Tinder*, No. BC550105 (Super. Ct. Cal. September 5, 2014), www.rezlaw.com/News-Events/06-30-14_Complaint_with_Exhibits-1.pdf.

13 Steven Bertoni, "Exclusive: Sean Rad Out as Tinder CEO. Inside the Crazy Saga," *Forbes*, November 4, 2014, www.forbes.com/sites/stevenbertoni/2014/11/04/exclusive-sean-rad-out-as-tinder-ceo-inside-the-crazy-saga/#6010891f3ccd; Kolhatkar, "The Tech Industry's Gender-Discrimination Problem."

14 Nick Bilton, "'Silicon Valley Has Its Own Unique Kind of Harassment': Will Technology Have Its #MeToo Moment?," *Vanity Fair*, December 15, 2017, www .vanityfair.com/news/2017/12/silicon-valley-has-its-own-unique-kind-of-harassment-will-technology-have-its-metoo-moment.

15 Catherine Ashcraft et al., *Women in Tech: The Facts: 2016 Update // See What's Changed and What Hasn't* (Denver, CO: National Center for Women & Information Technology, 2016), 11, www.ncwit.org/sites/default/files/resources/ncwit_women-in-it_2016-full-report_final-web06012016.pdf. See generally Mundy, "Why Is Silicon Valley So Awful to Women?"

16 See generally Emily Chang, *Brotopia: Breaking Up the Boys' Club of Silicon Valley* (New York, NY: Portfolio, 2018).

17 See Kolhatkar, "The Tech Industry's Gender-Discrimination Problem." See also Bilton, "'Silicon Valley Has Its Own Unique Kind of Harassment'."

18 Mundy, "Why Is Silicon Valley So Awful to Women?"

19 Bilton, "'Silicon Valley Has Its Own Unique Kind of Harassment'."

20 Debra S. Katz, "Thirty Million Women Can't Sue Their Employer Over Harassment. Hopefully That's Changing," *Washington Post*, May 17, 2018, www.washingtonpost .com/opinions/companies-are-finally-letting-women-take-sexual-harassment-to-court/2018/05/17/552ca876-594e-11e8-b656-a5f8c2a9295d_story.html?utm_term=.422bebb 03a38.

21 Klint Finley, "Tech Still Doesn't Take Discrimination Seriously," *Wired*, February 20, 2017, www.wired.com/2017/02/tech-still-doesnt-take-discrimination-seriously/.

22 See generally Vivian Anette Lagesen, "The Strength of Numbers: Strategies to Include Women into Computer Science," *Social Studies of Science* 37, no. 1 (February 2007): 1, 67.

23 See Biz Carson, "Inside Uber's Effort to Fix Its Culture Through a Harvard-Inspired 'University,'" *Forbes*, February 3, 2018, www.forbes.com/sites/bizcarson/2018/02/03/inside-ubers-effort-to-fix-its-culture-through-a-harvard-inspired-university/#3e98cd1a1695.

24 See Roselinde Torres, "The Rise of the Not-So-Experienced CEO," *Harvard Business Review*, December 26, 2014, https://hbr.org/2014/12/the-rise-of-the-not-so-experienced-ceo.

25 See Mundy, "Why Is Silicon Valley So Awful to Women?"

26 Alex Lindsey et al., "Two Types of Diversity Training That Really Work," *Harvard Business Review*, July 28, 2017, https://hbr.org/2017/07/two-types-of-diversity-training-that-really-work; Claire Cain Miller, "Sexual Harassment Training Doesn't Work. But Some Things Do," *New York Times*, December 11, 2017, www.nytimes.com/2017/12/11/upshot/sexual-harassment-workplace-prevention-effective.html.

27 Brendan L. Smith, "What It Really Takes to Stop Sexual Harassment," *Monitor on Psychology* (February 2018): 36, www.apa.org/monitor/2018/02/sexual-harassment .aspx; Carson, "Inside Uber's Effort to Fix Its Culture."

28 See Chai R. Feldblum and Victoria A. Lipnic, *Select Task Force on the Study of Harassment in the Workplace* (Washington, DC: U.S. Equal Employment Opportunity Commission, 2016), 68.

29 O'Brien and Segall, "Money, Power & Sexual Harassment."

30 See Feldblum and Lipnic, *Select Task Force*; Eric Gay, "Uber Report: Eric Holder's Recommendations for Change," *New York Times*, June 13, 2017, www .nytimes.com/2017/06/13/technology/uber-report-eric-holders-recommendations-for- change.html.

31 Robin Feldman, "Patent Demands & Startup Companies: The View from the Venture Capital Community," *Yale Journal of Law and Technology* 16 (2014): 236, 242.

32 See Kolhatkar, "The Tech Industry's Gender-Discrimination Problem." See also Erin Griffith, "How Venture Capitalists Got Away with Sexual Harassment," *Fortune*, July 21, 2017, www.fortune.com/2017/07/21/venture-capitalists-sexual-harass ment/.

33 See Paresh Dave and Jack Flemming, "Sexual Harassment Claims Prompt Venture Capitalists to Apologize, Change Policies and Head to Counseling," *Los Angeles Times*, July 3, 2017, www.latimes.com/business/technology/la-fi-tn-venture-capital- sexual-harassment-20170630-story.html.

34 See Alison Wistner, "The VC World Is Still a Boy's Club – Here's How to Change That," *Entrepreneur*, October 26, 2018, www.entrepreneur.com/article/321321.

35 See Jessica Fink, "Gender Sidelining and the Problem of Unactionable Discrimination," *Stanford Law and Policy Review* 29 (2018): 57, 100–01 (citing Christine Jolls, "Antidiscrimination Law's Effects on Implicit Bias," in *NYU Selected Chapters on Labor and Employment Law*, Vol. 3, *Behavioral Analyses of Workplace Discrimination*, ed. Mitu Gulati and Michael J. Yelnosky [Alphen aan den Rijn: Kluwer Law International, 2007], 69).

36 See Connie Kremer, "*McDonnell Douglas* Burden Shifting and Judicial Economy in Title VII Retaliation Claims: In Pursuit of Expediency, Resulting in Inefficiency," *University of Cincinnati Law Review* 85 (2017): 857, 859–60; Patricia A. Moore, "Parting Is Such Sweet Sorrow: The Application of Title VII to Post-Employment Retaliation," *Fordham Law Review* 62 (1993): 205, 206.

37 See Nathalie Molina Niño, "#decencypledge Needs Outcomes Not Optics," *LinkedIn*, June 24, 2017, www.linkedin.com/pulse/decencypledge-needs-outcomes- optics-nathalie-molina-ni%C3%B1o/?published=t.

38 See Reid Hoffman, "The Human Rights of Women Entrepreneurs," *LinkedIn*, June 23, 2017, www.linkedin.com/pulse/human-rights-women-entrepreneurs-reid- hoffman/.

39 See Niño, "#decencypledge."

40 Brandie M. Nonnecke, "Opinion: Fight Sexual Harassment in Technology Companies With – Technology," *Mercury News* (San Jose, CA), December 13, 2017, www.mercurynews.com/2017/12/13/opinion-fight-sexual-harassment-in-technology-com panies-with-technology/.

41 Maggie Roache, "Online Platforms Hope to Tackle Sexual Harassment in the Tech Industry," *Peninsula Press* (Stanford, CA), June 17, 2018, http://peninsulapress.com/ 2018/06/17/online-platforms-hope-to-tackle-sexual-harassment-in-the-tech-industry/.

42 Erin Griffith, "What Has Tech Done to Fix Its Harassment Problem?," *Wired*, January 22, 2018, www.wired.com/story/what-has-tech-done-to-fix-its-harassment-problem/.

43 See, e.g., Aaron Katersky and Morgan Winsor, "Women Accusing Uber Drivers of Sexual Assault Demand Their Stories Be Heard in Court, Not Arbitration," *ABC News*, April 26, 2018, https://abcnews.go.com/US/women-accusing-uber-drivers-sexual-assault-demand-stories/story?id=54747465; Sam Levin, "Airbnb Sued by Woman Who Says She Was Sexually Assaulted by 'Superhost,'" *Guardian*, July 27, 2017, www.theguardian.com/technology/2017/jul/27/airbnb-guest-sexual-assault-allega tion; Shivani Vora, "Airbnb Sued by Guest Who Says a Host Sexually Assaulted Her," *New York Times*, August 2, 2017, www.nytimes.com/2017/08/02/travel/airbnb-lawsuit-host-sexual-assault.html.

44 See Sarah Ashley O'Brien et al., "CNN Investigation: 103 Uber Drivers Accused of Sexual Assault or Abuse," *CNN Tech*, April 30, 2018, https://money.cnn.com/2018/04/ 30/technology/uber-driver-sexual-assault/index.html; see also Levin, "Airbnb Sued by Woman."

45 See generally David Lazarus, "Uber and Lyft See the Light on Sexual Assault, But They Could Do a Whole Lot Better," *Los Angeles Times*, May 18, 2018, www.latimes.com/ business/lazarus/la-fi-lazarus-uber-lyft-sexual-assault-arbitration-20180518-story.html.

46 See *Doe* v. *Uber Techs, Inc.*, 184 F. Supp. 3d 774 (N.D. Cal. 2016); *Cotter* v. *Lyft, Inc.*, 60 F. Supp. 3d 1067, 1078 (N.D. Cal. 2015). See generally Sterling A. McMahan, "Moving to Dismiss: Ridesharing and Assaults, and the Emerging Legal Frontier," *Trial Advocate Quarterly* (Spring 2018): 11, 13.

47 See Stephanie Francis Ward, "Judge Rejects Uber's Independent-Contractor Argument in Sexual Assault Tort Claim," *ABA Journal*, May 6, 2016, www.abajournal .com/news/article/judge_rejects_ubers_independent-contractor_argument_in_sexual_ assault_tort_ ("Plaintiffs in the tort claim also alleged negligent hiring, citing evidence that Aiello had a 2003 assault conviction Uber missed in his background check.").

48 This chapter also benefited greatly from the scholarship and work of numerous other authors. See Bibliography.

7

A Few Final Thoughts

We've arranged a civilization in which most crucial elements profoundly depend on science and technology.

—Carl Sagan[1]

The recent pandemic has made abundantly clear the overwhelming connection between the workplace and technology. With thousands of employees suddenly forced to work at home, a large swath of the workforce quickly received crash courses in videoconferencing and other related technologies. This virus has literally caused us as a society to take a step back and redefine what employment actually means. The virtual workplace is the blending of brick-and-mortar physical places of business with the advanced technologies that now make it possible for workers to perform their duties outside of the office. Taken a step further, there is now an entire platform-based industry where workers at the same company may never see one another, meet a supervisor, or even set foot in a corporate building. Trying to

Image Credit: AerialPerspective Images/Getty Images

regulate this area means attempting to apply decades-old employment laws to a context never conceived or contemplated by the legislatures that wrote those laws.

The on-demand economy continues to redefine work and the employment relationship. And the law struggles to keep up with the constant changes that are occurring in the technology sector. This book is designed to help reframe the existing employment laws in a way that makes more sense in a platform-based economy and in a technology industry that has literally changed overnight in response to COVID-19.

There are countless legal implications to the employment relationship, and the worker–employer relationship has been well litigated in many different respects. These legal implications are no different in the technology sector, as long as courts approach this industry in a flexible manner and not with an overly rigid adherence to the way workplace laws have been applied to brick-and-mortar facilities. While the prior precedent is quite helpful to understanding existing employment laws, we must allow the application of these laws to evolve to fit more modern businesses.

This book does not attempt to be exhaustive in its approach to these questions. Rather, it has focused the technology-based workplace questions on the primary ways that we often think about the employment relationship: the definition of who is an employee, the way workers organize together in an effort to negotiate with an employer, and some of the more recent issues of workplace harassment that have come to light. Similarly, this text has examined the more basic questions with respect to the litigation of workplace claims – coverage, pleading, and aggregation.

While each of these issues presents its own set of complexities, the one overarching difference between the platform-based worker and traditional brick-and-mortar employee is flexibility. Courts, litigants, and employers must all take a flexible approach to existing rules and regulations when considering more modern technology questions. This text identifies a number of indicia and factors to consider on different areas of the law in the technology sector. But at the end of the day, no single set of elements can completely capture the evolving nature of this quickly changing sector.

A pandemic has caused us all to rethink what is important and to remain flexible in our personal and professional lives. We must take a similarly flexible approach to establishing the contours of the technology industry itself, from how we define its workforce to how we make sure all workers and businesses are treated fairly. Technology today looks dramatically different from what it did a decade ago. Similarly, ten years from now advances will be made that were never even contemplated in the current marketplace. Flexibility is key, as the courts and legislatures must remain nimble and act quickly to keep pace and respond to the always evolving virtual workplace.

NOTE

1 Carl Sagan, *The Demon-Haunted World* (New York: Random House Publishers, 1996).

Selected Portions of Plaintiff's Complaint in
Bradshaw v. *Uber Technologies*[1]

2. Uber, a company valued at more than $50 billion, has and continues to take unfair advantage of its financially struggling Uber Drivers by terming them "Independent Transportation Providers."[2] Only in the counterfactual world could Uber Drivers be considered "independent."[3] Uber Drivers lack discretion in the performance of their employment relationship with Uber, and have no independence apart from Uber in performing their employment with Uber.[4]

3. Uber Drivers are able to secure fares only through Uber's mobile application, which governs every aspect of the Uber Drivers' transportation services for Uber.[5] When Uber restricts a Driver's access to Uber's mobile application, Uber effectively terminates the Driver, as the Driver is unable to work for Uber or Uber's users. Uber's misclassification of its Drivers as non-employees of the company has resulted in Uber Drivers' inability to earn minimum wage.[6]

4. Plaintiff alleges that he and other Uber Drivers are employees, and as employees, are entitled to basic wage protections such as expense reimbursement, overtime pay, rest- and meal-breaks, and other benefits that attach to employees that do not likewise attach to independent contractors.[7] Uber misclassifies its Drivers as independent contractors to evade these and other protections of Oklahoma law as well as the Fair Labor Standards Act.[8]

5. Moreover, Uber intentionally misrepresents to the public how it compensates its Drivers so that it can retain a disproportionate percentage of the fares generated by Uber Drivers.[9] Uber markets its rides as gratuity-included, but Uber does not remit the gratuity (or an amount in-kind) to its Drivers.[10] Uber effectively takes the tips.[11] To worsen the reality for these Drivers, Plaintiff and members of the putative class finance all

expenses related to their employment with Uber (e.g., gas, cost of insurance, deductibles, and vehicle maintenance, among others).[12]

18. Defendants employ(ed) Plaintiff and members of the Class exercised control over their wages, their hours, and their working conditions.[13]

19. Defendants regulate every aspect of Uber Drivers' job performance.[14]

20. As with other employers, Defendants required Plaintiff and Uber Drivers to submit to background checks, and to disclose banking information and residence, as well as social security numbers.[15]

21. Uber requires Plaintiff and Uber Drivers to register their cars with Uber and the vehicles cannot be more than ten years old.[16]

22. Uber Drivers do not pay Defendants to use Defendants' intellectual property, the mobile application. Uber Drivers do not, in the strictest sense, pay Uber a fee as consideration for use of Uber's mobile application.[17]

23. Rather, Defendants compensate their Uber Drivers based upon the employment arrangement that Uber unilaterally imposes upon its Drivers, as with any employment-based business model.[18]

24. Uber Drivers are not engaged in a business distinct from Uber's business.[19] The Uber application ensures this.[20] Through the application, Uber controls and directly manages Uber's entire transportation service, critically, inclusive of its Drivers.[21]

25. Plaintiff's and Uber Drivers' ability to earn income depends solely on Uber and not in any way on an Uber Driver's particular skill or acumen, or on any managerial or other discretionary job skill.[22]

After these general allegations about Uber drivers, the Bradshaw plaintiff included specific facts about his personal work relationship with Uber:

26. Plaintiff is a retired Oklahoma State Trooper.[23]

27. In February of 2014, Plaintiff began working for UberX. He is still currently employed as an Uber Driver.[24]

28. On average, Plaintiff drives thirty (30) hours each week and Uber compensates him on a weekly basis.[25]

29. In 2015, Plaintiff drove 40,000 miles.[26] He grossed $23,872.00, but after paying his employment-related expenses, which using the federal rate of 57.5 cents per mile, were $23,000, Plaintiff netted only $872.00 for the year, even though he worked 1,500 hours that year.[27] In other words, he made just 58 cents per hour.[28] In addition, the $23,000 for expenses did not include car washes, which cost him $300 per year, as well as satellite radio, which cost him $200 per year.[29]

31. When Plaintiff first started, after Uber retained its portion of the fare but before paying his employment-related expenses, Plaintiff earned between $500 and $600 per week.[30] Plaintiff's expenses, including gas, insurance, lease payments, and car repairs, were approximately 30% of any amount earned ($150 to $180 each week).[31]

32. For some time during his employment, Mr. Bradshaw worked in excess of 50 to 60 hours a week.[32] At all times, Uber failed to pay overtime compensation.[33]

33. The terms and conditions of Plaintiff's employment have changed drastically since he first was hired by Uber.[34] The changes were instituted by Uber, without any input from Plaintiff or other drivers.[35]

34. Initially, Plaintiff and other drivers earned $1.50 per mile.[36] Now, he and other Uber Drivers earn only .70 cents per mile.[37] Throughout his employment, Plaintiff has been subject to several price reductions implemented at the sole discretion of Uber.[38]

NOTES

1. Complaint, Bradshaw v. Uber Techs., Inc., No. CIV-16-388-R, 2017 WL 2455151 (W.D. Okla. June 6, 2017) [hereinafter *Bradshaw* Complaint].
2. *Bradshaw* Complaint, 1.
3. Ibid.
4. Ibid.
5. Ibid., 2.
6. Ibid.
7. Ibid.
8. Ibid.
9. Ibid.
10. Ibid.
11. Ibid., 2–3.
12. Ibid., 2–3.
13. Ibid., 6.
14. Ibid.
15. Ibid.
16. Ibid.
17. Ibid.
18. Ibid.
19. Ibid., 7.
20. Ibid.

21. Ibid.
22. Ibid.
23. Ibid.
24. Ibid.
25. Ibid.
26. Ibid.
27. Ibid.
28. Ibid.
29. Ibid.
30. Ibid., 7–8.
31. Ibid., 8.
32. Ibid.
33. Ibid.
34. Ibid.
35. Ibid.
36. Ibid.
37. Ibid.
38. Ibid.

Bibliography

"About Postmates," *Postmates*, www.postmates.com/about.

"About Us," *Doordash*, www.doordash.com/about/.

"About Us," *Grubhub*, www.about.grubhub.com/about-us/what-is-grubhub/default.aspx.

"About Us," *Handy*, www.handy.com/about.

"About Us," *Yelp*, www.yelp.com/about.

Ackerman, Bruce, *We the People, Vol. 2 Transformation* (Cambridge, MA: Belknap Press of Harvard University Press, 1998).

Aeppel, Timothy and Daniel Wiessner, "Unions Brace for Pro-Business Shift in Labor Policy under Trump," *Reuters*, November 9, 2016.

"AI for Your Business," *Crowdflower*, www.figure-eight.com.

Alexander, Janet Cooper, "Presentation at the Debates Over Group Litigation," in *Comparative Perspective Conference in Geneva, Switzerland, An Introduction to Class Action Procedure in the United States* (July 21–22, 2000) (abstract), www.law.duke.edu/grouplit/papers/classactionalexander.pdf.

Alleyne, Reginald, "Statutory Discrimination Claims: Rights 'Waived' and Lost in the Arbitration Forum," *Hofstra Labor Law Journal* 13 (1996): 381–432.

Alton, Larry, "Four Ways the On-Demand Economy Is Changing the Face of Business," *Forbes*, December 30, 2016.

Andrias, Kate, "The New Labor Law," *Yale Law Journal* 126 (2016): 2–101.

Arnow-Richman, Rachel, "Just Notice: Re-Reforming Employment at Will," *University of California at Los Angeles Law Review* 58 (2010): 1–72.

"Apply Now," *Lyft*, www.lyft.com/drive-with-lyft.

Ashcraft, Catherine et al., *Women in Tech: The Facts: 2016 Update // See What's Changed and What Hasn't* (Denver, CO: National Center for Women & Information Technology, 2016).

Barbaro, Michael and Ashley Parker, "Candidates Will Hail a Ride, but Not Necessarily the Uber Labor Model," *New York Times*, July 16, 2015.

Barenberg, Mark, "Democracy and Domination in the Law of Workplace Cooperation: From Bureaucratic to Flexible Production," *Columbia Law Review* 94 (1994): 753–983.

"The Political Economy of the Wagner Act: Power, Symbol, and Workplace Cooperation," *Harvard Law Review* 106 (1993): 1379–496.

Bargiacchi, Alexsandra and Laura Ivey* and Mark Larson**, "Sexual Harassment in the Workplace: #Metoo, Women, Men, and the Gig Economy" (*Edison Research and **Marketplace, 2018).

Barron, Myra H., "Who's an Independent Contractor? Who's an Employee?," *Labor Lawyer* 14 (1999): 457–73.

Barzilay, Arianne Renan and Anat Ben-David, "Platform Inequality: Gender in the Gig-Economy," *Seton Hall Law Review* 47 (2017): 393–432.

Bauer, David, "The Misclassification of Independent Contractors: The Fifty-Four Billion Dollar Problem," *Rutgers Journal of Law and Public Policy* 12 (2015): 138–78.

Beaird, J. Ralph, "Employer and Consultant Reporting under the LMRDA," *Georgia Law Review* 20 (1986): 533–64.

"Become a Dasher," *Doordash*, www.doordash.com/dasher/apply/.

"Become a Soothe Therapist," *Soothe*, www.soothe.com/apply.

"Become a Zeel Massage Therapist," *Zeel*, www.zeel.com/zmt.

Befort, Stephen F., "Revisiting the Black Hole of Workplace Regulation: A Historical and Comparative Perspective of Contingent Work," *Berkeley Journal of Employment and Labor Law* 24 (2003): 153–78.

Belknap, Michal R., "The New Deal and the Emergency Powers Doctrine," *Texas Law Review* 62 (1983): 67–109.

Bellstrom, Kristen, "You Won't Believe How Many Women in Tech Say They've Faced Sexual Harassment," *Fortune*, January 11, 2016.

Benner, Katie, "Women in Tech Speak Frankly on Culture of Harassment," *New York Times*, June 30, 2017.

Bercovici, Jeff, "Why the Next Uber Wannabe Is Already Dead," *Inc.com*, November 2015.

Bernstein, Irving, "Americans in Depression and War," in *A History of the American Worker*, ed. Richard B. Morris (Princeton, NJ: Princeton University Press, 1983).

Bertoni, Steven, "Exclusive: Sean Rad Out as Tinder CEO. Inside the Crazy Saga," *Forbes*, November 4, 2014.

Bertrand, Marianne and Sendhil Mullainathan, "Are Emily and Greg More Employable than Lakisha and Jamal? A Field Experiment on Labor Market Discrimination," *American Economic Review* 94 (2004): 991–1013.

Bilton, Nick, "'Silicon Valley Has Its Own Unique Kind of Harassment': Will Technology Have Its #MeToo Moment?," *Vanity Fair*, December 15, 2017.

Binder, Denis, "Sex Discrimination in the Airline Industry: Title VII Flying High," *California Law Review* 59 (1971):1091–112.

Bingham, Lisa B., "Employment Arbitration: The Repeat Player Effect," *Employee Rights and Employment Policy Journal* 1 (1997): 189–220.

Bird, Jane, "How the Tech Industry Is Attracting More Women," *Financial Times*, March 9, 2018.

Blanchflower, David G. and Alex Bryson, "Changes Over Time in Union Relative Wage Effects in the UK and the US Revisited," in *International Handbook of Trade Unions*, ed. John T. Addison and Claus Schnabel (Cheltenham: Edward Elgar, 2003).

Blank, Joshua D. and Eric A. Zacks, "Dismissing the Class: A Practical Approach to the Class-Action Restriction on Legal Services Corporation," *Pennsylvania State Law Review* 110 (2005): 1–40.

Bloomberg News, "California Judge Sides with Ex-Uber Driver Over Arbitration Clause," *Washington Post*, September 21, 2015.

Bock, Richard A., "Secondary Boycotts: Understanding NLRB Interpretation of Section 8(b)(4)(b) of the National Labor Relations Act," *University of Pennsylvania Journal of Labor and Employment Law* 7 (2005): 905–70.

Bodie, Matthew T., "Information and the Market for Union Representation," *Virginia Law Review* 94 (2008): 1–78.

"Participation as a Theory of Employment," *Notre Dame Law Review* 89 (2013): 661–726.

"Workers, Information, and Corporate Combinations: The Case for Nonbinding Employee Referenda in Transformative Transactions," *Washington University Law Review* 85 (2007): 871–930.

Bohlen, Celestine, "Making Gains for Women in STEM Fields Will Take More Effort," *New York Times*, November 20, 2018.

Bone, Robert G., "*Twombly*, Pleading Rules, and the Regulation of Court Access," *Iowa Law Review* 94 (2009): 873–936.

Bosilkovski, Igor, "Silicon Valley Billionaire Reid Hoffman Condemns Sexual Harassment in the Venture Capital World," *Forbes*, June 23, 2017.

Boston, William, "No Progress/or VW, Auto Workers Union in Resolving U.S. Labor Dispute," *Wall Street Journal*, June 9, 2016.

"VW and UAW to Meet for Talks on Car Maker's Chattanooga Plant," *Wall Street Journal*, May 1, 2016.

Brake, Deborah L. and Joanna L. Grossman, "The Failure of Title VII as a Rights-Claiming System," *North Carolina Law Review* 86 (2008): 859–936.

Brame, Megan, "Combating Sexual Harassment in the Tech Industry," *Huffington Post*, March 9, 2017.

Brantner, Paula, "Unions Create Associate Membership Programs to Help Maintain Their Strength," *Today's Workplace*, September 17, 2004.

Bronsteen, John, "Against Summary Judgment," *George Washington Law Review* 75 (2007): 522–71.

Brookins, Robert, "Mixed-Motives, Title VII, and Removing Sexism from Employment: The Reality and the Rhetoric," *Alabama Law Review* 59 (1995): 1–138.

Brudney, James J., "Neutrality Agreements and Card Check Recognition: Prospects for Changing Paradigms," *Iowa Law Review* 90 (2005): 819–86.

Bryson, Alex and Richard B. Freeman, "Worker Needs and Voice in the US and the UK" (National Bureau of Economic Research, Working Paper No. 12310, 2006).

"Build Your Own City: Spend Time Making Money," *Zirx*, zirx.com/agents/.

Burdick, Ruth, "Principles of Agency Permit the NLRB to Consider Additional Factors of Entrepreneurial Independence and the Relative Dependence of Employees When Determining Independent Contractor Status under Section 2(3)," *Hofstra Labor and Employment Law Journal* 15 (1997): 75–136.

Cagle, Susie, "There's No Such Thing as 'The Gig Economy'," *Pacific Standard*, July 28, 2015.

Calamur, Krishnadev, "New Volkswagen Policy Oks Interactions with Unions at U.S. Factory," *The Two-Way*, NPR, November 12, 2014

Campbell, Charles B., "A 'Plausible' Showing after *Bell Atlantic Corp. v. Twombly*," *Nevada Law Journal* 9 (2008): 1–31.

Cao, Jing and Eric Newcomer, "Uber and Union Agree to Form Drivers Guild in New York City," *Bloomberg*, May 10, 2016.

Carboni, Megan, "A New Class of Worker for the Sharing Economy," *Richmond Journal of Law and Technology* 22 (2016): 1–56.

Carlson, Richard R., "Why the Law Still Can't Tell an Employee When It Sees One and How It Ought to Stop Trying," *Berkeley Journal of Employment and Labor Law* 22 (2001): 295–368.

Carson, Biz, "Inside Uber's Effort to Fix Its Culture through a Harvard-Inspired 'University'," *Forbes*, February 3, 2018.

"The Lawyer Fighting for Uber and Lyft Employees Is Taking the Fight to Four More Companies," *Business Insider*, July 1, 2015.

Casteel, Kathryn, "Sexual Harassment Isn't Just a Silicon Valley Problem," *FiveThirtyEight*, July 13, 2017.

Chang, Emily, "Brotopia: Breaking up the Boys' Club of Silicon Valley" (excerpt), *Fortune*, February 6, 2018.

Chepaitis, Daniel J., "The National Labor Relations Act, Non-Paralleled Competition, and Market Power," *California Law Review* 85 (1997): 769–820.

Cherry, Miriam A., "Working for (Virtually) Minimum Wage: Applying the Fair Labor Standards Act in Cyberspace," *Alabama Law Review* 60 (2009): 1077–110.

Chu, Patrick, "Labor Cases Filed against Shyp, Washio, Postmates," *San Francisco Business Times*, July 1, 2015.

Claire, "How Partnering with Uber Can Spark Small Business & Entrepreneurship," *Uber*, June 30, 2016.

Clegg, Sherry E., "Employment Discrimination Class Actions: Why Plaintiffs Must Cover All Their Bases after the Supreme Court's Interpretation of Federal Rule of Civil Procedure 23(a)(2) in *Wal-Mart v. Dukes*," *Texas Tech Law Review* 44 (2012): 1087–120.

Clermont, Kevin M., "Litigation Realities Redux," *Notre Dame Law Review* 84 (2009): 1919–74.

Clermont, Kevin M. and Stephen C. Yeazell, "Inventing Tests, Destabilizing Systems," *Iowa Law Review* 95 (2010): 821–62.

Colby, Charles and Kelly Bell, "The On-Demand Economy Is Growing, and Not Just for the Young and Wealthy," *Harvard Business Review*, April 14, 2016.

Coleman, Charles D., "Is Mandatory Employment Arbitration Living Up to Its Expectations – A View from the Employer's Perspective," *ABA Journal of Labor and Employment Law* 25 (2010): 227–40.

Coley, Timothy J., "Getting Noticed: Direct and Indirect Power-Allocation in the Contemporary American Labor Market," *Catholic University Law Review* 59 (2010): 965–1000.

Colvin, Alexander J. S., "Empirical Research on Employment Arbitration: Clarity Amidst the Sound and Fury?," *Employee Rights and Employment Policy Journal* 11 (2007): 405–48.

Connolly, Scott J., "Individual Liability of Supervisors for Sexual Harassment under Title VII: Courts' Reliance on the Rules of Statutory Construction," *Boston College Law Review* 42 (2001): 421–54.

Corbett, Christianne and Catherine Hill, *Solving the Equation: The Variables for Women's Success in Engineering and Computing* (Washington, DC: American Association of University Women, 2015).

Corbett, William R., "Waiting for the Labor Law of the Twenty-First Century: Everything Old Is New Again," *Berkeley Journal of Employment and Labor Law* 23 (2002): 259–306.

Corbyn, Zoe and Emily Chang, "Why Sexism Is Rife in Silicon Valley," *Guardian*, March 17, 2017.

Craig, Robin Kundis, "Notice Letters and Notice Pleading: The Federal Rules of Civil Procedure and the Sufficiency of Environmental Citizen Suit Notice," *Oregon Law Review* 78 (1999): 105–202.

"The Criminal Justice System: Statistics," *RAINN*, www.rainn.org/statistics/criminal-justice-system.

Crolley, Axton, "Strippers, Uber Drivers, and Worker Status in South Carolina," *South Carolina Law Review* 69 (2018): 945–76.

Dasteel, Jeffrey H. and Ronda McKaig, "What's Money Got to Do with It?: How Subjective, Ad Hoc Standards for Permitting Money Damages in Rule 23(b)(2) Injunctive Relief Classes Undermine Rule 23's Analytical Framework," *Tulane Law Review* 80 (2006): 1881–904.

Dau-Schmidt, Kenneth G., "Promoting Employee Voice in the American Economy: A Call for Comprehensive Reform," *Marquette Law Review* 94 (2011): 765–836.

Dave, Paresh and Jack Flemming, "Sexual Harassment Claims Prompt Venture Capitalists to Apologize, Change Policies and Head to Counseling," *Los Angeles Times*, July 3, 2017.

Davey, Monica, "Unions Suffer Latest Defeat in Midwest with Signing of Wisconsin Measure," *New York Times*, March 9, 2015.

Davey, Monica and Julie Bosman, "In Victory for Unions, Law on Dues Is Struck Down in Wisconsin," *New York Times*, April 8, 2016.

Davidson, Patricia, "The Definition of 'Employee' under Title VII: Distinguishing between Employees and Independent Contractors," *University of Cincinnati Law Review* 53 (1984): 203–30.

Davidson, Paul, "Decline of Unions Has Hurt All Workers: Study," *USA Today*, August 30, 2016.

De Stefano, Valerio, "The Rise of the 'Just-in-Time Workforce': On-Demand Work, Crowdwork, and Labor Protection in the 'Gig-Economy'," *Comparative Labor Law and Policy Journal* 37 (2016): 471–504.

DeBonis, Mike and Kelsey Snell, "House GOP Discusses Obamacare Replacement Ideas – But Doesn't Call Them a Plan," *Washington Post*, February 16, 2017.

DeFelice, Manon, "Want More Women in Tech Jobs? Create a Culture of Flexibility & Entrepreneurship," *Forbes*, May 17, 2018.

DeSilver, Drew, "American Unions Membership Declines as Public Support Fluctuates," *Pew Research Center*, February 20, 2014.

Diakopoulos, Nicholas, "How Uber Surge Pricing Really Works," *Washington Post*, April 17, 2015.

Dilts, Elizabeth, "U.S. Fast-Food Workers Rally for Higher Minimum Wage," *Chicago Tribune*, December 5, 2013.

Dobbin, Frank and Alexandra Kalev, "Training Programs and Reporting Systems Won't End Sexual Harassment. Promoting More Women Will," *Harvard Business Review*, November 15, 2017.

Dodson, Scott, "Beyond *Twombly*," *Civil Procedure & Federal Courts Blog*, May 18, 2019, https://lawprofessors.typepad.com/civpro/2009/05/beyond-twombly-by-prof-scott-dodson.html;

Dodson, Scott, "Pleading Standards after *Bell Atlantic Corp.* v. *Twombly*," *Virginia Law Review in Brief* 93 (2007): 135–44.

Dolan, Matthew and Kris Maher, "Unions Dealt Blow in UAW's Home State," *Wall Street Journal*, December 12, 2012.

"Driver App," *Uber*, www.uber.com/drive/partner-app/.

"Driving Jobs vs Driving with Uber," *Uber*, www.uber.com/driver-jobs/.

Duff, Michael C., "ALT-Labor, Secondary Boycotts, and toward a Labor Organization Bargain," *Catholic University Law Review* 63 (2014): 837–78.

Dulaney, Chelsey, "Uber Ruling Adds More Drivers to Class-Action Suit," *Wall Street Journal*, December 9, 2015.

Editorial Board, "Defining 'Employee' in the Gig Economy," *New York Times*, July 18, 2015.

EEOC, "Holistic Approach Needed to Change Workplace Culture to Prevent Harassment, Experts Tell EEOC," Press Release, October 31, 2018.

Eidelson, Josh, "Uber Found an Unlikely Friend in Organized Labor," *Bloomberg*, October 27, 2016.

"Union-ish: VW and UAW Are Odd Bedfellows at a Southern U.S. Plant," *Bloomberg Businessweek*, February 19, 2015, 21.

Eisenberg, Theodore and Charlotte Lanvers, "Summary Judgment Rates over Time, across Case Categories, and across Districts: An Empirical Study of Three Large Federal Districts" (Cornell Law School, Research Paper No. 08-022, 2008), www.ssrn.com/abstract=1138373.

"Elephant in the Valley," www.elephantinthevalley.com/.

E-mail from Joe S. Cecil, Sr. Research Assoc., Fed. Judicial Ctr., to Joseph Seiner, Assistant Professor of Law, University of South Carolina (May 19, 2008, 22:07:36 EST) (on file with author).

E-mail from Joe S. Cecil, Sr. Research Assoc., Fed. Judicial Ctr., to Joseph Seiner, Assistant Professor of Law, University of South Carolina (June 20, 2008, 16:24:17 EST) (on file with author).

E-mail from Joe S. Cecil, Sr. Research Assoc., Fed. Judicial Ctr., to Joseph Seiner, Assistant Professor of Law, University of South Carolina (September 24, 2008, 10:07:00 EST) (on file with author).

E-mail from Managing Editor, Jury Verdict Research, to Joseph Seiner, Assistant Professor of Law, University of South Carolina (May 27, 2009 08:55:00 EST) (on file with author).

Epstein, Richard A., "Class Actions: Aggregation, Amplification, and Distortion," *University of Chicago Legal Forum* (2003): 475–518.

"In Defense of the Contract at Will," *University of Chicago Law Review* 51 (1984): 947–82.

"Uber and Lyft in California: How to Use Employment Law to Wreck an Industry," *Forbes*, March 16, 2015.

Erickson, Christopher L. et al., "Justice for Janitors in Los Angeles and Beyond: A New Form of Unionism in the Twenty-First Century?," in *The Changing Role of Unions: New Forms of Representation*, ed. Phanindra V. Wunnava (New York: M. E. Sharpe, 2004).

Estlund, Cynthia L., "Are Unions a Constitutional Anomaly?," *Michigan Law Review* 114 (2015): 169–234.

"The Black Hole of Mandatory Arbitration," *North Carolina Law Review* 96 (2018): 679–710.

"Citizens of the Corporation? Workplace Democracy in a Post-Union Era," in *Corporations and Citizenship*, ed. Greg Urban (Philadelphia: University of Pennsylvania Press, 2014).

"Employment Rights and Workplace Conflict: A Governance Perspective," in *The Oxford Handbook of Conflict Management in Organizations*, ed. William K. Roche et al. (Oxford: Oxford University Press, 2014).

"The Ossification of American Labor Law," *Columbia Law Review* 102 (2002): 1527–612.

Regoverning the Workplace: From Self-Regulation to Co-Regulation (New Haven, CT: Yale University Press, 2010).

"Why Workers Still Need a Collective Voice in the Era of Norms and Mandates," in *Research Handbook on The Economics of Labor and Employment Law*, ed. Cynthia L. Estlund and Michael L. Wachter (Cheltenham: Edward Elgar, 2012).

Estreicher, Samuel, "Employee Involvement and the 'Company Union'·Prohibition: The Case for Partial Repeal of Section 8(a)(2) of the NLRA," *New York University Law Review* 69 (1994): 125–61.

"Freedom of Contract and Labor Law Reform: Opening Up the Possibilities for Value-Added Unionism," *New York University Law Review* 71 (1996): 827–50.

"Nonunion Employee Representation: A Legal/Policy Perspective," in *Nonunion Employee Representation: History, Contemporary Practice, and Policy*, ed. Bruce E. Kaufman and Daphne Gottlieb Taras (New York: M. E. Sharpe, 2000).

"Strategy for Labor Revisited," *St. John's Law Review* 86 (2012): 413–30.

Evans, Michelle, "Establishing Employee or Independent Contractor Status," *American Jurisprudence Proof of Facts, 3rd Series* 108 (2009).

Fairman, Christopher M., "Heightened Pleading," *Texas Law Review* 81 (2002): 551–626.

Faiz, Siddiqui, "New York Considering Setting Minimum Wage for Uber, Lyft Drivers," *Washington Post*, July 2, 2018.

"Uber Launches New Features Aimed at Improving Driver Experience," *Washington Post*, June 7, 2016.

Farleigh, Jenna G., "Splitting the Baby: Standardizing Issue Class Certification," *Vanderbilt Law Review* 64 (2011): 1585–632.

Farmer, Miles B., "Mandatory and Fair? A Better System of Mandatory Arbitration," *Yale Law Journal* 121 (2012): 2346–94.

Feldblum, Chai R. and Victoria A. Lipnic, *Select Task Force on the Study of Harassment in the Workplace* (Washington, DC: U.S. Equal Employment Opportunity Commission, 2016).

Feldman, Robin, "Patent Demands & Startup Companies: The View from the Venture Capital Community," *Yale Journal of Law and Technology* 16 (2014): 236–84.

Fink, Jessica, "Gender Sidelining and the Problem of Unactionable Discrimination," *Stanford Law and Policy Review* 29 (2018): 57–106.

Finley, Klint, "Tech Still Doesn't Take Discrimination Seriously," *Wired*, February 20, 2017.

Fisk, Catherine L., "Workplace Democracy and Democratic Worker Organizations: Notes on Worker Centers," *Theoretical Inquiries in Law* 17 (2016): 101–30.

Fitzpatrick, Brian T., "The End of Class Actions?," *Arizona Law Review* 57 (2015): 161–200.

Foote, Doug, "Forty Thousand Workers in Albuquerque Get a Raise This Week (You Built That)," *Working America Main Street Blog*, January 3, 2013.

Foster, Natalie, "Uber's Major Step Forward for Workers," *CNN*, May 25, 2016.

Fowler, Susan, "Reflecting on One Very, Very Strange Year at Uber," *SusanJFowler*, February 19, 2017.

Frankel, Alison, "The Supreme Court's Next Big Class Action Controversy: Ascertainability," *Reuters*, January 4, 2016.

"Freelancer Discounts," *Freelancers Union*, www.freelancersunion.org/discounts/#/all.

Freeman, Richard B., "From the Webbs to the Web: The Contribution of the Internet to Reviving Union Fortunes" (National Bureau of Economic Research, Working Paper No. 11298, 2005).

Freeman, Richard B. and Joel Rogers, *What Workers Want* (Ithaca, NY: Cornell University Press, 1999).

Fried, Meredith J., "Helping Employers Help Themselves: Resolving the Conflict between the Fair Credit Reporting Act and Title VII," *Fordham Law Review* 69 (2000): 209–42.

Friedenthal, Jack H. et al., *Civil Procedure*, 5th ed. (St. Paul, MN: West Academic, 1999).

Frizell, Sam, "Uber Just Answered Everything You Want to Know About Your Driver," *Time*, January 22, 2015.

Garden, Charlotte, "Labor Values Are First Amendment Values: Why Union Comprehensive Campaigns Are Protected Speech," *Fordham Law Review* 79 (2011): 2617–68.

Gay, Eric, "Uber Report: Eric Holder's Recommendations for Change," *New York Times*, June 13, 2017.

George, B. Glenn, "Revenge," *Tulane Law Review* 83 (2008): 439–94.

Getman, Julius, "The National Labor Relations Act: What Went Wrong; Can We Fix It?," *Boston College Law Review* 45 (2003): 125–46.

Glynn, Timothy P., "Taking the Employer out of Employment Law? Accountability for Wage and Hour Violations in an Age of Enterprise Disaggregation," *Employee Rights and Employment Policy Journal* 15 (2011): 201–36.

Godard, John and Carola Frege, "Labor Unions, Alternative Forms of Representation, and the Exercise of Authority Relations in U.S. Workplaces," *Industrial and Labor Relations (ILR) Review: The Journal of Work and Policy* 66 (2013): 142–68.

Goldman, Lee, "Trouble for Private Enforcement of the Sherman Act: *Twombly*, Pleading Standards, and the Oligopoly Problem," *Brigham Young University Law Review* 2008 (2008): 1057–102.

Goldstein, Bruce et al., "Enforcing Fair Labor Standards in the Modern American Sweatshop: Rediscovering the Statutory Definition of Employment," *University of California at Los Angeles Law Review* 46 (1999): 983–1164.

Gorman, Tricia and Rebecca Ditsch, "Q&A: The Uber Settlement and Its Impact on Worker Classification in the Gig Economy," *Westlaw Journal Employment* 30 (2016): 6–7.

Gosselin, Peter and Ariana Tobin, "Cutting 'Old Heads' at IBM," *ProPublica*, March 22, 2018.

Gottheil, Thomas I. M., "Not Part of the Bargain: Worker Centers and Labor Law in Sociohistorical Context," *New York University Law Review* 89 (2014): 2228–64.

Gray, Kathleen, "Anti-Union Bills Pass Michigan House of Representatives," *Detroit Free Press*, December 7, 2016.

Grebeldinger, Susan K, "How Can a Plaintiff Prove Intentional Employment Discrimination if She Cannot Explore the Relevant Circumstances: The Need for Broad Workforce and Time Parameters in Discovery," *Denver University Law Review* 74 (1996): 159–206.

Green, Michael Z., "Proposing a New Paradigm for EEOC Enforcement after 35 Years: Outsourcing Charge Processing by Mandatory Mediation," *Dickinson Law Review* 105 (2001): 305–64.

Greenhouse, Steven, "Bill Easing Unionizing Is under Heavy Attack," *New York Times*, January 8, 2009.

"On Demand, and Demanding Their Rights," *American Prospect*, June 28, 2016.

"Labor Federation Forms a Pact with Day Workers," *New York Times*, August 10, 2006.

"Tackling Concerns of Independent Workers," *New York Times*, March 23, 2013.

"Wisconsin's Legacy for Unions," *New York Times*, February 22, 2014.

Gregg, Remington A., "Hey, Tech Industry: In the #MeToo Era, Forced Arbitration Must End," *Hill*, February 20, 2018.

Griffith, Erin, "How Venture Capitalists Got Away with Sexual Harassment," *Fortune*, July 21, 2017.

"What Has Tech Done to Fix Its Harassment Problem?," *Wired*, January 22, 2018.

Grodin, Joseph, "Toward a Wrongful Termination Statute for California," *Hastings Law Journal* 42 (1990): 135–64.

Groff, Amy L. et al., "Platforms Like Uber and the Blurred Line between Independent Contractors and Employees: Facing the Challenges to Employment Law Presented by Seemingly Intermediary Platforms of the Modern On-Demand Economy," *Computer Law Review International* 16 (2015): 166–71.

Guynn, Jessica, "Here's Why Women, Hispanics and Blacks Are Leaving Tech," *USA Today*, April 27, 2017.

Hadfield, Gillian, "World Needs Twenty-first Century Regulation to Police Gig Economy," *Financial Times*, November 22, 2017.

Hall, Jonathan, "In the Driver's Seat: A Closer Look at the Uber Partner Experience," *Uber*, January 22, 2015.

Hall, Jonathan V. and Alan B. Krueger, "An Analysis of the Labor Market for Uber's Driver-Partners in the United States" (National Bureau of Economic Research, Working Paper No. 22843, 2016).

Hamed, Karen R. et al., "Creating a Workable Legal Standard for Defining an Independent Contractor," *Journal of Business Entrepreneurship and Law* 4 (2010): 93–118.

"Handling Internal Discrimination Complaints about Disciplinary Action," *Equal Employment Opportunity Commission*, www.eeoc.gov/employers/smallbusiness/checklistsinternal_complaints_about_disciplinary_action.cfm.

Hannon, Kendall W., "Much Ado About *Twombly*? A Study on the Impact of *Bell Atlantic Corp.* v. *Twombly* on 12(b)(6) Motions," *Notre Dame Law Review* 83 (2008): 1811–46.

Harris, Seth D. and Alan B. Krueger, "A Proposal for Modernizing Labor Laws for Twenty-First-Century Work: The 'Independent Worker'" (Hamilton Project Discussion Paper No. 2015-10 December 2015).

Hart, Melissa, "Will Employment Discrimination Class Actions Survive?," *Akron Law Review* 37 (2004): 813–46.

Hartnett, Edward A., "Taming *Twombly*, Even after *Iqbal*," *University of Pennsylvania Law Review* 158 (2010): 473–516.

Harvey, Philip, "Joblessness and the Law before the New Deal," *Georgetown Journal on Poverty Law and Policy* 6 (1999): 1–42.

Hatamyar, Patricia W., "The Tao of Pleading: Do *Twombly* and *Iqbal* Matter Empirically?," *American University Law Review* 59 (2010): 553–633.

Haviz, Hiba, "How Legal Agreements Can Silence Victims of Workplace Sexual Assault," *Atlantic*, October 18, 2017.

Heckscher, Charles C., *The New Unionism: Employee Involvement in the Changing Corporation* (New York: Basic Books, 1988).

Hennessey, Kathleen, "The 'Gig Economy' Gets the Campaign Treatment," *Los Angeles Times*, July 13, 2015.

Hersch, Joni, "A Workers' Lobby to Provide Portable Benefits," in *Emerging Labor Market Institutions for the Twenty-First Century*, ed. Richard B. Freeman et al. (Cambridge, MA: National Bureau of Economic Research, 2005).

Hesson, Ted, "NLRB Argues against Uber," *Politico*, November 3, 2016.

Hiatt, Jonathan P. and Laurence E. Gold, "Employer–Employee Committees: A Union Perspective," in *Nonunion Employee Representation: History, Contemporary Practice, and Policy*, ed. Bruce E. Kaufman and Daphne Gottlieb Taras (New York: M. E. Sharpe, 2000).

Hill, Adriene, "Freelancers Piece Together a Living in the Temp Economy," *New York Times*, March 24, 2014.

Hillman, Robert A., "Drafting Chapter 2 of the ALI's Employment Law Restatement in the Shadow of Contract Law: An Assessment of the Challenges and Results," *Cornell Law Review* 100 (2015): 1341–68.

Hirsch, Barry T. and David A. Macpherson, "Union Membership and Coverage Database from the Current Population Survey: Note," *Industry and Labor Relations Review* 56 (2003): 349–54.

"Union Membership and Coverage Database, Union Membership, Coverage, Density, and Employment by Industry," *Unionstats*, http://unionstats.gsu.edu/Ind_U_2017.htm.

Hirsch, Jeffrey M., "Employee or Entrepreneur?," *Washington and Lee Law Review* 68 (2011):353–68.

Hirsch, Jeffrey M. and Barry T. Hirsch, "The Rise and Fall of Private Sector Unionism: What Next for the NLRA?," *Florida State University Law Review* 34 (2007): 1133–80.

Hirsch, Jeffrey M. and Joseph Seiner, "A Modern Union for the Modern Economy," *Fordham Law Review* 86 (2018): 1727–84.

Hoffman, Lonny S., "Burn Up the Chaff with Unquenchable Fire: What Two Doctrinal Intersections Can Teach Us about Judicial Power over Pleadings," *Boston University Law Review* 88 (2008): 1217–70.

Hoffman, Reid, "The Human Rights of Women Entrepreneurs," *LinkedIn*, June 23, 2017.

Holland, Scott, "Drivers Deliver Class Action Saying GrubHub Needs to Treat Them as Employees, Not Contractors," *Cook County Record*, July 11, 2016.

Huet, Ellen, "Homejoy Shuts Down, Citing Worker Misclassification Lawsuits," *Forbes*, July 17, 2015.

Huffman, Max, "The Necessity of Pleading Elements in Private Antitrust Conspiracy Claims," *Pennsylvania Journal of Business and Employment Law* 10 (2008): 627–62.

Hwang, Tim and Madeleine Clare Elish, "The Mirage of the Marketplace," *Slate.com*, July 27, 2015.

Hyde, Alan, "Employee Caucus: A Key Institution in the Emerging System of Employment Law," *Chicago-Kent Law Review* 69 (1993): 149–94.

"Employee Organization in Silicon Valley: Networks, Ethnic Organization, and New Unions," *University of Pennsylvania Journal of Labor and Employment Law* 4 (2002): 493–528.

"Employment Law after the Death of Employment," *University of Pennsylvania Journal of Labor and Employment Law* 1 (1998): 99–116.

"New Institutions for Worker Representation in the United States: Theoretical Issues," *New York Law School Law Review* 50 (2006): 385–416.

"IAM District 15 Announces Groundbreaking Deal with Uber in NYC," *International Association of Machinists and Aerospace Workers*, May 12, 2016, www.goiam.org/news/iam-district-15-announces-groundbreaking-deal-with-uber-in-nyc/.

Ides, Allan, "*Bell Atlantic* and the Principle of Substantive Sufficiency under Federal Rule of Civil Procedure 8(a)(2): Toward a Structured Approach to Federal Pleading Practice," *F.R.D. (Federal Rules Decisions)* 243 (2007): 604–39.

"Independent Contractors," *Workplace Fairness*, www.workplacefairness.org/independent-contractors.

"Independent Drivers Guild," www.drivingguild.org.

Ip, Greg, "As the Gig Economy Changes Work, So Should Rules," *Wall Street Journal*, December 9, 2015.

Isaac, Mike and Michael J. de la Merced, "Uber Turns to Saudi Arabia for $3.5 Billion Cash Infusion," *New York Times*, June 1, 2016.

Isaac, Mike and Noam Scheiber, "Uber Settles Cases with Concessions, but Drivers Stay Freelancers," *New York Times*, April 21, 2016.

Isaac, Mike and Natasha Singer, "California Says Uber Driver Is Employee, Not a Contractor," *New York Times*, June 17, 2015.

Isaac, Mike et al., "Seattle Considers Measure to Let Uber and Lyft Drivers Unionize," *New York Times*, December 13, 2015.

Isadore, Chris, "Uber Settles Disputes with Thousands of Drivers ahead of Its IPO," *CNN Business*, May 9, 2019.

Issacharoff, Samuel and Erica Worth Harris, "Is Age Discrimination Really Age Discrimination?: The ADEA's Unnatural Solution," *New York University Law Review* 72 (1997): 780–840.

Jaconi, Mike, "The 'On-Demand Economy' Is Revolutionizing Consumer Behavior – Here's How," *Business Insider*, July 13, 2014.

Johnson, Benjamin D., "There's No Place like Work: How Modern Technology Is Changing the Judiciary's Approach to Work-at-Home Arrangements as an ADA Accommodation," *University of Richmond Law Review* 49 (2015): 1229–64.

Johnson, Craig, "Crowdsourcing Supplier Settles Class Action Lawsuit," *Staffing Industry Analysts*, July 8, 2015.

"Join the Saucey HQ," *Saucey*, www.saucey.com/careers.

"Join the Valet Team," *Luxe*, www.luxe.com/valet.

"Join Vint," *Vint*, www.joinvint.com/.

Jolls, Christine, "Antidiscrimination Law's Effects on Implicit Bias," in *NYU Selected Chapters on Labor and Employment Law*, Vol. 3, *Behavioral Analyses of Workplace Discrimination*, ed. Mitu Gulati and Michael J. Yelnosky (Alphen aan den Rijn: Kluwer Law International, 2007).

Jones, Jeffrey M., "Approval of Labor Unions Holds Near Its Low, at 52%," *Gallup*, August 31, 2011.

  "New High of 55% of Americans Foresee Labor Unions Weakening," *Gallup*, September 1, 2011.

Joyce, Amy, "Labor Web Site Keeps Tabs on Business," *Washington Post*, November 18, 2005.

Jury Verdict Research, *Employment Practice Liability: Jury Award Trends and Statistics* (Eagan, MN: Thomson Reuters, 2008).

Kabaservice, Geoffrey, "When Republicans Take Power," *New York Times*, November 2016.

Kahn-Freund, Otto, *Labor and the Law*, 2nd ed. (London: Stevens & Sons, 1977).

Kantor, Jodi, "Working Anything but Nine to Five," *New York Times*, August 13, 2014.

Karmasek, Jessica, "Boston Plaintiffs Attorney Targets Startup Companies in Class Actions," *Legal Newsline*, May 27, 2016.

Katersky, Aaron and Morgan Winsor, "Women Accusing Uber Drivers of Sexual Assault Demand Their Stories Be Heard in Court, Not Arbitration," *ABC News*, April 26, 2018.

Katz, Debra S., "Thirty Million Women Can't Sue Their Employer over Harassment. Hopefully That's Changing," *Washington Post*, May 17, 2018.

Kaufman, Bruce E., "Does the NLRA Constrain Employee Involvement and Participation Programs in Nonunion Companies?: A Reassessment," *Yale Law and Policy Review* 17 (1999): 729–812.

Kedmey, Dan, "This Is How Uber's 'Surge Pricing' Works," *Time*, December 15, 2014.

Kelly, Heather, "Uber's Never-Ending Stream of Lawsuits," *CNN*, August 11, 2016.

Kendall, Marisa, "Uber Battling More than 70 Lawsuits in Federal Courts," *Mercury News*, July 4, 2016.

Kennedy, Elizabeth, "Freedom from Independence: Collective Bargaining Rights for 'Dependent Contractors'," *Berkeley Journal of Employment and Labor Law* 26 (2005): 143–80.

Kessler, Sarah, "The Gig Economy Won't Last Because It's Being Sued to Death," *Fast Company*, February 17, 2015.

Khazan, Olga, "The More Gender Equality, the Fewer Women in STEM," *Atlantic*, February 18, 2018.

Kim, Pauline T., "Bargaining with Imperfect Information: A Study of Worker Perceptions of Legal Protection in an At-Will World," *Cornell Law Review* 83 (1997): 105–60.

King Jr., Joseph H., "Limiting the Vicarious Liability of Franchisors for the Torts of Their Franchisees," *Washington and Lee Law Review* 62 (2005): 417–86.

Klein, Adam Klein et al., "Individualized Justice in Class and Collective Actions," in *Beyond Elite Law: Access to Civil Justice in America*, ed. Samuel Estreicher and Joy Radice (New York: Cambridge University Press, 2016).

Klonoff, Robert H., "The Decline of Class Actions," *Washington University Law Review* 90 (2013): 729–838.

Kokalitcheva, Kia, "Home Cleaning Startup Homejoy Bites the Dust – Literally," *Fortune*, July 17, 2015.

"Uber Strikes Deal with New York City Union to Create Driver Guild," *Fortune*, May 10, 2016.

Kolhatkar, Sheelah, "The Tech Industry's Gender-Discrimination Problem," *New Yorker*, November 13, 2017.

Kolodny, Lora, "Homejoy Raises $38M for House Cleaning on Demand," *Wall Street Journal*, December 5, 2013.

Koppel, Nathan, "Job-Discrimination Cases Tend to Fare Poorly in Federal Court," *Wall Street Journal*, February 19, 2009.

Korb, Elaine M. and Richard A. Bales, "A Permanent Stop Sign: Why Courts Should Yield to the Temptation to Impose Heightened Pleading Standards in § 1983 Cases," *Brandeis Law Journal* 41 (2002): 267–96.

Kosoff, Maya, "Two Workers Are Suing a Cleaning Startup Called Handy over Alleged Labor Violations," *Business Insider*, November 12, 2014.

Koysza, David Hill, "Preventing Defendants from Mooting Class Actions by Picking Off Named Plaintiffs," *Duke Law Journal* 53 (2003): 781–806.

Kremer, Connie, "*McDonnell Douglas* Burden Shifting and Judicial Economy in Title VII Retaliation Claims: In Pursuit of Expediency, Resulting in Inefficiency," *University of Cincinnati Law Review* 85 (2017): 857–76.

Kritikos, A. J., "A Lawsuit to Break the Gig Economy," *Wall Street Journal*, September 20, 2015.

Kruppstadt, Thomas K., "Determining Whether a Physician Is a United States Employee or an Independent Contractor in a Medical Malpractice Action under the Federal Tort Claims Act," *Baylor Law Review* 47 (1995): 223–48.

"Labor Unions," *Gallup*, www.news.gallup.com/poll/12751/labor-unions.aspx.

Lacy, D. Aaron, "The Most Endangered Title VII Plaintiff?: Exponential Discrimination against Black Males," *Nebraska Law Review* 86 (2008): 552–94.

Lagesen, Vivian Anette, "The Strength of Numbers: Strategies to Include Women into Computer Science," *Social Studies of Science* 37, no. 1 (February 2007): 67–92.

Lahey, Joanna N., "Age, Women, and Hiring: An Experimental Study," *Journal of Human Resources* (Winter 2008): 30–56.

Lazarus, David, "Uber and Lyft See the Light on Sexual Assault, but They Could Do a Whole Lot Better," *Los Angeles Times*, May 18, 2018.

Lee, Dayne, "Bundling 'Alt-Labor': How Policy Reform Can Facilitate Political Organization in Emerging Worker Movements," *Harvard Civil Rights-Civil Liberties Law Review* 51 (2016): 509–36.

Leonard, James, "The Equality Trap: How Reliance on Traditional Civil Rights Concepts Has Rendered Title I of the ADA Ineffective," *Case Western Reserve Law Review* 56 (2005): 1–64.

LePrince-Ringuet, Daphne, "Talent Isn't Keeping Women Away from Science. Sexism, Stereotypes and Bad Science Are," *Wired*, August 31, 2018.

LeRoy, Michael H., "Employee Participation in the New Millennium: Redefining a Labor Organization under Section 8(a)(2) of the NLRA," *Southern California Law Review* 72 (1999): 1651–724.

Levin, Sam, "Airbnb Sued by Woman Who Says She Was Sexually Assaulted by 'Superhost'," *Guardian*, July 27, 2017.

"Sexism, Racism and Bullying Are Driving People out of Tech, US Study Finds," *Guardian*, April 27, 2017.

Levine, Dan, "In US Driver Lawsuit, Uber Must Live with Class Action Order for Now," *Reuters*, November 17, 2015.

Levine, David I., *Reinventing the Workplace: How Business and Employees Can Both Win* (Washington, DC: Brookings Institution, 1995).

Levs, Josh, "Analysis: Why America's Unions Are Losing Power," *CNN*, December 12, 2012.

Li, Shan, "On-Demand Laundry Start-Up Washio Shuts down," *Los Angeles Times*, August 30, 2016.

Liedtke, Michael and Johana Bhuiyan, "After Worker Protest, Google Stops Requiring Arbitration in Sexual Misconduct Cases," *Los Angeles Times*, November 8, 2018.

Lien, Tracey, "GrubHub, DoorDash and Caviar Face Lawsuits over Worker Misclassification," *Los Angeles Times*, September 23, 2015.

"Meet the Attorney Suing Uber, Lyft, GrubHub and a Dozen California Tech Firms," *Los Angeles Times*, January 24, 2016.

"Uber Sued by Drivers Excluded from Class-Action Lawsuit," *Los Angeles Times*, January 4, 2016.

Linder, Marc, "Dependent and Independent Contractors in Recent U.S. Labor Law: An Ambiguous Dichotomy Rooted in Simulated Statutory Purposelessness," *Comparative Labor Law and Policy Journal* 21 (1999): 187–230.

The Employment Relationship in Anglo-American Law (New York: Greenwood Press, 1989).

Lindsey, Alex et al., "Two Types of Diversity Training That Really Work," *Harvard Business Review*, July 28, 2017.

Liptak, Adam, "9/11 Case Could Bring Broad Shift on Civil Suits," *New York Times*, July 20, 2009.

"Case About 9/11 Could Lead to a Broad Shift on Civil Lawsuits," *New York Times*, July 21, 2009.

Lobel, Orly, "The Gig Economy & the Future of Employment and Labor Law," *University of San Francisco Law Review* 51 (2017): 51–74.

Lobel, Orly and Anne Marie Lofaso, "Systems of Employee Representation: The US Report," in *Systems of Employee Representation at the Enterprise: A Comparative Study*, ed. Roger Blanpain et al. (New York: Kluwer Law International, 2012).

Lorenzetti, Laura, "Everything to Know About the Uber Class Action Lawsuit," *Fortune*, September 2, 2015.

Ludden, Jennifer, "The End of 9-to-5: When Work Time Is Anytime," *NPR*, March 16, 2010.

Macey, Barry A., "Response to Theodore J. St. Antoine and Michael C. Harper," *Indiana Law Journal* 76 (2001): 135–42.

MacMillan, Douglas, "Uber Agrees to Work with a Guild for Its Drivers in New York City," *Wall Street Journal*, May 10, 2016.

"Uber Drivers Suit Granted Class-Action Status," *Wall Street Journal*, September 1, 2015.

Maher, Kris and Amy Merrick, "Ohio Vote Puts Curbs on Unions in Reach," *Wall Street Journal*, March 3, 2011.

Mahoney, Tara and Allison Drutchas, "Could Your Employee Participation Program Be Illegal? Two Laws You Should Know," *Society of Human Resource Management*, June 9, 2016.

Malamud, Deborah C., "The Last Minuet: Disparate Treatment after *Hicks*," *Michigan Law Review* 93 (1995): 2229–324.

Malin, Martin H., "The Canadian Auto Workers-Magna International, Inc. Framework of Fairness Agreement: A U.S. Perspective," *St. Louis University Law Journal* 54 (2010): 525–64.

Maltby, Lewis L. and David C. Yamada, "Beyond 'Economic Realities': The Case for Amending Federal Employment Discrimination Laws to Include Independent Contractors," *Boston College Law Review* 38 (1997): 239–74.

Malveaux, Suzette M., "How Goliath Won: The Future Implications of *Dukes* v. *Wal-Mart*," *Northwestern University Law Review Colloquy* 106 (2011): 34–52.

"The Jury (or More Accurately the Judge) Is Still Out for Civil Rights and Employment Cases Post-Iqbal," *New York Law School Law Review* 57 (2012–13): 719–746, https://scholar.law.colorado.edu/articles/994.

Manjoo, Farhad, "Grocery Deliveries in Sharing Economy," *New York Times*, May 21, 2014.

Marculewicz, Stefan J. and Jennifer Thomas, "Labor Organizations by Another Name: The Worker Center Movement and Its Evolution into Coverage under the NLRA and LMRDA," *Engage*, October 2012, 79–98.

Matwyshyn, Andrea M., "Silicon Ceilings: Information Technology Equity, the Digital Divide and the Gender Gap among Information Technology Professionals," *Northwestern Journal of Technology and Intellectual Property* 2 (2003): 35–75.

McCabe, David, "Labor, Tech Unite Behind Push for 'On Demand' Worker Rights," *Hill*, November 15, 2015.

McGinley, Ann C., "Credulous Courts and the Tortured Trilogy: The Improper Use of Summary Judgment in Title VII and ADEA Cases," *Boston College Law Review* 34 (1993): 203–56.

McGinty, Tom and Brody Mullins, "Political Spending by Unions Far Exceeds Direct Donations," *Wall Street Journal*, July 10, 2012.

McMahan, Sterling A., "Moving to Dismiss: Ridesharing and Assaults, and the Emerging Legal Frontier," *Trial Advocate Quarterly* (Spring 2018): 11–14.

Means, Benjamin and Joseph A. Seiner, "Navigating the Uber Economy," *University of California at Davis Law Review* 49 (2016): 1511–46.

Memorandum from Colton Tully-Doyle, former Uber Driver, to author (July 30, 2015) (on file with author).

Memorandum from Joe Cecil & George Cort, Research Div., Fed. Judicial Ctr., to Judge Michael Baylson, Advisory Comm. on Civil Rules 4 (August 13, 2008) (on file with author).

Meyerson, Harold, "Labor Wrestles with Its Future," *Washington Post*, May 8, 2013.

Miano, Gabe, "How Freelancers Can Thrive in 2015's Gig Economy," *Forbes*, November 18, 2014.

Miller, Arthur R., "From *Conley* to *Twombly* to *Iqbal*: A Double Play on the Federal Rules of Civil Procedure," *Duke Law Journal* 60 (2010): 1–130.

"The Preservation and Rejuvenation of Aggregate Litigation: A Systemic Imperative," *Emory Law Journal* 64 (2014): 293–328.

Miller, Claire Cain, "Sexual Harassment Training Doesn't Work. But Some Things Do," *New York Times*, December 11, 2017.

Miller, Kevin J., "Welfare and the Minimum Wage: Are Workfare Participants 'Employees' under the Fair Labor Standards Act?," *University of Chicago Law Review* 66 (1999): 183–212.

"Misclassification of Employees as Independent Contractors," *U.S. Department of Labor*, www.dol.gov/whd/workers/misclassification/.

Mishel, Lawrence, "Unions, Inequality, and Faltering Middle-Class Wages," *Economic Policy Institution*, August 29, 2012.

et al., "Wage Stagnation in Nine Charts," *Economic Policy Institution*, January 2015.

Moore, James Wm. et al., *Moore's Federal Practice*, § 23.02, vol. 5, 3rd ed. (New York: Matthew Bender, 1998).

Moore, Patricia A., "Parting Is Such Sweet Sorrow: The Application of Title VII to Post-Employment Retaliation," *Fordham Law Review* 62 (1993): 205–24.

Morpurgo, Julia, "Should Class Be Dismissed? The Advantages of a One-Step Class Certification Process in Unpaid Intern FLSA Lawsuits," *Cardozo Law Review* 36 (2014): 765–804.

Moskowitz, Seymour, "Save the Children: The Legal Abandonment of American Youth in the Workplace," *Akron Law Review* 43 (2010): 107–62.

Mosley, Deanne M. and William C. Walter, "The Significance of the Classification of Employment Relationships in Determining Exposure to Liability," *Mississippi Law Journal* 67 (1998): 613–44.

Mullenix, Linda S., "Ending Class Actions as We Know Them: Rethinking the American Class Action," *Emory Law Journal* 64 (2014): 399–450.

Mundy, Liza, "Why Is Silicon Valley So Awful to Women?," *Atlantic*, April 2017.

"My Employer Says I Am an Independent Contractor. What Does This Mean?," *Communications Workers of America*, www.cwa-union.org/about/rights-on-job/legal-toolkit/my-employer-says-i-am-independent-contractor-what-does-mean.

Naduris-Weissman, Eli, "The Worker Center Movement and Traditional Labor Law: A Contextual Analysis," *Berkeley Journal of Employment and Labor Law* 30 (2009): 232–335.

Neumark, David, "Sex Discrimination in Restaurant Hiring: An Audit Study," *Quarterly Journal of Economics* 111 (1996): 915–41.

Newcomb, Alyssa, "#MeToo: Sexual Harassment Rallying Cry Hits Silicon Valley," *NBC News*, October 23, 2017.

"Silicon Valley Grapples with How to Fix a Sexist Culture," *NBC News*, July 26, 2017.

Niño, Nathalie Molina, "#decencypledge Needs Outcomes Not Optics," *LinkedIn*, June 24, 2017.

Nonnecke, Brandie M., "Opinion: Fight Sexual Harassment in Technology Companies with – Technology," *Mercury News* (San Jose, CA), December 13, 2017.

O'Brien, Sara Ashley, "The Uber Effect: Instacart Shifts Away from Contract Workers," *CNN Money*, June 22, 2015.

O'Brien, Sara and Laurie Segall, "Money, Power & Sexual Harassment," *CNN Tech*, money.cnn.com/technology/sexual-harassment-tech/.

O'Brien, Sarah Ashley et al., "CNN Investigation: 103 Uber Drivers Accused of Sexual Assault or Abuse," *CNN Tech*, April 30, 2018.

O'Conner, Clare, "Billion-Dollar Bumble: How Whitney Wolfe Herd Built America's Fastest-Growing Dating App," *Forbes*, November 14, 2017.

O'Connor, Lydia, "Yelp Reviewers File Class-Action Lawsuit Claiming They Are Unpaid Writers," *Huffington Post*, October 31, 2013.

O'Neil, Luke, "Surviving the Gig Economy," *Boston Globe*, August 31, 2014.

Occhialino, Anne Noel and Daniel Vail, "Why the EEOC (Still) Matters," *Hofstra Labor and Employment Law Journal* 22 (2005): 671–708.

Ohanesian, Nicholas M., "Does 'Why' or 'What' Matter: Should Section 302 Apply to Card Check Neutrality Agreements?," *University of Memphis Law Review* 45 (2014): 249–80.

Opfer, Chris, "Gig Worker Organizers Find Hurdle in Antitrust Laws" (Antitrust and Trade Regulation Report, BNA No. 110, November 25, 2016).

Opfer, Chris and Jasmine Ye Han, "Worker Centers May Get Closer Look under Trump" (Daily Labor Report, BNA No. 30, February 15, 2017).

Oreskovic, Johanna, "Capturing Volition Itself: Employee Involvement and the TEAM Act," *Berkeley Journal of Employment and Labor Law* 19 (1998): 229–95.

Oswalt, Michael M., "Improvisational Unionism," *California Law Review* 104 (2016): 597–670.

Overly, Steven, "Uber Hires Eric Holder to Investigate Sexual Harassment Claims," *Washington Post*, February 21, 2017.

"Packing Expert," *Shyp*, jobs.lever.co/shyp/eaoc0a39–7a0e-4b79–9540-6920c89d8cd2.

Pager, Devah, "The Use of Field Experiments for Studies of Employment Discrimination: Contributions, Critiques, and Directions for the Future," *Annals of the American Academy of Political and Social Science* (January 2007): 104–33.

Pare, Mike, "Labor Groups Support New VW Policy as Volkswagen Opens Way for Talks, Meetings with UAW and ACE," *Times Free Press* (TN), November 13, 2014.

Parker, Kim and Cary Funk, "Women Are More Concerned Than Men about Gender Discrimination in the Tech Industry," *Pew Research Center*, October 10, 2017.

Patrick, Dorrian, "Gig Workers and Job-Related Bias: Are Protections on the Way?," (Daily Labor Report, BNA No. 243, December 19, 2016).

Paul, Sanjukta M., "The Enduring Ambiguities of Antitrust Liability for Worker Collective Action," *Loyola University of Chicago Law Journal* 47 (2016): 969–1048.

Pawlenko, Kye D., "Reevaluating Inter-Union Competition: A Proposal to Resurrect Rival Unionism," *University of Pennsylvania Journal of Labor and Employment Law* 8 (2006): 651–706.

Pearce II, John A. and Jonathan P. Silva, "The Future of Independent Contractors and Their Status as Non-Employees: Moving on From a Common Law Standard," *Hastings Business Law Journal* 14 (2018): 1–36.

Perry, Robin, "Proving the Existence of an Employment Relationship," *American Jurisprudence Proof of Facts*, 3rd Series (1993).

Peters, Laura, "Uber Expands into the Area," *Newsleader*, December 28, 2015.

Phillip, Abby, "Read the Most Surprising Allegations from the Tinder Sexual Harassment Lawsuit," *Washington Post*, July 1, 2014.

Picchi, Aimee, "One Startup Reconsiders the Merits of the 'Gig Economy'," *CBS Moneywatch*, June 23, 2015.

"Platform Overview," *figure eight*, www.figure-eight.com/platform/ (formerly Crowdflower).

Plouffe, David, "David Plouffe Remarks on Creation of Independent Drivers Guild," *Uber*, May 10, 2016.

Poletti, Therese, "Uber Drivers' Class-Action Lawsuit Endangers Much More than Uber," *Marketwatch*, September 1, 2015.

Polivka, Anne E., "A Profile of Contingent Workers," *Monthly Labor Review* (October 1996): 10–21.

"Positions at Instacart," *Instacart*, www.instacart.com/shoppers.

Press Release, U.S. Department of Labor, Bureau of Labor Statistics, *Employer Costs for Employee Compensation – September 2015* (December 9, 2015).

Press Release, Volkswagen, Volkswagen Chattanooga Establishes Community Organization Engagement Policy (November 12, 2014), www.media.vw.com/en-us/releases/396.

Primack, Dan, "Top of the Morning," *Axios Pro Rata*, www.axios.com/newsletters/axios-pro-rata-30ed724c-d7e7-4b55-9d69-40752b60aa2e.html.

Przeworski, Adam, *Capitalism and Social Democracy* (Cambridge: Cambridge University Press, 1985).

Pullen, John Patrick, "Everything You Need to Know About Uber," *Time*, November 4, 2014.

"Q&A: Robots, Uber and the Role of Government," *Financial Times*, June 25, 2015.

Quigly, Fran, *If We Can Win Here: The New Front Lines of the Labor Movement* (Ithaca, NY: Cornell University Press, 2015).

Quraishi, Asifa, "From a Gasp to a Gamble: A Proposed Test for Unconscionability," *University of California at Davis Law Review* 25 (1991): 187–228.

Rabinowitz, Randy S. and Mark M. Hager, "Designing Health and Safety: Workplace Hazard Regulation in the United States and Canada," *Cornell International Law Journal* 33 (2000): 373–434.

Ramsey, Mike, "UAW Files Unfair Labor Practice Charge against VW for Not Bargaining," *Wall Street Journal*, December 22, 2015.

"UAW Wins Vote at VW Chattanooga Plant as Some Workers Vote to Unionize," *Wall Street Journal*, December 7, 2015.

Randazzo, Matthew, "Students Shouldn't Live in STEM Deserts," *U.S. News & World Report,* May 10, 2017.

Redish, Martin H. and Andrianna D. Kastanek, "Settlement Class Actions, the Case-or-Controversy Requirement and the Nature of the Adjudicatory Process," *University of Chicago Law Review* 73 (2006): 545–616.

Redmond, Sean P., "Supreme Court Considers NLRA Case ("Mulhall Case")," *U.S. Chamber of Commerce,* January 18, 2013.

Reinicke, Carmen, "These Are the Soft Skills Tech Employers Are Most Looking for in New Hires," *CNBC,* November 5, 2018.

Report on the Economic Well-Being of U.S. Households in 2017 (Washington, DC: Board of Governors of the Federal Reserve System, 2018).

Reuters, "Auto Union Urges Volkswagen to Accept Labor Board Ruling on Chattanooga Plant," *Fortune,* September 1, 2016.

Reuters, "Judge Expands Driver Class-Action Lawsuit against Uber," *New York Post,* December 9, 2015.

Reuters, "Volkswagen Is Challenging UAW's Union Strategy," *Fortune,* September 26, 2016.

Richards, J. Douglas and Benjamin D. Brown, "Predominance of Common Questions – Common Mistakes in Applying the Class Action Standard," *Rutgers Law Journal* 41 (2009): 163–86.

Risen, Tom, "Hillary Clinton Boosts Workers, Blasts Uber," *U.S. News and World Report,* July 13, 2015.

Roache, Maggie, "Online Platforms Hope to Tackle Sexual Harassment in the Tech Industry," *Peninsula Press* (Stanford, CA), June 17, 2018.

Rogers, Brishen, "Libertarian Corporatism Is Not an Oxymoron," *Texas Law Review* 94 (2016): 1623–46.

"The Social Costs of Uber," *University of Chicago Law Review Dialogue* 82 (2015): 85–102.

Rogers, Kate, "What the Uber, Lyft Lawsuits Mean for the US Economy," *CNBC,* March 16, 2015.

Romberg, Jon, "Half a Loaf Is Predominant and Superior to None: Class Certification of Particular Issues under Rule 23(c)(4)(A)," *Utah Law Review* (2002): 249–334.

Rosenberg, Janet et al., "Now that We Are Here: Discrimination, Disparagement, and Harassment at Work and the Experience of Women Lawyers," *Gender and Society* 7 (1993): 415–33.

Rosenblatt, Joel, "Ex-Twitter Engineer Seeks to Show Women Can Climb Only So High," *Bloomberg,* October 23, 2017.

"Uber's $100 Million Driver Pay Settlement Rejected by Judge," *Bloomberg,* August 18, 2016.

Rosenblatt, Joel and Pamela MacLean, "Uber Judge Taps Brakes on California Drivers' Suit Outcome," *Bloomberg,* December 22, 2015.

Rosenfeld, David, "Worker Centers: Emerging Labor Organizations – Until They Confront the National Labor Relations Act," *Berkeley Journal of Employment and Labor Law* 27 (2006): 469–514.

Rosenthal, Lawrence D., "Motions for Summary Judgment When Employers Offer Multiple Justifications for Adverse Employment Actions: Why the Exceptions Should Swallow the Rule," *Utah Law Review* (2002): 335–80.

Rubenstein, William B., *Newberg on Class Actions*, § 1:9, vol. 1, 5th ed. (Eagan, MN: West, 2011).

Sachs, Benjamin, "Minority Unionism (Sort of) Comes to VW Chattanooga," *Onlabor*, November 12, 2014.

Sahadi, Jeanne, "How Companies Are Changing Old Ways to Attract Young Workers," *CNN Money*, July 23, 2015.

"When an Independent Contractor Is Really an Employee," *CNN*, July 16, 2015.

Schawbel, Dan, "How Technology Created a Lonely Workplace," *MarketWatch*, December 2, 2018.

Scheiber, Noam, "As Freelancers' Ranks Grow, New York Moves to See They Get What They're Due," *New York Times*, October 27, 2016.

"Growth in the 'Gig Economy' Fuels Work Force Anxieties," *New York Times*, July 12, 2015.

Scheiber, Noam and Mike Isaac, "Uber Recognizes New York Drivers' Group, Short of a Union," *New York Times*, May 10, 2016.

Scheindlin, Shira A. and John Elofson, "Judges, Juries, and Sexual Harassment," *Yale Law and Policy Review* 17 (1999): 813–52.

Schmidt, Ronald A., "The Plaintiffs Burden in Title VII Disparate Treatment Cases: Discrimination Vel Non – *St. Mary's Honor Center* v. *Hicks*, 113 S. Ct. 2742 (1993)," *Nebraska Law Review* 73 (1993): 953–96.

Schneider, Elizabeth M., "The Changing Shape of Federal Civil Pretrial Practice: The Disparate Impact on Civil Rights and Employment Discrimination Cases," *University of Pennsylvania Law Review* 158 (2010): 517–70.

Schuck, Peter H., "Legal Complexity: Some Causes, Consequences, and Cures," *Duke Law Journal* 42 (1992): 1–52.

Schultz, Vicki, "Open Statement on Sexual Harassment from Employment Discrimination Law Scholars," *Stanford Law Review Online* 71 (2018): 17–48.

Schwab, Stewart J., "Life-Cycle Justice: Accommodating Just Cause and Employment at Will," *Michigan Law Review* 92 (1993): 8–62.

Schwochau, Susan, "The Labor Exemptions to Antitrust Law: An Overview," *Journal of Labor Research* 21 (2000): 535–55.

Secunda, Paul M., "The Wagner Model of Labor Law Is Dead – Long Live Labor Law," *Queen's Law Journal* 38 (2013): 580–86.

et al., *Mastering Labor Law* (Durham, NC: Carolina Academic Press, 2014).

Segall, Laurie, "Startup Offers Anonymous Harassment Reporting Tool," *CNN Money*, November 16, 2017.

Seiner, Joseph A., "After Iqbal," *Wake Forest Law Review* 45 (2010): 179–230.

"Commonality and the Constitution: A Framework for Federal and State Court Class Actions," *Indiana Law Journal* 91 (2016): 455–92.

"The Discrimination Presumption," *Notre Dame Law Review* 94 (2019): 1115–60.

"Disentangling Disparate Impact and Disparate Treatment: Adapting the Canadian Approach," *Yale Law and Policy Review* 25 (2006): 95–142.

"Harassment, Technology, and the Modern Worker," *Employee Rights and Employment Policy Journal* 23 (2019): 85–114.

"The Issue Class," *Boston College Law Review* 56 (2015): 121–58.

"Platform Pleading: Analyzing Employment Disputes in the Technology Sector," *Washington Law Review* 94 (2019): 1947–86.

"Plausibility and Disparate Impact," *Hastings Law Journal* 64 (2012): 287–324.

"Plausibility beyond the Complaint," *William & Mary Law Review* 53 (2012): 987–1038.

"Pleading Disability," *Boston College Law Review* 51 (2010): 95–150.

"Punitive Damages, Due Process, and Employment Discrimination," *Iowa Law Review* 97 (2012): 473–520.

The Supreme Court's New Workplace (New York: Cambridge University Press, 2017)

"Tailoring Class Actions to the On-Demand Economy," *Ohio State Law Journal* 78 (2017): 21–72.

"The Trouble with *Twombly*: A Proposed Pleading Standard for Employment Discrimination Cases," *University of Illinois Law Review* 2009 (2009): 1011–60.

"Understanding the Unrest of France's Younger Workers: The Price of American Ambivalence," *Arizona State Law Journal* 38 (2006): 1053–110.

"Weathering *Wal-Mart*," *Notre Dame Law Review* 89 (2014): 1343–82.

Selyukh, Alina, "Uber Surge Price? Research Says Walk a Few Blocks, Wait a Few Minutes," *NPR*, October 29, 2015.

Sewell, Abby, "Protesters Out in Force Nationwide to Oppose Wisconsin's Anti-Union Bill," *Los Angeles Times*, February 26, 2011.

Sharkey, Catherine M., "The Future of Classwide Punitive Damages," *University of Michigan Journal of Law Reform* 46 (2013): 1127–50.

Sherman, Erik, "How the U.S. Just Knee-Capped the 'Gig Economy'," *Inc.* July 17, 2015.

"Uber Faces New Class Action Suit by Drivers," *Forbes*, May 4, 2016.

Shreve, Gene R. and Peter Raven-Hansen, *Understanding Civil Procedure*, 4th ed. (New York: LexisNexis, 2009).

Siegel, Stephen A., "Lochner Era Jurisprudence and the American Constitutional Tradition," *North Carolina Law Review* 70 (1991): 1–112.

Silk, Stephanie S., "More Decentralization, Less Liability: The Future of Systemic Disparate Treatment Claims in the Wake of *Wal-Mart* v. *Dukes*," *University of Miami Law Review* 67 (2013): 637–60.

Smith, Ben, "Uber Executive Suggests Digging Up Dirt on Journalists," *Buzzfeed*, November 17, 2017.

Smith, Brendan L., "What It Really Takes to Stop Sexual Harassment," *Monitor on Psychology* 49 (February 2018): 36–51.

Smith, Douglas G., "The *Twombly* Revolution?," *Pepperdine Law Review* 36 (2009): 1063–100.

Smith, Jenna C., "'Carving at the Joints': Using Issue Classes to Reframe Consumer Class Actions," *Washington Law Review* 88 (2013): 1187–226.

Solomon, Brian, "America's Most Promising Company: Instacart, the $2 Billion Grocery Delivery App," *Forbes*, January 21, 2015.

"Washio, the On-Demand Laundry Startup, Washes Out," *Forbes*, August 30, 2016.

Solomon, Lewis D., "The Microelectronics Revolution, Job Displacement, and the Future of Work: A Policy Commentary," *Chicago-Kent Law Review* 63 (1987): 65–96.

Soper, Taylor, "Seattle Councilmember Who Created Uber Union Law: 'We Can Be Pro-Innovation, but also Pro-Worker'," *GeekWire*, December 17, 2015.

Spencer, A. Benjamin, "Class Actions, Heightened Commonality, and Declining Access to Justice," *Boston University Law Review* 93 (2013): 441–92.

"Iqbal and the Slide toward Restrictive Procedure," *Lewis and Clark Law Review* 14 (2010): 185–202.

"Plausibility Pleading," *Boston College Law Review* 49 (2008): 431–94.

"Pleading Civil Rights Claims in the Post-*Conley* Era," *Howard Law Journal* 52 (2008): 99–166.

"Understanding Pleading Doctrine," *Michigan Law Review* 108 (2009): 1–36.

St. Antoine, Theodore J., "Mandatory Employment Arbitration: Keeping It Fair, Keeping It Lawful," *Case Western Reserve Law Review* 60 (2010): 629–44.

Stancil, Paul, "Balancing the Pleading Equation," *Baylor Law Review* 61 (2009): 90–173.

Stangler, Cole, "Why the Uber, Lyft Driver Union Push Could Disrupt the Gig Economy," *International Business Times*, December 18, 2015.

State Minimum Wages: 2016 Minimum Wage by State (Washington, DC: National Conference of State Legislatures, 2016).

Steinberger, Ben Z., "Redefining Employee in the Gig Economy: Shielding Workers from the Uber Model," *Fordham Journal of Corporate and Financial Law* 23 (2018): 577–96.

Steinman, Adam N., "The Pleading Problem," *Stanford Law Review* 62 (2010): 1293–360.

Steinmetz, Katy, "Exclusive: See How Big the Gig Economy Really Is," *Time*, January 6, 2016.

"Homejoy, Postmates, and Try Caviar Sued over Labor Practices," *Time*, March 19, 2015.

"Judge Lets Drivers' Class Action Lawsuit against Uber Go Forward," *Time*, September 1, 2015.

Stemler, Abbey, "The Myth of the Sharing Economy and Its Implications for Regulating Innovation," *Emory Law Journal* 67 (2017): 197–242.

Stewart, Richard B., "The Discontents of Legalism: Interest Group Relations in Administrative Regulation," *Wisconsin Law Review* (1985): 655–86.

Stokowski, Laura A., "Nurses Are Talking About: Working the Night Shift," *Medscape*, January 11, 2013.

Stone, Katherine V. W., "Legal Protections for Atypical Employees: Employment Law for Workers without Workplaces and Employees without Employers," *Berkeley Journal of Employment and Labor Law* 27 (2006): 251–86.

From Widgets to Digits: Employment Regulation for the Changing Workplace (New York: Cambridge University Press, 2004).

Suk, Julie C., "Procedural Path Dependence: Discrimination and the Civil–Criminal Divide," *Washington University Law Review* 85 (2008): 1315–72.

Sullivan, Charles A., "Circling Back to the Obvious: The Convergence of Traditional and Reverse Discrimination in Title VII Proof," *William and Mary Law Review* 46 (2004): 1031–136.

"Plausibly Pleading Employment Discrimination," *William and Mary Law Review* 52 (2011): 1613–78.

Summers, Clyde W., "Employee Voice and Employer Choice: A Structured Exception to Section 8(a)(2)," *Chicago-Kent Law Review* 69 (1993): 129–48.

Sundararajan, Arun, "The 'Gig Economy' Is Coming. What Will It Mean for Work?," *Guardian*, July 25, 2015.

Surowiecki, James, "Gigs with Benefits," *New Yorker*, July 6, 2015.

Sussman, Edna and John Wilkinson, "Benefits of Arbitration for Commercial Disputes," *Dispute Resolution Magazine*, March 2012.

Tarantolo, Danielle, "From Employment to Contract: Section 1981 and Antidiscrimination Law for the Independent Contractor Workforce," *Yale Law Journal* 116 (2006): 170–216.

Tavernise, Sabrina, "Ohio Turns Back a Law Limiting Unions' Rights," *New York Times*, November 9, 2011.

Tellerman, Shanna, "Recruiting and Retaining Female Tech Talent Is a Challenge – Here's How We Did It," *Entrepreneur*, February 22, 2018.

The New Model of Representation: An Overview of Leading Worker Centers (Washington, DC: U.S. Chamber of Commerce, 2014).

"There's an App for That," *Economist*, December 30, 2014.

"This Map Shows Which Cities Have the Highest Minimum Wages," *Time*, May 21, 2015.

Thomas, Suja A., "The New Summary Judgment Motion: The Motion to Dismiss under *Iqbal* and *Twombly*," *Lewis and Clark Law Review* 14 (2010): 15–42.

"Why the Motion to Dismiss Is Now Unconstitutional," *Minnesota Law Review* 92 (2008): 1851–90.

Thompson, Matt, "The Class-Action Lawsuit against Uber Is a Case to Watch," *Atlantic*, September 7, 2015.

Thoreau, Henry D., *Walden*, ed. J. Lyndon Shanley (Princeton, NJ: Princeton University Press, 1971 [1854]).

Tice, Saritha Komatireddy, "Recent Development: A 'Plausible' Explanation of Pleading Standards: *Bell Atlantic Corp. v. Twombly*, 127 S. Ct. 1955 (2007)," *Harvard Journal of Law and Public Policy* 31 (2008): 827–40.

Ticona, Julia and Alexandra Mateescu, "How Domestic Workers Wager Safety in the Platform Economy," *Fast Company*, March 29, 2018.

Tom, Jean, "Is a Newscarrier an Employee or an Independent Contractor? Deterring Abuse of the 'Independent Contractor' Label via State Tort Claims," *Yale Law and Policy Review* 19 (2001): 489–514.

Torpey, Elka and Andrew Hogan, "Working in a Gig Economy," *Bureau of Labor Statistics*, May 2016.

Torres, Roselinde, "The Rise of the Not-So-Experienced CEO," *Harvard Business Review*, December 26, 2014.

"Trade Union Density," OECD, 2017.

Troy, Leo and Neil Sheflin, *U.S. Union Sourcebook: Membership, Finances, Structure, Directory* (West Orange, NJ: Industrial Relations Data and Information Services, 1985).

"U.S. Equal Employment Opportunity Comm'n, Charge Statistics," *EEOC*, www.eeoc.gov/.

"U.S. Equal Employment Opportunity Comm'n, Title VII of the Civil Rights Act of 1964 Charges," *EEOC*, www.eeoc.gov/eeodstatistics/enforcement/titlevii.cfm.

U.S. Government Accountability Office, *Employee Misclassification: Improved Outreach Could Help Ensure Proper Worker Classification* (Washington, DC: GAO-07-859T, 2007).

"Uber Cities," *Uber*, www.uber.com/cities/.

"Uber Drivers," *Uber Law Suit*, www.uberlawsuit.com.

"Uber Moves: Columbia, SC," *Uber*, www.uber.com/cities/columbia.

"The Unicorn List," *Fortune*, January 19, 2016.

Vora, Shivani, "Airbnb Sued by Guest Who Says a Host Sexually Assaulted Her," *New York Times*, August 2, 2017.

Wachter, Michael L., "Labor Unions: A Corporatist Institution in a Competitive World," *University of Pennsylvania Law Review* 155 (2007): 581–634.

"The Striking Success of the National Labor Relations Act," in *Research Handbook on the Economics of Labor and Employment Law*, ed. Cynthia L. Estlund and Michael L. Wachter (Cheltenham: Edward Elgar, 2012).

Wakabayashi, Daisuke, "Uber Eliminates Forced Arbitration for Sexual Misconduct Claims," *New York Times*, May 15, 2018.

Wakabayashi, Daisuke and Jessica Silver-Greenberg, "Facebook to Drop Forced Arbitration in Harassment Cases," *New York Times*, November 9, 2018.

et al., "Google Walkout: Employees Stage Protest over Handling of Sexual Harassment," *New York Times*, November 1, 2018.

Ward, Ettie, "The After-Shocks of *Twombly*: Will We 'Notice' Pleading Changes?," *St. John's Law Review* 82 (2008): 893–920.

Ward, Stephanie Francis, "Judge Rejects Uber's Independent-Contractor Argument in Sexual Assault Tort Claim," *ABA Journal*, May 6, 2016.

Warner, Mark R, "Asking Tough Questions About the Gig Economy," *Washington Post*, June 18, 2015.

Watchman, Gregory R., "Safe and Sound: The Case for Safety and Health Committees under OSHA and the NLRA," *Cornell Journal of Law and Public Policy* 4 (1994): 65–126.

Weber, Lauren, "New Data Spotlights Changes in the U.S. Workforce," *Wall Street Journal*, May 28, 2015.

Weil, David, *Administrator's Interpretation No. 2015-1. The Application of the Fair Labor Standards Act's "Suffer or Permit" Standard in the Identification of Employees Who Are Misclassified as Independent Contractors* (Washington, DC: U.S. Department of Labor, 2015).

Weiler, Paul C., "A Principled Reshaping of Labor Law for the Twenty-First Century," *University of Pennsylvania Journal of Labor and Employment Law* 3 (2001): 177–206.

Weisul, Kimberly, "Yes, Sexual Harassment in Tech Is Really That Bad, 78 Percent of Female Founders Say," *Inc.*, December 6, 2017.

"What Is Instacart?," *Instacart*, www.instacart.com/help/section/200758544#204426950.

"Where to Drive: Houston," *Uber*, www.driveuberhouston.com/peakhours/.

White, Gillian, "When Will Labor Laws Catch up with the Gig Economy?," *Atlantic*, December 9, 2015.

Whitney, Heather M., "Rethinking the Ban on Employer-Labor Organization," *Cardozo Law Review* 37 (2016): 1455–522.

Wickre, Karen, "Corporate Boards Are Complicit in Sexual Harassment," *Wired*, December 6, 2017.

Willborn, Steven L. et al., *Employment Law: Cases and Materials*, 5th ed. (New Providence, NJ: LexisNexis, 2012)

Williams III, Frank V., "Reinventing the Courts: The Frontiers of Judicial Activism in the State Courts," *Campbell Law Review* 29 (2007): 591–736.

Williams, Joan C., "The Five Biases Pushing Women out of STEM," *Harvard Business Review*, March 24, 2015.

Wilson, Reid, "Seattle Becomes First City to Cap Uber, Lyft Vehicles," *Washington Post*, March 18, 2014.

Winning, Lisa, "It's Time to Prioritize Diversity across Tech," *Forbes*, March 13, 2018.

Wistner, Alison, "The VC World Is Still a Boy's Club – Here's How to Change That," *Entrepreneur*, October 26, 2018.

Wood, Robert W., "FedEx Settles Independent Contractor Mislabeling Case for $228 Million," *Forbes*, June 16, 2015.

Worstall, Tim, "Uber Reduces Capital Concentration and Increases the Number of Capitalists," *Forbes*, August 2, 2015.

Wright, Charles Alan et al., *Federal Practice and Procedure*, § 1790, vol. 7AA, 3rd ed. (St. Paul, MN: Thomson West, 2005).

Wuolo, Gabrielle, "New Tool Lets Freelancers Rate Clients and Companies," *FreelancersUnion*, May 31, 2011.

Wyman, Katrina Miriam, "Problematic Private Property: The Case of New York Taxicab Medallions," *Yale Journal on Regulation* 30 (2013): 125–88.

Yelnosky, Michael J., "Salvaging the Opportunity: A Response to Professor Clark," *University of Michigan Journal of Law Reform* 28 (1994): 151–96.

Young, Mary Beth, "Learning to Discern Rather Than Judge," *National Catholic Report*, March 11, 2005.

Zaleski, Katharine, "The Maddeningly Simple Way Tech Companies Can Employ More Women," *New York Times*, August 15, 2017.

Index

CPSIA information can be obtained
at www.ICGtesting.com
Printed in the USA
LVHW081132210821
695698LV00005B/208